MAN AND WAR

MAN AND WAR

by
Plinio Prioreschi

Philosophical Library
New York

The three Goya etchings are reprinted from *The Complete Etchings of Goya*, copyright © 1943, 1971 by Crown Publishers, Inc. Used by permission of Crown Publishers, Inc.

The Durer woodcuts are reprinted from *The Complete Woodcuts of Albrecht Durer*, edited by Dr. Willy Kurt, published 1963 by Dover Publications, Inc., and are used with kind permission of the publisher.

Library of Congress Cataloging-in Publication Data

Prioreschi, Plinio.
  Man and war.

  1. War.   2. War—Moral and ethical aspects.
3. Man.   I. Title.
U21.2.P655   1986   303.6'6   85-31033
ISBN 0-8022-2510-1

Copyright 1987 by Philosophical Library, Inc.
200 West 57 Street, New York, N.Y. 10019
All rights reserved
Manufactured in the United States of America

To Gordon and Luisa

E pensando io come queste cose procedino, giudico il mondo sempre essere stato ad uno medesimo modo...

Machiavelli
Discorsi, II

TABLE OF CONTENTS

	Introduction	xiii
Chapter 1	The Nature of War	3
	What is War?	3
Chapter 2	The Soldier	15
	a) Warrior	15
	b) Sufferer	30
	c) Hero and Beast	47
Chapter 3	War, Famine, and Pestilence	67
	a) *A peste...*	67
	b) *...fame...*	70
	c) *...et bello...*	72
Chapter 4	Prisoners and Military Occupation	81
	a) The Prisoner	81
	b) Military Occupation	94

Chapter 5	Laws of War and Peace 109	
	a) Rules of War	109
	b) Dreams of Perpetual Peace	129
Chapter 6	Ethics and War Crimes 143	
	a) Ethics and War	143
	b) War Criminals	170
Chapter 7	Just War and Pacifism 195	
	a) The Just War Doctrine	195
	b) Pacifism: Another Dream	215
Chapter 8	Power and Decline 227	
	a) Power	227
	b) Decline	240
Chapter 9	Progress and Hope 263	
	a) Is There Progress?	263
	b) Is There Hope?	280

Conclusions 297

Notes 307

Index 331

LIST OF ILLUSTRATIONS

Albrecht Dürer — Cain Kills Abel	2
Albrecht Dürer — Death and the Landsknecht	14
Albrecht Dürer — The Four Riders of the Apocalypse	66
Goya — Bitter Presence (From Los Desastres De La Guerra)	80
Albrecht Dürer — Astronomer	108
Goya — The Way Is Hard (From Los Desastres De La Guerra)	142
Goya — What a Tailor Can Do! (From Los Caprichos)	194
Albrecht Dürer — The Fall of Icarus	226
Albrecht Dürer — Samson Killing the Lion	262

ACKNOWLEDGMENTS

I want to thank the administration of Creighton University for their support, the staff of the Creighton Alumni Library and of the Creighton Health Sciences Library (especially Sister Raymarie Lickteig) for their help in obtaining references, and my friends with whom I have often debated the issues discussed in the book.

INTRODUCTION

In this book we shall discuss war from various points of view, and we shall try to judge the many issues examined, if not with absolute impartiality—an impossible feat—at least "sine ira et studio."[1]

Unfortunately, it is difficult to be impartial when discussing this subject. Compare, for example, our attitude toward war and cancer: both are scourges that have afflicted humanity for ages; both, so far, have defied all attempts at prevention; both have caused death and terrible suffering for an immense number of human beings; and both have been the object of much study in an effort to understand and finally control them.[2] Yet we can talk coldly and in a detached manner about cancer, but we do not seem to be able to do so about war and problems related to it. We become indignant or upset talking about the arms race, the Vietnam war, disarmament, a freeze in the production of nuclear weapons, supplying arms to Central America, etc., and our ability to reason logically is decreased. This happens even to people who are usually rigorous in other circumstances. Here is an example.

In "Mathematical Games," in a recent number of the *Scientific American*,[3] the author comments on a lottery, previously proposed in the same journal, which resulted in many readers trying, in effect, to outdo each other by writing in their entries, the largest possible number. He reports that some entered the Avogadro's number, others the Googol, others the Googolplex, he then continues:

> Some of them exploited such powerful concepts of mathematical logic and set theory that to evaluate which one was the largest became a serious problem, and it is not even clear that I, or for that matter anyone else, would be able to determine which is the largest integer submitted. I was strongly reminded of the lunacy and pointlessness of the current arms race in which two sides vie with each other to produce arsenals so huge that not even teams of experts can say which one is the larger....

Evidently, concerning the arms race, what disturbs the author is not the fact that experts cannot agree (there are many fields where this is the rule more than the exception), but that the United States and Russia are engaged in a contest that, to him, is as pointless as the one in which some of the readers of the journal had just indulged, and pointless for the same reason.

The inanity of a competition to express the largest number resides in the fact that each side can alternatively put forward a number larger than the other side so that the contest could continue *ad infinitum*. The author's criticism of the arms race is based on the same argument, so are the denunciations that appear now and then in the press, and so are those that we all endure during cocktail conversations: "What is the use of our developing a better missile or a faster airplane? The other side will simply match it and build a better one. Then we will build a still better one and they will match that too...."

The argument is based on the unspoken assumption that, as in the case of the competition discussed above concerning numbers, the "supply," and therefore the capacity of each side to match the increments of the other, is without limit. Clearly this is not the case. In the arms race, the capacity to match and surpass is not unlimited and each side counts on the other's running out of breath first—the American Government relying on the lesser technical capabilities of the Russians and the Russian Government on the weaker will of the Americans.

The arms race may be pointless and lunatic but if it is, it is not for the same reason as a contest to express the biggest integer.

Similar difficulties with our emotions are encountered when we discuss means and ends. For all honest, law-abiding citizens the proposition "the end justifies the means" evokes feelings of righteous indignation and conjures images of devilish cunning and treachery. It is associated with despicable leaders and politicians, with the poisons of the Borgias and, naturally, with the black-robed, sulfur-smelling figure of Machiavelli. How often has it been said or implied by journalists, commentators, politicians, and other honorable men that the world would be a much better place if the human mind would abjure, curse, and detest such a proposition! Yet it is quite obvious that the proposition is not only valid but also applied routinely to many human activities, and that it is commonly accepted, *de facto*, even by the most honest and law-abiding citizens.

To begin with, we must clearly understand what its precise meaning is. The end justifies the means signifies, of course, that if an end is important enough any necessary means used to achieve it is justified or, which amounts to the same, that given a certain means, no matter how reprehensible, there is always, at least in theory, an end of sufficient importance to justify it. It is obvious, however, that the reprehensibility of the means must be clearly outweighed by the desirability of the end. It follows, therefore, that it would be unacceptable to use any means (e.g., bank robbery) to achieve an end that may be simply desirable (e.g., acquisition of money).

If the end is sufficiently important, however, it always justifies the means. A few examples will illustrate the point. Killing is justified in self-defense. The police sharpshooter is justified in killing the highjacker who is in the process of blowing up the airplane with the hostages. The surgeon is justified in maiming his patient by amputating the leg with the cancerous growth and so on.

These examples are taken from common events. Ends that would justify even more horrible means can easily be imagined. An insane highjacker has in his possession a nuclear bomb and has commandeered an airplane, with all its passengers, to fly to a metropolitan center, where he intends to detonate the nuclear device. The estimated number of deaths, if he succeeds, is two million. The only possible way to avoid the catastrophe is to destroy the airplane (unavoidably with all the passengers). Estimated number of deaths for this course of action: one hundred. The choice is clear.[4]

In fact, the same principle is not only applied in the dramatic examples mentioned above, but also by practically everybody in the common occurrences of daily life. The man who deprives himself and his family of small luxuries to make a larger payment on his new home, the student who accepts an unpleasant summer job to pay his tuition, the worker who renounces part of his salary to pay his union dues—all are other examples of the application of the same principle, although in these cases the ends are not as compelling and the means are simply disagreeable or unpleasant rather than ethically repugnant.

There are two main causes for the rejection, in theory, of the principle that the end justifies the means. First, because, most often, it is understood as meaning that any means is justified to achieve what is in one's own interests. This is, of course, a misunderstanding. As stated before, for the principle to be acceptable, there must be proportionality between the desirability of the end and the reprehensibility of the means. Suppose that my child needs a coat and that I do not have the money to buy one. Even if we all agree that it is proper and desirable to obtain a coat for one's own children, it is evident that if I were to kill somebody to obtain that coat, the lack of proportionality between the means and the end would make the act unacceptable. On the other hand, if serious suffering is caused to my child because of the lack of the garment and I, not having other means to obtain it, decide to steal one from a department store, the act might become acceptable and justifiable.

The other cause for rejection is the "Pauline teaching that we may not do evil that good may come."[5] If this means that no good can come from evil acts, the proposition is without proof, and arguments to the contrary can be easily found:

> Thus, it is not enough to argue that one may never do evil so that good may come because the good will not come (only the evil), or that the evil act will corrupt the actor and thereby defeat his ends (however desirable in themselves), or that the means cannot be separated from the ends but are themselves the ends in the very process of coming into existence. It is not enough to argue in this manner if only for the reason that each of these familiar contentions is open to question....experience shows that good may come of evil, that the use of evil means does not always corrupt the actor, and that it is much too simple to conceive of means as themselves the ends of action in the very process of coming into existence....[this last] point... smacks of sophistry, it is like saying that selling groceries is equivalent to owning a Rembrandt if somebody is selling groceries to earn the money to buy a Rembrandt.[6]

A clear understanding of the proportionality between means and ends helps to solve problems that would appear at first sight insoluble. Here is an example that has been used in discussions about ethics, the so-called case of Jim and Pedro:

> Latin America. An army captain, Pedro, has twenty Indians tied up against a wall. He is about to shoot them when Jim, an English botanist, happens along. Pedro offers Jim a choice: you shoot one of the Indians or I shoot them all. Jim has very good reason to believe that heroics, e.g., turning the gun on Pedro, will save no lives; and knows that Pedro is, though a brute, a man of his word who can be trusted to release the nineteen Indians if Jim will shoot the twentieth. What should Jim do?
> ...Let us suppose that the twenty Indians whom Pedro is

proposing to kill have done nothing that could be adduced as evidence that they deserve to be killed as a punishment (or even that they deserve some lesser penalty). Let us also assume that the twenty Indians do not know which one of their number will be singled out for execution if Jim accedes to Pedro's offer and that therefore, very reasonably, the Indians implore Jim to accept the offer. Finally, let us assume that Jim knows that the Indians are not guilty of anything for which Pedro is proposing to punish them, and knows that the Indians want him to take up Pedro's terms.

...The point we wish to make about Jim is that if one views him straight, and preserves one's caring about people from such systematizing simplifications of the emotions as utilitarianism and Kantian philosophy, he plainly has an impossible problem. As some would put it, whatever he does he is damned.[7]

Indeed Jim's situation is difficult. However, because we are dealing with a purely hypothetical scenario created to clarify a point, we have the possibility of changing it so that it will be easier to analyze the underlying difficulties.

Suppose now that the twenty Indians are replaced by a much larger number. At first sight one would think that this would not radically change the situation; what difference would it make if the number of Indians is changed to one hundred, or even five hundred? If we keep increasing the number, however, we note that the situation does indeed change. Suppose that the twenty Indians are replaced with all the human beings living on earth. The choice of Jim now is: either kill one person or see humanity wiped out. It is evident that now the choice becomes clear; it is still painful, of course, but it is clear.[8]

On the other hand, if we go in the other direction and reduce the number of Indians, it is evident that it becomes more and more difficult for Jim to accept Pedro's proposal. Imagine that the number of Indians is now two. Jim has now the choice of killing one human being to save another or letting both of them die. Immediately the temptation on Jim's part to say, "Pedro, you are an abominable individual and I do not want to get involved in your horrible schemes," becomes very strong.

After all, it is clearly the responsibility of Pedro to face his conscience and ethical problems. If the existence of humanity were at stake, however, it becomes obvious that this last course of action would be unthinkable.

It must be underlined that by stating that Jim should kill one human being to save humanity we are not passing judgment on the ethical value of his act, we are simply introducing necessity in the algebraic relation of end and means. The degree of necessity may become so overwhelming (as when the existence of humanity is in jeopardy, for example) that it may transcend all ethical considerations. This clarifies the utilitarian position. If we agree that Jim should kill one innocent to save humanity, or nine-tenths of humanity, can we say the same for eight-tenths? Or six-tenths? Where is the dividing line? We do not know, of course, but the point is made that a quantitative element has to be considered.

Why do we feel that the situation is different when the lives of very large numbers of human beings are at stake? Because, perhaps unwittingly, we apply the principal that the end justifies the means. In other words, we feel that the life of an innocent human being could be too high a price for the life of another, at least in those circumstances, but not for the life of all (or of a sufficiently large number of) human beings. By increasing the number of Indians we make the end more and more important until, when the very existence of humanity is at stake, it becomes overwhelming.

When the human species was young and countries and civilizations did not yet exist, men coalesced into groups that eventually became increasingly larger and more complex social units. In the process they acquired different names. In this book we will use the word *group* to indicate a number of human beings that have in common goals, interests, language, and culture; sometimes we use the term as a synonym for *country*. The advantage of simplicity may perhaps excuse the neglect of the more subtle, undoubtedly more orthodox, and more discriminating meanings and use of terms like bodies politic, nation, state, community, and society.[9]

xx MAN AND WAR

War has a tremendous impact on society. All aspects of man's life are affected by it, from his forms of government (changing republics to monarchies and vice versa) to his mental status (suicides decrease during wars), to his social doctrines (the establishment of Communist and Fascist societies was related to the effects of war), to the progress of his technology (stimulated by the war effort). All these effects are beyond the scope of this book and we shall discuss here only elements that seem to be more immediately related to war.

MAN AND WAR

Albrecht Dürer — *Cain Kills Abel*

Chapter 1

> ... non potendo gli uomini assicurarsi
> se non con la potenza...[1]
>
> Machiavelli,
> *Discorsi*, I, 1

THE NATURE OF WAR

What Is War?

The oldest cave paintings show men with weapons in their hands. The oldest poems sing of battles and warriors. The most ancient histories tell of wars, conquests, and destruction. The oldest city yet discovered, Jericho, shows that, around 7000 B.C., man was fortifying his cities with walls, towers, and moats in preparation for war.[2] From the beginning of the Golden Age (after the last Persian War, 480-479 B.C.) to the Macedonian domination (Battle of Chaeronea, 338 B.C.), Athens was at war on the average of two years out of every three.[3] From the time of the kings until Augustus, the

4   MAN AND WAR

Temple of Janus (which was opened in time of war and closed in peace) was shut on only two occasions, once after the war with Carthage and once after the Battle of Actium. In the summer of 1983, at least 15 small wars and 20 or more lesser conflicts were being fought; since 1945, more than 10 million people have died in more than 300 wars.[4] From the oldest times to our days, man has fought almost continuously.

Only phenomena anchored deeply in the nature of things last that long. Many have recognized this. For example, Hobbes saw war as man's natural state, from which he was released only when he agreed to surrender his liberty to fight his neighbor to the supreme power of the state, the Leviathan[5]; and Quinton says:

> La guerre n'est point un dèfi à la nature. Il n'est point contre nature pour le mâle de tuer son semblable. La loi qui régit les rapports des mâles a l'intérieur d'une même espèce est une loi de meurtre et de risque. La guerre est un chapitre de l'amour.[6]

The causation of war has been the object of much study and speculation. Wright reviews the opinions of scientists, historians, and "practical men," the latter group comprising politicians, publicists, and jurists:

> ...the scientifically minded have attributed war (a) to the difficulty of maintaining stable equilibrium among the uncertain and fluctuating political and military forces within the state system; (b) to the difficulty of utilizing the sources and sanctions of international law so as to make it an effective instrument for determining the changing interests of states, the changing values of humanity, and the just settlement of international disputes; (c) to the difficulty of so organizing political power that it can maintain order in a universal society, not threatened by other societies external to itself; and (d) to the difficulty of making peace a more important symbol in world public opinion than particular symbols which may locally, temporarily, or generally favor war. In short, scientific investigators, giving due consideration to both the historical inertia and the inventive genius of mankind, have tended to

attribute war to immaturities in social knowledge and control, as one might attribute epidemics to insufficient medical knowledge or to inadequate public health services....

...Historians have...sought to demonstrate causes by drawing from a detailed knowledge of the antecedents of a particular war events, circumstances, and conditions which can be related to the war by practical, political, and juristic commonplaces about human motives, impulses, and intentions. When they have written of the causes of war in a more general way, they have meant simply a classification of the causes of the particular wars in a given period of history....

...Practical men...suggest that wars arise in the following situations: (a) Men and governments find themselves in situations where they believe they must fight or cease to exist, and so they fight from necessity. (b) Men or governments want something—wealth, power, social solidarity—and, if the device of war is known to them and other means have failed, they use war as a rational means to get what they want. (c) Men and governments have a custom of fighting for an ideology which requires fighting in the presence of certain stimuli, and so in appropriate situations they fight. (d) Men and governments feel like fighting because they are pugnacious, bored, or the victims of frustrations or complexes, and accordingly they fight spontaneously for relief or relaxation.[7]

By others, war has been attributed to causes either fatuous:

Margaret Mead, for example, makes these comparisons [between war and some obsolete institutions like duelling and trial by ordeal] in defining war as a social invention and concludes that just as duelling and trial by ordeal went out of fashion when methods more congruent with the institutions and feelings of the period were invented, so the ingrained habit of war can be replaced by a better invention, provided only that "the people must recognize the defects of the old invention, and someone must make a new one."[8]

or superficial:

"I have always heard it said," wrote Luigi da Porto, an

6　MAN AND WAR

Italian historian of the sixteenth century, "that peace brings riches; riches bring pride; pride brings anger; anger brings war; war brings poverty; poverty brings humanity; humanity brings peace; peace, as I have said, brings riches, and so the world's affairs go round."[9]

Also, there is no lack of definitions of war by famous men, who, incapable of understanding the mechanisms responsible, took refuge in satire. Here is an example from Voltaire:

> A l'heure où je vous parle, il y a cent mille fous de notre espèce couverts de chapeaux, qui tuent cent mille autres animaux couverts de turbans pour quelque tas de boue grands comme votre talon.... Il ne s'agit que de savoir s'ils appartiendront à un certain homme qu'on nomme Sultan ou à un autre qu'on nomme, je ne sais pourquoi, Cé sar.... Presque aucun de ces animaux n'a jamais vu l'animal pour lequel ils s'é gorgent.[10]

Considering the amount of suffering that war has caused over the centuries, we must conclude that only the most profound of natural drives could have compelled man to inflict upon himself such terrible punishment. The explanation that invokes a specific sado-masochistic trait characteristic of man must be rejected because, as discussed below, something closely resembling primitive warfare has been described among animals. Yet, in the human subconscious, a drive for war must exist, a drive powerful enough to overcome all the others that would restrain him from engaging in armed conflict. For example, man is naturally inclined to avoid hardship, pain, insecurity, and sorrow, and to seek ease, pleasure, security, and happiness. Yet war invariably brings the former and destroys the latter. Man instinctively seeks self-preservation and war endangers his life, man cherishes property and war destroys it. A most powerful drive toward war must indeed be at work. In addition, as it is present also in animals, such a drive must be one of the most fundamental and primitive.

It has been suggested[11] that fundamental drives, in terms of the end object, are food, sex, dominance, self-preservation, home territory, activity, independence, and society. All of them, however (with the possible exception of activity and independence), can be considered manifestations of an even more fundamental instinct: self-perpetuation. Food, self-preservation, home territory, and society are necessary for the survival of the individual, while sex and dominance (with its sexual prerogatives) assure self-perpetuation through descendants, as discussed below.

This fundamental super-drive for self-perpetuation, so powerful as to be responsible for most of the others, is the only one that can override those, mentioned above, that urge man toward peace. In other words, it is the drive that is also responsible for war. War, therefore, is an expression of man's struggle to avoid death; that is to say, the main motivation of war is the fear of annihilation, which is the negative image of man's unbounded desire to survive.

It is paradoxical that what brings death and destruction should be the result of man's struggle to avoid death and destruction; obviously, this must be due to a process that "translates" war into survival.

Let us consider the following series of concepts: oneself, family, country, civilization, humanity, earth, solar system, universe, God. It is a sequence of increasingly larger entities that could be considered a set of lines of defense and of retreat in an effort to achieve immortality by the animal that, alone, knows of the inevitability of death.

Youth assumes invulnerability and immortality. Soon, however, the realization that death is inevitable makes it necessary to retreat from the first line of defense (the individual), to the second (the family). Although one must die, the family may survive. In this way, individuality is diluted but descendants mean survival.[12] Through them one's name may not perish for centuries. Given enough time, however, families become extinct and the mind rightly perceives that the end is simply postponed for a relatively short period. Therefore, rear positions are created on which the need for survival can fall back: country and civilization. What is lost in terms of further

8 MAN AND WAR

dilutions of individuality is gained in length of survival. An individual lives a few decades, a family may exist for a few centuries, but a country may last for many centuries and a civilization perhaps for millennia. History, however, teaches that countries and civilizations decay and die and a new position is needed in the rear: humanity. There is further dilution of individuality but further gains in terms of survival. We are now in the hundreds of thousands or millions of years. Is the need for survival now satisfied? Is humanity the bastion from which we can successfully repel the assaults of time? Hardly. Fossils of extinct species suggest that humanity is not immortal. As a result the planet and the solar system become new positions for retreat. Humanity could perish but solace is given by the thought that on earth the signs of man would live. And even if earth were to be vaporized, the sun would still remain as the star of man. Forever. Almost forever. Science relentlessly kills our dreams. We know that even the stars one day will be extinguished. So the last bastion is reached: the universe may die engulfed in infinite entropy but God will really exist forever and in Him some reminiscence of man will remain. With the idea of God the need for survival reaches the ultimate, impregnable position. Hence death will bring sorrow to the believer but not despair.

In this chain of mental steps for self-reassurance, as stated before, man progressively gains in length of survival and loses in terms of individuality. It is true that many religions reassure the believer that his individuality will survive eternity but, while this may satisfy the intellect of the devout, it would appear that it is not enough for the subconscious forces that control the behavior of man. Such forces maintain their pressure so that the struggle for immortality continues at all levels at all times: the energy source for self-preservation and for love toward family, fatherland, civilization, nature, and religion is operating incessantly. In other words, the various lines of defense (oneself, family, country, civilization, humanity, earth, solar system, universe, God) are all held at the same time. They are fronts on which simultaneous battles are fought constantly.

In spite of temporary deviations and exceptions, it is a matter of common observation that man has a particular attachment to the land where, by mere chance, he happens to be born (we call it fatherland even if the term nowadays is out of fashion) and to the socio-cultural milieu to which—equally by chance—he happens to belong (we call it culture or civilization).

Consider, for example, Western civilization. Being the direct heir of the Greco-Roman civilization, it runs in an unbroken line from Homer to Vergil to Dante to Shakespeare to Goethe to more recent poets, and from Alexander to Caesar to Charlemagne to Louis XIV to the present leaders of the Western World. Like all civilizations, it was created with hardship and toil and it will continue to exist as long as we are prepared to support it with toil and sacrifice. One could ask: "Why would we do it? We could enjoy Dante and Vergil even if Western civilization were to collapse, and Caesar and Louis XIV may not be worth our admiration and respect anyway."

The answer is to be found in our longing to survive our death. A civilization is the sum total of what has survived from all its men and women who have ever lived. When, today, we use a Latin word or a word that is derived from Latin, it is not only something of Cicero that survives but also of the uncounted farmers of ancient Latium. Similarly, a verse of Homer or a line of Tacitus with which we may be familiar contributes to the immortality not only of the authors but also of the medieval monks who copied the manuscripts, of the unknown makers of parchment, of the innumerable readers and commentators—in other words, of our ancestors. Similarly, when in the far future somebody mentions Athens or Milan or New York or tries to remember whether Hitler came before Napoleon or vice versa, or comes across a word from our time, a little part of us, dead long before, will still be alive.

Something of us will survive as long as our civilization exists. This concept is expressed in the famous verses of Horace:

> Non omnis moriar multaque pars mei

> vitabit Libitinam: usque ego postera
> crescam laude recens. Dum Capitolium
> scandet cum tacita virgine pontifex,
> dicar....[13]

What we have said about civilization is also valid for individual countries. If a certain language is spoken by many foreigners or if the cultural presence of a given country is felt in other parts of the world for a long time, those who created that language, the citizens of that country, will survive longer in the minds of men. The same applies to structures and buildings that survive the centuries and that are identified with ancient peoples. Hadrian's Wall, Baalbek, the Pyramids, the Parthenon make the Romans, the Egyptians, the Greeks "less mortal" than the peoples who disappeared without trace.

These are the roots of patriotism and nationalism. This is why, when we study ancient history, we are on the side of the Greeks at Marathon and of the Romans in the Punic Wars. Throughout history, men have been ready to suffer, toil, fight, and die so that their country, their civilization, and therefore they, themselves, might survive.

If we assume that war is the expression of an inner drive embedded in the genetic endowment of man, we must expect to find violent conflict among the most primitive groups and even among those close cousins of man that we call primates.

War was indeed common among primitive groups and various circumstances (climate, availability of food, tribal customs, etc.) influenced its frequence and intensity:

> ...[Among the primitives we can distinguish] the most unwarlike people who fight only in defense; the moderately warlike who fight for sport, ritual, revenge, personal prestige, or other social purposes; the more warlike who fight for economic purposes (raids on herds, extension of grazing lands, booty, slaves); and the most warlike of all who, in addition, fight for political purposes (extension of empire, political prestige, maintenance of authority of rulers)...out of the warlike peoples

arose civilization, while the peaceful collectors and hunters were driven to the end of the earth, where they are gradually being exterminated or absorbed.[14]

Even if the immediate purpose for a given conflict was a raid on herds, booty, or the acquisition of slaves, the overall subconscious purpose of armed conflict was the preservation of the group. Hoijer concludes a study of the causes of primitive war with the following statement:

> In striving to remain a tribal entity and to preserve itself physically, the group must perfect a strong social organization and a powerful war machinery. Needless to say, these strivings are unconscious. If they fail, they lose their group identity, if, indeed, they are not annihilated altogether. Those who succeed establish strong tribal organizations whose lives can only be maintained by hostility—warfare becomes the necessary means of preserving group identity, in primitive society.[15]

It is interesting to note that, in spite of the suffering and destruction that war has always caused, it had, paradoxically, a civilizing effect among primitive people because it developed social virtues and social organization.[16] Marrett says:

> It is a commonplace of anthropology that at a certain stage of evolution—the half-way stage, so to speak—war is a prime civilizing agency; in fact, that, as Bagehot puts it, "civilization begins, because the beginning of civilization is a military advantage." The reason is not far to seek. "The compact tribes win," says Bagehot. Or as Spencer more elaborately explains, "From the beginning, the conquest of one people over another has been, in the main, the conquest of the social man over the anti-social man."[17]

As for violence among primates, examples of murder, infanticide, cannibalism, and even primitive warfare have been described among gorillas and chimpanzees.

Dian Fossey, interestingly, believed that an instinct of lineage perpetuation is the cause of infanticide among gorillas:

> Though victims usually die almost instantly as the result of one severe and crushing skull bite, accompanied by a deep bite in the lower groin, the initial concept of gorilla killing gorilla was too horrid for me to accept. Yet I now believe infanticide is the means by which a male instinctively seeks to perpetuate his own lineage by killing another male's progeny in order to breed with the victim's mother.[18]

Jane Goodall, in a work describing murder, cannibalism, and war among chimpanzees, reports the first known extermination of a chimp community by another:

> War and kidnapping, killing and cannibalism: how inappropriate—how jarring—those words seemed as I stood in a tree's shade looking out across the glinting waters of Lake Tanganyika.... And I knew that some of our chimpanzees, so gentle for the most part, could on occasion become savage killers, ruthless cannibals, and that they had their own form of primitive warfare...by 1977 all adult males of the Kahama community had been killed or had disappeared, the first known extermination of one chimp community by another.[19]

Moreover, war is a general biological phenomenon that is not limited to man and the primates; it has been shown to be well distributed throughout the animal kingdom:

> C'est ainsi que le rat asiatique est parvenu à éliminer complètement les races qui existaient auparavant en Europe. Un peu partout on a signalé des faits du même ordre. La fourmi argentine, partout où elle s'installe et prospère, parvient à supprimer toutes les autres espèces de fourmis qui se trouvaient primitivement dans les régions envahies par elle....l'opposition entre deux espèces voisines et concurrentes, revêt l'aspect d'un état de guerre quasi perpétuel. Tous les moyens sont bons pour provoquer la destruction de l'espèce adverse. En dehors des violences, l'un des principaux moyens de parvenir à cette fin est l'accaparement de toutes les sources d'aliments, l'expulsion de

l'espèce la moins forte de toutes les zones d'habitat sain, fertile et avantageux où elle est supplantée par l'espèce la plus forte...C'est ainsi que chaque lion a son domain particulier dans lequel il ne tolère aucune intrusion. D'autres animaux ont tendance à accaparer pour leur usage propre un territoire de pâture ou de chasse et à y dominer par la force....Mais c'est chez les fourmis que l'on trouve les penchants guerriers les plus caractérisés.[20]

The translation of the instinct of survival into war is evidently an irrational phenomenon which must be mediated through the most primitive parts of our central nervous system. In other words, the fact that this translation still takes place indicates that our ferine past is not far away. War among animals, including our cousins, the gorilla and chimpanzee, reminds us of this.

The point is readily appreciated if one views the 4.5 billion years that have passed since the earth formed as being a single year, with each day lasting for 12.3 million years. On such time scale the earth's first forms of life—primitive plants resembling modern single-cell algae—appeared in the seas in early May. Many-celled forms of life, however, did not arise until early November. By about November 20 primitive fishes were swimming in the planet's waters. Toward the end of the month their descendants ventured onto the land. By December 7 reptiles had become the dominant terrestrial animals, and by mid-December the first mammals had appeared. At about 5:00 P.M. on the last day of the year two early hominids left their footprints in a fresh fall of volcanic ash on the Laetoli Plain of Kenya. Our own genus, Homo, did not appear until about an hour before midnight—some 500,000 years ago.[21]

Only if we assume that the motivation for war is part of our biological heritage can we understand how it is possible that man, an intelligent being, could have engaged continuously, from the beginning, in such an activity.

Albrecht Dürer — *Death and the Landsknecht*

Chapter 2

> Donde si vede spesso, se alcuno disegna nello esercizio del soldo prevalersi, che subito...da ogni civile uso si disforma; perché non crede poter vestire un abito civile colui che vuole essere espedito e pronto a ogni violenza...[1]
>
> Machiavelli,
> *Dell' Arte della Guerra, Proemio*

THE SOLDIER

(a) Warrior

For primitive man, at the very beginning, the difference between killing animals like or unlike himself was probably not very distinct. It is easy to imagine that for a primitive human being still close to non-human ancestors, killing, eating, mating, and eliminating body wastes were simply needs that had to be satisfied.

Later, when his mind started to seek causes, he created entities that could be designated as causes. Traces of this can still be found in primitive societies of our days. For the Dani of New Guinea, for example, armed conflict is "demanded" by the ghosts:

> The fifty thousand or more Dani of the Grand Valley are divided into some dozen alliances, each a potential enemy of the other.... The greatest of these pressures [to fight] is exerted by the ghosts, but there are other influences, such as the goading of women who want their men to revenge the death of a husband, son, or brother. The major inducement, however, is the Dani's sense of obligation to the ghosts. [Ghosts are the shades of deceased relatives and friends.] It is assumed that until the ghosts are avenged the people themselves will suffer. The ghosts may trouble them with accidents, sickness, blights upon their crops, droughts, floods, or any of a multitude of other distresses. For Dani warriors the risks involved in fighting an occasional battle, or even joining the far more dangerous occasional raiding parties, which are a more promising way to kill an enemy, are not nearly as great as those to be encountered were they to ignore the demands of unavenged ghosts.[2]

When the group became more important and more organized, its members began to "specialize." Some among the strongest were hunters and warriors; hunters when beasts were the object of the killing, warriors when men were. Later, the warrior became the soldier. Among humans, the division of labor was not as rigid as in other species—for example, insects—and therefore the soldier was not a soldier for his entire life but only for periods that varied according to time and circumstances.

The purpose of the soldier was to be ready to fight wars. In combat, his duty was (to use modern terminology) to reduce as much as possible the enemy's capacity to wage war—in other words, to destroy enemy property and manpower. In the process of doing so he risked his life. While the modern soldier, in time of war, has to endure deprivation and hardship unthinkable in civilian life, for primitive man the distinction between civilian and military life was blurred and war was no hardship. On the contrary, battle offered him the possibility of immediate satisfaction of his needs through pillage and rape.

In historical times, the characteristics of armies varied greatly in different periods, from bands of able-bodied men hastily assembled to fight a sudden enemy attack, to the Roman imperial army, which was the earliest of the world's standing armies in which the soldiers were regularly recruited, systematically trained, cared for, and finally pensioned off by the state.[3] The Roman remained for centuries the example and the standard against which all other armies were measured, if not in terms of details of organization, surely in terms of military efficiency and capability. It was the army that conquered an immense empire and maintained "the immeasurable majesty of the Roman peace."[4]

The Roman soldier has been the object of admiration and awe since success and victory started to be the almost constant companions of the legions. His valor and endurance have become legendary. It has been underlined that during a march he would carry equipment weighing as much as sixty pounds, including food for more than two weeks, pickaxe with bronze sheath, chain, rope, leather thong, saw, hook, stakes for entrenchments, wicker basket (for moving earth)—plus, of course, sword, javelins, armor, and helmet. Cicero spoke of "the toil, the great toil of the march..." and Gibbon suggested that the weight that he carried "would oppress the delicacy of a modern soldier."[5] The Roman soldier went without breakfast, and ate mainly farinaceous foods,[6] especially in the form of bread or porridge made from wheat that he himself ground on stone mills carried with the *impedimenta* of the legion and cooked over hot stones or embers.[7] The wheat ration—unground—was a bushel a month.[8] As for meat, although he ate it, he considered a diet consisting only of meat to be a hardship. Tacitus says, "...per inopiam et labores fatiscebant, carne pecudum propulsare famem adacti,"[9] and Caesar, "...ut complures dies frumento milites caruerint et pecores ex longinquoribus vicis adacto extremam famem sustentarent...."[10]

18   MAN AND WAR

The Roman soldier used to drink water mixed with vinegar—the mixture offered to Jesus on the cross.

Flavius Josephus, a man who indeed appreciated power, says about the Roman soldier:

> This vast empire of theirs has come to them as a prize of valor, and not as a gift of fortune.
>
> For their nation does not wait for the outbreak of war to give men their first lesson in arms. They do not sit with folded hands in peacetime only to put them in motion in the hour of need. On the contrary, as though they had been born with weapons in hand, they never have a truce from training, never wait for emergencies to arise. Moreover their peace maneuvers are no less strenuous than veritable warfare. Each soldier daily throws all his energy into his drill, as though he were in action. Hence that perfect ease with which they sustain the shock of battle. No confusion breaks their customary formation, no panic paralyzes, no fatigue exhausts them. And as their opponents cannot match these qualities, victory is the invariable and certain consequence. Indeed, it would not be wrong to describe their maneuvers as bloodless combats and their combats as sanguinary maneuvers....
>
> By their military exercises the Romans instill into their soldiers fortitude not only of body but also of soul. Fear too plays its part in their training. For they have laws which punish with death not merely desertion of the ranks, but even a slight neglect of duty. And their generals are held in even greater awe than the laws. For the high honors with which they reward the brave prevent the offenders whom they punish from regarding themselves as treated cruelly.
>
> This perfect discipline makes the army an ornament of peacetime and in war welds the whole into a single body—so compact are their ranks, so alert their movements in wheeling to right or left, so quick their ears for orders, their eyes for signals, their hands to act upon them. Prompt as they consequently are in action, none are slower than they in succumbing to suffering, and never have they been known in any predicament to be beaten by numbers, by ruse, by difficulties of ground, or even by fortune—for they feel surer of victory than of fortune's power. Where counsel thus precedes active opera-

tions, where the leader's plan of campaign is followed up by so efficient an army, no wonder that the empire has extended its boundaries on the east to the Euphrates, on the west to the ocean, on the south to the most fertile tracts of north Africa, on the north to the Danube and the Rhine.

One might say without exaggeration that, great as are their possessions, the people that won them are greater still. If I have dwelt at some length on this topic, my intention was not so much to extol the Romans as to console those whom they have vanquished—and to deter others who may be tempted to revolt.[11]

Such is the admiration for the Roman legionary that it has been suggested that he conquered the empire in spite of the ineptitude of his generals, who continued to deploy the legion in the usual way (in the center with the Roman cavalry on the right and the allied cavalry on the left) even after Hannibal had shown its inadequacy.[12]

Following, however, what seems to be a recurrent historical pattern, the profession of soldier came to be despised by the young Romans of the late Empire. In the fourth century A.D., many of the youth in Italy and the provinces chose to cut off the fingers of their right hand to escape military service. The practice became so common that specific words were created in the Latin language: the verb was *murcare* and the practitioners were called *murci*.[13] At that time, inevitably, the invincible Roman legionary began to be defeated more and more often and the glory of serving the eagles was, until the end of the empire, for others than the descendants of Romulus.

During the Middle Ages, war and soldiers continued to play a prominent role, in spite of the triumph of Christianity, a religion of peace and love. According to the colorful simile of the time that used the recurrent religious symbol of the shepherd and the flock, the clergyman were the shepherds, the knights the dogs, and the people the sheep. The function of the shepherds was to look after the salvation of the flock, of the dogs to defend it, and of the sheep to have their souls saved, be defended, and pay for it all. Not that the people were not asked to fight; the peasants in fact were fighting and dying, but only when allowed to, and in an inglorious sort of way because

> ...the glory of death in the battlefield was reserved to the armored man on horseback [that is, the nobleman]; and though common men were permitted to come to his assistance in some extreme cases, this was regarded as abnormal and monstruous. If they perished by his side, it was viewed with lusty mockery as a joke. Describing the Battle of Senlis in 1418, a French chronicler said: "There was a captain who had a crowd of footmen who all died, and there was great laughter because they were all men of poor estate."[14]

In other circumstances the fighting of peasants was not considered funny at all: in 1078 peasants of southern Germany who had fought for their Emperor, Henry IV, were, after their defeat, "castrated by the feudal armies for their presumption in bearing tools reserved for the knighthood."[15]

Wearing a sword was a sign of noble birth and of belonging to a privileged social class. The vanity of man often found ways to correct the occasional mistakes of Mother Nature, who may have caused a noble man to be born in a bourgeois family. In the eighteenth century, for example, swords were rented at the gates of the park of Versailles to anyone who wanted to walk there, as long as he had the money to pay the rent and was properly dressed.[16]

The profession of arms was for the nobleman, who depended on the labor of the peasants for support. The relationship was not, however, altogether parasitical because, in exchange, the nobleman was obliged to undertake military service—that is, to pay the *impôt du sang*, the tax of blood.[17] As stated before, this did not mean that the peasant never had to bear arms. When called by the *seigneur*, or later by the king, every adult male had to defend the village, the province, or the country. Even ecclesiastics occasionally participated. For example, in Dole, besieged by the French army in 1636, a Capuchin monk served in the artillery, and Carmelites and Dominicans worked on the defensive earthworks.[18] The peasants bearing arms were not exactly soldiers, however; they were *ad hoc* fighters who were called, when necessity arose, to fight not only the enemy, but also outlaws, wolves, and even epidemics by establishing quarantine zones.[19] We must wait for the institution of permanent armies to note the rise of a class of men who spent the greater parts of their lives in the profession of arms. Nevertheless, it has been estimated that, at the end of the reign of Louis XIV, one Frenchman out of six would very likely have been called to arms at least once in his life.[20]

In Christian Europe, up to the seventeenth century, because of the association of noble birth and the bearing of arms, society was permeated with a military spirit that eventually led to the establishment of a class of professional soldiers. In the Moslem world, professional soldiers were created earlier. The janissaries of the sultan's guard, for example, were usually children taken from Christian families, raised as Moslems, and turned into formidable fighters freed from all material cares.

The knights and the *ad hoc* peasant fighters of the feudal period were suitable for small skirmishes between barons, but not for the king when the need for large armies arose. When confronted with the necessity of keeping men in the army for prolonged periods of time and even in peacetime, it became necessary to find some form of inducement so that the men would not find the long service unbearable. Since time immemorial, money has been singularly capable of making man endure the most unpleasant circumstances, if not with a smile, at least with patience and forbearance. It is not surprising, therefore, that money was used early in the game, first in the form of land grants, then of currency.

> Such early forms are to be seen in Sicily, under the Emperor Frederick II, in England during the Scottish and French wars, and in France around 1300. Payment became the rule in the permanent armies, in which all members—officers and men, whether fulfilling military obligations or serving as mercenaries—received some wages.[21]

It is to be noted that, in the main Europe languages, the word for "soldier" does not derive from *miles,* the Latin equivalent, but from *soldus* (sold, *solde*), a variation of *solidus*—a Roman gold coin. In fact, the terms "soldier," *soldat, soldato,* and *soldado* originally referred to fighting men who received a *solde* or wage.

Recruitment of mercenaries by means of professional war contractors reached a peak in Italy in the fifteenth century with the *condotta.* The *condottiere* recruited the captains, who then signed up their own men. Some, like Colleoni and Sforza, became major figures in the politico-military scene of the time. The men recruited by the contractor were from many backgrounds, often from the lowest strata of society, looking for wars in which to fight and, naturally, to loot. Some were peasants ruined by war—like Simplicissimus, Grimmelshausen's hero—but the army also represented a refuge for criminals who wanted to avoid prosecution and vent some of their instincts in the brutalities of war, for men threatened by lawsuits, for others who desperately needed the enlistment bonus to pay debts, and for those who wished to avoid all kind of bondage in the confusion and lack of restraints so common in time of war.

> Enlistment was also a means of escaping from miserable poverty, and recruiting was easiest in time of scarcity or famine. The record of enlistment bonuses provides a true indicator in this respect: [in France] in 1693-94 and in 1710 men enlisted without even asking for the bonus (the *argent du roi*). They simply hoped to survive by enlisting...Psychological misery became an increasingly important factor. Widowers, orphans, uprooted foreign vagrants, especially men from the countryside who had not succeeded in finding positions in the cities, looked to the army for human contact and support....[21]

The army, in other words, also played, at times, a positive social role. This was also the time when camp followers were particularly numerous. From time immemorial, armies have been followed by crowds of non-combatants, from the *calones* of the *De Bello Gallico* to the prostitutes, parasites, and black-marketeers surrounding the American troops in Vietnam. In certain historical periods, the number of such followers swelled to large dimensions. Before the Thirty Years War a regiment of 3,000 men was followed by about 4,000 noncombatants. At the end of the war, there were 40,000 men enlisted in the Imperial-Bavarian army and they were followed by a train of 100,000 wives, whores, servants, children, and other camp-followers.[22]

> In the camp at Langenau in 1630, there were 368 horsemen, 600 horses, 66 women, 78 girls, 307 stableboys, and 24 children. This was an appendix that took no part in the actual fighting but appeared on the scene again soon after the battle was over in order to take from the dead whatever had been left behind by the victorious soldier.[23]

The activities of the camp-followers were not limited to the robbing of the dead; having to feed themselves, they often organized "raids" in the areas along the route followed by the army. This was often well regarded by the commander because it solved, or at least helped to solve, the supply problems of some of the fighting units.[24]

Among the mercenaries, ethnic groups evolved with their characteristic forms of armament and methods of fighting. The most prominent were the *Lansquenets* of Germanic origin, the Gascons, the Scots, and Albanians, and the Hussars from Hungary.[25] The mercenary soldiers were bound to the captain by contract, oral if not written, and by the payment of a certain sum at the time of hiring. In addition, wages were to be paid regularly during the campaign. In practice, of course, wages often were not paid and this generated strikes, desertions, and mutinies—as, for example, in the Spanish army in the Netherlands between 1572 and 1607.

During the Thirty Years War, armies used to try to lure enemy soldiers with special bonuses and higher wages.[26] It is easy to understand that in such circumstances peace was

24 MAN AND WAR

feared and considered a scourge by some, and war greeted with relief. In other cases, however, enlistment was tantamount to slavery and death:

> ...conditions of service in the eighteenth-century Russian army were little different from those of serfdom. It was indeed customary for Russian village priests to say the Mass for the Dead on the departure of youths nominated for military service, since the term was for life and their families were resigned by experience to abandon hope of seeing them again.[27]

Evidently the importance of the *condottieri*, their personal prestige, and their strength were not compatible with the strong monarchies that were becoming more and more the centers around which European politics was revolving. Sweden was the first country to organize a permanent army. In 1544 the government instituted an annual census of men with the purpose of calling up one of five or six whenever it should be necessary. When the soldier was at war, it was the duty of his neighbors to cultivate his land and to support his family.[28] By the end of the seventeenth century, several countries, Spain and England among them, had organized local forces on a national scale, although in principle still distinct from the regular army.[29]

Support for the formation of regular armies was based not only on possible antagonism between the central government and the semi-independent *condottieri* but also on the belief of many (e.g., Machiavelli) that permanently enlisted regulars, especially if from the national territory, would have a higher degree of loyalty and therefore would be better warriors. The victory of the Spaniards over the French at Pavia in 1525 seemed to confirm the decisive nature of the "military revolution" of the sixteenth century started by Spain when it began to replace mercenaries with permanently enlisted regulars.[30] The superiority of national armies was confirmed by the successes of Gustavus Adolphus of Sweden, whose soldiers were not only regular but recruited exclusively from among Swedes.[31] By the time of Charles V, the era of the *condottieri* was over.[32]

Although sixteenth and seventeenth century Christian Europe was imbued with militaristic spirit, Italy was somewhat of an exception. Even if it was the land of the *condottieri*, it was also the land of the Renaissance, and the writer, the poet, and the artist were more prominent than the *condottiero*[33]—an indication of a high level of civilization, but also of the general decline that was to follow, and that in fact had already started after the death of Lorenzo il Magnifico in 1492. The Italians, like the Romans of the late Empire before them, refused to engage in such uncomfortable and uncivilized activity as the bearing of arms, and the people no longer contributed to defense other than with tax money.[33] Although Venice still had an army and was able to maintain its independence until the time of Napoleon, Florence and the Church States had only a few foreign mercenary troops; city militias increasingly became police forces. Armies became foreign to the country, and Italians who wanted a military career went to serve in Spain, France, or Germany.[34] Italy was condemned to play a secondary role on the international scene by the very causes that made her, at the time, the most civilized country in Europe. The relation between decline and degree of intellectual refinement will be discussed in Chapter 8.

As long as fighting was the prerogative of the noblemen only, the rules of the game were clear: when the conflict was over, the gentlemen would return to their estates and, if maimed, would show the honorable scars as proof that they had paid their "blood tax." The king did not feel that he had any financial obligation toward them—first, because they did not need financial help, and second, because it was all part of the "blood tax."

When the common people started to carry the main burden of war, things changed dramatically in this respect. The maimed soldier who was dismissed was usually destitute. The only way he could survive was by begging, unless his handicap was such that he was not prevented from finding some menial job. After the sixteenth century, the gentlemen who went in the army often were also destitute, and therefore the fate of the maimed nobleman was sometimes the same as that of the common man. In Italy the multitude composed of those wrecks left by the wars was called "the dead army."[35]

As the "dead army" became more and more numerous, the problem had to be faced and a solution attempted. At first the normal channels were used. In the Catholic countries, charity was teh responsibility of the monastery; in the Protestant countries, of the charitable institutions that had taken over church property. The monasteries started to take in the former soldiers as lay brothers or oblates and very soon, as was to be expected, this started to cause serious problems. The ex-soldiers did not possess those attributes of virtue, self-discipline, and asceticism that were expected from members of monastic religious communities. In addition, their number grew to such an extent that the monasteries preferred to pay a pension to the oblates so that they could live outside the monastery. The situation became impossible also for the Protestant charitable institutions that could not handle the enormous influx generated by the Thirty Years War.[36]

At this point the governments had no choice but to intervene—first with the idea that, because of the great generosity of this or that ruler, a great favor was going to be bestowed on the ex-soldiers, and later with the recognition that it was the least that could be done for those who were disabled at the service of their country. After a lapse of fifteen centuries, the *res publica* again started to take care of its veterans.

In England, in the reign of Elizabeth I, pensions of ten pounds for common soldiers and twenty for lieutenants were instituted.[37] In Spain the first hospital to house disabled and elderly soldiers was founded at Malines in 1585; in Sweden, Queen Christine founded a similar hospital in Vodsterna in 1647; and the *Invalides* in France was created in 1670-74 by Louis XIV.[38] Eventually foundations like the *Invalides* were created in England (Chelsea, 1692), and later in almost all European countries.

After the principle that the state was to take care of disabled veterans was established, the abundance of wars soon created a surplus of disabled ex-soldiers, and the problem that had previously confronted the monasteries arose again. Hospitals became overcrowded; at the *Invalides*, for example, those who were capable of serving in sedentary positions were sent with garrison forces to various forts in the kingdom.[39] This measure proved to be insufficient to solve the problem, and eventually admission to the *Invalides* was often converted into a pension paid to these veterans in their own homes. Twenty-five years of service qualified them for the equivalent of regular pay, and sixteen for half-pay. A uniform was issued to them every seven years.[40]

One of the elements that induce man to become a warrior is patriotism. Primitive man had to contend with a harsh environment full of dangers of all sorts. He attacked animals and other humans for food and loot, and often was himself in the position of being attacked. Together with the bellicosity necessary to carry on his attacks he must have developed, quite early, a need for defense—not only his own defense, but the defense of the group as well. As a member of a group that controlled a certain amount of territory, he developed the concept of the fatherland, and eventually came to describe his attachment and positive feelings toward the group and its controlled territory with the term patriotism.

Originally, of course, the concept of what we now call fatherland was limited to the village or to the small area that belonged to the group, often a small geographical unit no larger than the area that could be crossed on foot in one day.[41] The distrust of foreigners, together with the bond established by common language and way of life, contributed to the coalescence of subgroups and to the enlargement of the frame of the fatherland.

Patriotism became a force that contributed to the preservation of the group. On occasion, it would burst forth with renewed vigor and engulf a whole nation. This happened, for example, to Revolutionary France in the early 1790's, when patriotic fervor and national solidarity, created by the political convulsions of the time, produced the phenomenon of the "nation at arms" in which "every citizen was a soldier and every soldier a citizen." This made France an almost invincible country where

> ...not just adult male citizens but just about everybody else were prepared for involvement in the national war effort; a *patrie* whose *enfants* seemed to be potentially available for its military purposes in hitherto unimaginable numbers, and with a hitherto unprecedented spirit..."La Marseillaise" says it all.[42]

The phenomenon was so striking and effective, in terms of increasing the military capability of the country, that subsequent French Governments (as well as all the other European ones) have tried to reproduce it ever since, but without such spectacular success.

The French army at the time was composed exclusively of national soldiers, and its success suggested to reformers in Prussia in 1798 a reduction by one half of the number of foreigners in its army—who still amounted to about 50 per cent of the privates—and the naturalization of the rest of them.[43] At the time the process of replacing foreigners with nationals, which had begun in the sixteenth century, was not yet completed.

Of course, not all national soldiers behaved like patriots. Desertion, for example, which has been a constant problem in all armies since the beginning of history, continued, although in certain times and circumstances it was worse than in others. Its immediate causes were many: from the *mal du pays* (homesickness) that affected men who came from remote communities speaking obscure dialects and who therefore felt isolated from their comrades, to a very productive raid that made the deserter think that he could now "retire" and live happily as a civilian.[44]

Frequently associated with the army and the soldier, especially since the Middle Ages, has been the concept of "honor." Chivalry dictated the rules and a tradition that was kept alive for centuries with variations related to time and place. It was usually an aristocratic code in which the simple foot soldier had no place, and which, in spite of Cervantes' devastating portrayal of chivalry, survived until the last century, when duels to defend stained honor were still fought.

> Attempts of various governments to interfere in such affairs of honor, in the interest of military efficiency, were furiously resented.... Public opinion turned more and more against the duel; as early as the 1690's, Defoe urged that it be punished and a challenger be denied the character of gentleman.
> The more feudal spirit of the French nobleman led to a greater insistence upon self-determination in that respect. It is said that in the first eighteen years of the reign of Henry IV [that is, from 1589 to 1607], around four thousand gentlemen had been killed in duels. As the Absolute Monarchy strove to put down this lordly pride, it attacked the duel system. Louis XIII had two noblemen of high rank beheaded on account of a duel and, from the mid-seventeenth century on, increasing edicts prohibited such affairs, often putting them on a level with ordinary brawling. Under Louis XIV, when the edicts were actually applied with punishment as well as threat, dueling became for a time almost extinct, though by the end of Louis XV's reign it so far revived that there was said to be more of it in France than in all the rest of Europe put together. The reasons for mortal combat were often trifling, a remark on one's dress, a struggle over a theater seat, merely to try out the courage of a newcomer to a regiment.... At times, the disputes set regiments at odds: on one occasion, fifty men of one regiment were fighting an equal number of another on the *glacis* of Maubeuge; when they were separated, two men were dead and thirty-seven wounded.[45]

Later, the idea of honor, which impelled gentlemen to kill each other for the silliest of reasons, shifted its focus from the soldier's immediate surroundings to war. Around the end of the eighteenth century, it became necessary to convince the combatants that the war they were fighting was honorable, legitimate, and just. The concept of "just war" (see Chapter 7) was resuscitated to convince both soldiers and civilians once again to endure the hardships of war because their side was "right."

> In the armies of the Absolutism [i.e., of the absolute kings of the times before the American and French Revolutions], soldiers were expected to fight without "a just cause," but such a cause had to be supplied to the forces fighting against [those armies]. They had to be persuaded that the wars they were waging were just, useful, honorable, and advantageous.[46]

For example, the Americans accused the British of being the first to fire at Lexington and they often described stories of British cruelty in their newspapers. In the same vein Napoleon took great care to show how the enemies of France were always the aggressors.[47]

> Marshal Ney, according to a biographer of 1911, "developed this beautiful idea that the French soldier does not fight well except for a cause thought by him to be interesting and just." And he issued an order to his generals in 1805 that "the intelligence and the nature of the French armies demand that they be well informed about the cause that obliges them to fight, and only when the aggression is legitimate can one expect marvels of valor from them."[48]

Modern propaganda was born.

(b) Sufferer

The word "soldier" evokes in our mind images that vary according to personal experiences and historical circumstances. Usually, however, although those images may include the soldier-warrior, the soldier-killer, the soldier-criminal, the soldier-hero, the soldier-liberator, the soldier-oppressor, etc., very rarely do they include the soldier-sufferer. Concerning suffering, the soldier is more often considered a purveyor than a victim of it. Yes, of course, thinking of our boys at the front we may think of the cold, the mud, and the bad food; when indulging in historical reminiscences we may even go so far as to wonder how those men of the past could have submitted to such harsh military life. In spite of that, however, the soldier is not usually seen as a human being who, throughout history, has endured terrible suffering.

While, for millennia, the social status of the officer has oscillated between fair and excellent, the status of the private has always been low except in special cases—as, for example, in Sparta, where each hoplite was accompanied by a helot, who would carry his baggage and fulfill the functions of a servant.[49]

One of the sources of suffering for the soldier was officers' abuse, which has been a common phenomenon in history; we can find examples in antiquity and in modern times. In the Roman army of the first century:

> Flagitatum ut vacationes praestari centurionibus solitae remitterentur; namque gregarius miles ut tributum annuum pendebat. Quarta pars manipuli sparsa per commeatus aut in ipsis castris vaga, dum mercedem centurioni exolveret.... Tum locupletissimus quisque miles labore ac saevitia fatigari donec vacationem emeret.[50]

In the army of Frederick the Great (where it was held that the soldier must fear his officers more than his enemies),[51] and in the British Army at the time of Waterloo:

> Floggings were inflicted by the drummers of the regiment, under the superintendence of the drum-major and the adjutant. The culprit was bound by his extended arms to two of three sergeant's halberds, planted in the ground in a triangle, and lashed together at the top. The strokes were inflicted at the tap of a drum beaten in slow time. Each of the wielders of the cat retired after having given twenty-five lashes. The surgeon was always present to certify that the man's life was not in danger by the further continuance of the punishment, and the prisoner was taken down the moment that the medical man declared that he could stand no more. Often this interference saved the culprit from the end of his punishment....he might never be

called upon to undergo the balance. But in grave cases the prisoner was merely sent into hospital till he was sufficiently convalescent to endure the payment of the remainder of his account. Inhuman commanding officers sometimes refused to allow for any abatement, even when the crime had not been a very serious one, and insisted that the whole sentence should be executed even if the culprit had to go twice into hospital before it was completed.[52]

On occasion, the officers themselves were victims of the mindless rigidity of their superiors:

...in June 1916, an infantry company commanded by Lieutenant Herduin was defending a position near Verdun. The Germans attacked, broke through, and Herduin's company suffered severe casualties. From Verdun itself it looked as if Herduin's position had been overrun. So the French artillery was ordered to shell it. Under heavy fire, and with another German assault in the offing, Herduin was faced with three choices: annihilation, surrender, or evacuation of the position. In the event Herduin opted for the third course, and with some difficulty managed to get the sorry remnants of his company back to Verdun. Two days later he and the only other surviving officer were ordered to report to their regimental headquarters. They were told that the brigade commander had ordered their execution, on the ground that they had abandoned their position to the enemy. Nineteen men's lives had been saved but Herduin's part in this was not seen as initiative. So both officers were executed by a firing squad.[53]

More often, however, it was war that exacted its terrible price from the solider:

The wounded men between the trenches had to perish miserably. Nobody dared help them as the opposing side kept up its fire. They perished slowly, quite slowly. Their cries died away after long hours, one after the other. One man after the other had lain down to sleep, never to awake again. Some we could hear for days; night and day they begged and implored [someone] to assist them, but nobody could help. Their cries became softer and softer until at last they died away—all suffering had ceased. There was no possibility of burying the dead. They remained where they fell for weeks. The bodies began to decompose and spread pestilential stenches, but nobody dared to come and bury the dead.... The French tried the Red Cross flag. We laughed and shot it to pieces. The impulse to shoot down the "enemy" suppressed every feeling of humanity, and the "red cross" had lost its significance when raised by a Frenchman. Suspicion was nourished artificially, so that we thought the "enemy" was only abusing the flag; and that was why we wanted to shoot him and the flag to bits.[54]

Although the above refers to the First World War, it is a scene that, except for details, has repeated itself thousands of times since the beginning of man. Until the discovery of anesthesia in the nineteenth century, the fate of the wounded soldier was to suffer terrible pain. In the case quoted it was man's perversity that prevented the helping of the wounded, but, for many centuries, it was also man's ignorance. The lack of anesthesia and antisepsy made the treatment of wounds a horrible torture that, often, was worse than neglect.

Certain medical practices of the past make us shudder. For example, in the Middle Ages the crossbow was sometimes used to extract arrows or other foreign bodies firmly embedded in the body of the victim. Probably the theory was that if the great strength of the weapon was necessary to drive the arrow in, it was also necessary to drive it out. The practice consisted of attaching the embedded arrow to a rope that was connected with the crossbow so that the missile could be "fired in reverse."[55] The damage produced must have been considerable.

A fatal misconception, transmitted down the centuries from the time of Galen, greatly retarded progress in the treatment of wounds: the idea that pus was *bonum et laudabile*, good and laudable. We know today that pus is a sign of infection and that its presence, except in the most superficial abrasions, is to be considered a complication that requires energetic treatment. The modern surgeon carefully cleans the wound and then closes it with sutures so that it is not in contact with the contaminated external environment and is therefore protected from infection; in addition, the margins being brought together, the process of healing and cicatrization is easier and faster because the gap between the margins is reduced. When the healing process takes place in these conditions (clean, sutured wound, with no infection), we say that it is "by first intention." If the wound is not sutured, it inevitably gets infected, the gap between the margins is much larger, the healing process is longer, and we say that the wound may heal "by second intention." In this case the scar is, of course, bigger.

Obviously the modern surgeon always tries to obtain healing "by first intention." Not so in the past. Because from time immemorial wounds were always infected and therefore full of pus, it was felt that the purulent discharge was a necessary step in the healing process. It was also observed that not all kinds of pus were the same. The abundant, yellow, creamy kind was most often followed by healing, but other kinds (pale-whitish, bloody and watery, scanty—those associated with tubercular infection, gangrene, or a non-localized process) were often a sign that the wound would not heal or that the patient would die. Hence the usual pus (the abundant yellow, creamy kind) resulting from common, localized infections was *bonum et laudabile*. In fact, its formation in the wound was often encouraged by the application of various substances.

Some surgeons of the thirteenth and early fourteenth centuries, particularly those trained in Bologna, advocated immediate suture and healing "by first intention,"[56] and Bruno da Longoburgo was the first to mention healing "by first and second intention." Unfortunately, under the influence of Guy de Chauliac, the advice of the surgeons of Bologna (who also advocated the washing of the wounds with wine, an antiseptic) was not heeded,[57] and the old idea of *pus bonum et laudabile*, with the open treatment, prevailed until the eighteenth century. As recently as the first part of the nineteenth century, Dominique Larrey, the famous French surgeon, still believed that pus was necessary for wound healing and advocated the use of powder of cantarides to promote it; having noted that the application of alcohol dried up the wound, he concluded that it was a poor remedy.[58]

Larrey's aversion to topical alcohol for wounds was shared many years later (1867) by his son, Hippolyte Larrey, when he and Velpeau, acting as a commission for the French Imperial Society of Surgery, rejected the plea of Marc Sée and Labbé. These two, motivated by their own favorable experience with the use of alcohol in wound management as well as Nelaton's, urged recognition of its topical application to wounds as a sovereign remedy against infection and hospital gangrene.[59]

Another pernicious belief that retarded progress in wound management and caused terrible suffering for many unfortunate men was the one that regarded gunshot lesions as poisoned. Because it was known that poisons were often destroyed by boiling liquids, it was the practice of military surgeons to pour scalding oil in the gaping wounds. It was the great sixteenth-century French surgeon Paré who, having one evening, after a particularly bloody battle, run out of scalding oil, noticed the next day that the soldiers who had not been treated with it were much better off than their unfortunate comrades:

> At last my oil lacked and I was constrained to apply in its place a digestive made of the yolks of eggs, oil of roses, and turpentine. That night I could not sleep at my ease, fearing by lack of cauterization that I should find the wounded on whom I had failed to put the said oil dead or empoisoned, which made me rise very early to visit them, where, beyond my hope, I found those upon whom I had put the digestive medicament feeling little pain, and their wounds without inflammation or swelling, having rested fairly well throughout the night; the others to whom I had applied the said boiling oil I found feverish, with great pain and swelling about their wounds. Then I resolved with myself never more to burn thus cruelly poor men wounded by gunshot.[60]

Even without scalding oil the suffering of the wounded was terrible:

36 MAN AND WAR

> In the Wars I was called to see a poor souldier who had his Arm shot off near the Shoulder. The bruised and shattered Stump seemed to his chirurgeon to be gangrened, and accordingly he dresst him with Aegiptiac...from which sharp dressing the wound gleeted, and, by reason of the Pain, inflamed. He had roared some days through the vehemency of the Pain. When I came to him, I saw a great Trembling of the Part, and a frequent twitching upwards of the Tendons and Musculous flesh in the Stump; also the Flesh in the whole Stump was of a whitish color, as if it had been scalded. I dressed him up with Anodynes...then anointed the Parts about, as the Neck and Spine, with unguent....I also blistered the Legs and Thighs; But it was too late, he died howling.[61]

As for the drugs used, they were terribly inadequate. Not having any idea of the patho-physiology of the wounds, the imagination (sometimes the sick imagination) of man was the only criterion used in the choice of substances for their treatment.[62] Here is an example of the state of ignorance, in this field, in the sixteenth century:

> Charles IX had been presented with a bezoar stone. These so-called stones are concretions which are found in the intestinal tract of certain animals. Introduced into medicine by the Arabs, they were held in great esteem as universal antidotes. Charles IX was very proud of his bezoar stone. He spoke of it to Paré, who told him that there was no such thing as a universal antidote. Paré suggested that its efficiency could easily be tested on some rascal who had been sentenced to be hung. The king sent for his provost and asked him if he had any prisoner who merited hanging. "He told him that he had in his prison a cook who had stolen two silver plates from his master and that the next day was to be hanged and strangled. The king told him he wished to experiment with a stone which they said was good against all poisons, and that he should ask the said cook after his condemnation if he would take a certain poison, and that they would at once give him an antidote; to which the said cook very willingly agreed, saying that he liked much better to die of said poison in the prison than to be strangled in view of the people. And then an apothecary gave him a certain poison in a

drink and at once the bezoar stone. Having these two good drugs in his stomach he took to vomiting and purging, saying that he was burning inside, and calling for water to drink, which was not denied him. An hour later, having been told that the cook had taken this good drug, I prayed Monsieur de la Trousse (the provost) to let me see him, which he accorded, accompanied by three of his archers, and found the poor cook on all fours, going like an animal, his tongue hanging from his mouth, his eyes and face flaming, retching in a cold sweat, bleeding from his ears, nose, and mouth. I made him drink about one half sextier of oil, thinking to aid him and save his life, but it was no use because it was too late, and he died miserably, crying it would have been better to have died on the gibbet. He lived about seven hours." Paré performed an autopsy which showed that he had died of gastroenteritis from corrosive sublimate poisoning.[63]

The history of man's struggle against disease, physical suffering, and damage inflicted on his body by war or by hostile environment—in other words, the history of medicine—has pages full of heroism, devotion, sacrifice, blunders, chicanery, and compassion, but, until quite recently, the pages of success were rare. Until late in the nineteenth century the treatment of wounds, far from being beneficial, quite often caused harm, at best was innocuous, and only rarely accomplished more than what nature, if left alone, would have done.

The famous case of Alexis St. Martin as reported by his physician, Doctor William Beaumont,[64] can be considered an example of wound treatment in the first half of the nineteenth century:

> Alexis St. Martin...was a Canadian, of French descent...about eighteen years of age, of good constitution, robust and healthy. He had been engaged in the service of the American Fur Company, as a voyageur, and was accidentally wounded by the discharge of a musket, on the 6th of June, 1822.
> The charge, consisting of powder and duck shot, was received in the left side of the youth, he being at a distance of not more than one yard from the muzzle of the gun. The contents entered

> posteriorly, and in an oblique direction, forward and inward, literally blowing off integuments and muscles of the size of a man's hand, fracturing and carrying away the anterior half of the sixth rib, fracturing the fifth, lacerating the lower portion of the left lobe of the lungs, the diaphragm, and perforating the stomach.
>
> The whole mass of materials forced from the musket, together with fragments of clothing and pieces of fractured ribs, [was] driven into the muscles and cavity of the chest.
>
> I saw him twenty-five or thirty minutes after the accident occurred, and, on examination, found a portion of the lung, as large as a turkey's egg, protruding through the external wound, lacerated and burnt; and immediately below this, another protrusion, which, on further examination, proved to be a portion of the stomach, lacerated through all its coats, and pouring out the food he had taken for his breakfast, through an orifice large enough to admit the forefinger.

A serious wound even by modern standards. The most grave aspect was the large opening of the chest wall with the danger of massive pneumothorax (entry of air into the chest cavity) and immediate death. At the time, there was no way of treating such a complication, which, fortunately, did not occur in this case.[65] Doctor Beaumont proceeded in his treatment:

> In attempting to return the protruded portion of the lung, I was prevented by a sharp point of the fractured rib, over which it had caught by its membranes; but by raising it with my finger, and clipping off the point of the rib, I was able to return it into its proper cavity, though it could not be retained there, on account of the incessant efforts to cough.

Here Doctor Beaumont, by clipping the sharp point of the fractured rib, prevented complications that could have resulted from further damage to the exposed lung. This may have been the only beneficial measure in the treatment of this case. Now the next main danger was infection, the forever-present scourge of old surgery. In this case it was particularly to be feared because both the thoracic and the peritoneal cavities

The Soldier 39

were open and therefore susceptible to infection by gastric content and the non-sterile finger of the physician probing the wound and attempting to replace the viscera into their "proper cavity."

> The projecting portion of the stomach was nearly as large as that of the wound. It passed through the lacerated diaphragm and external wound, mingling the food with the bloody mucus blown from the lungs.
> After cleansing the wound from the charge and other extraneous matter, and replacing the stomach and lungs as far as practicable, I applied the carbonated fermenting poultice, and kept the surrounding parts constantly wet with a lotion of muriate of ammonia and vinegar; and gave internally the aq. acet. am. with camphor, in liberal quantities.

We are not aware of modern studies concerning the therapeutic value of these old remedies[66] and therefore their value cannot be assessed with certitude; it would appear, however, that they were at best innocuous. Very likely a clean bandage would have produced the same results by protecting the wound from the external environment and would not have run the risk of infecting the pleural and peritoneal cavities with non-sterile liquids. The medications administered by mouth were also ineffective at best.

Doctor Beaumont continues:

> Under this treatment a strong reaction took place in about twenty-four hours, accompanied with high arterial excitement, fever, and marked symptoms of inflammation of the lining membranes of the chest and abdomen, great difficulty in breathing, and distressing cough.
> He was bled to the amount of eighteen or twenty ounces, and took a cathartic. The bleeding reduced the arterial action, and gave relief. The cathartic had no effect, as it escaped from the stomach through the wound.[67]

If, at this crucial stage, the "inflammation of the lining membranes of the chest and abdomen"—that is, the pleuritis and peritonitis—was to become generalized, the patient would die; as it happened, it remained localized and he survived in spite of the bleeding that was supposed to have given relief and that, in fact, probably gave that impression because it made the patient weaker and therefore quieter.

Even if the mortal pleuritis and peritonitis did not occur, the infection of the wound and its complications still endangered the life of the patient:

> On the fifth day a partial sloughing of the integuments and muscles took place. Some of the protruded portions of the lung, and lacerated parts of the stomach, also sloughed, and left a perforation into the stomach, plainly to be seen, large enough to admit the whole length of my forefinger into its cavity; and also a passage into the chest, half as large as my fist, exposing to view a part of the lung, and permitting the free escape of air and bloody mucus at every respiration.
> A violent fever continued for ten days, running into a typhoid type, and the wound became very fetid.[68]

Fortunately, the infection remained localized and the general condition started to improve.

> On the eleven day, a more extensive sloughing took place, the febrile symptoms subsided, and the whole surface of the wound assumed a healthy and granulating appearance.[69]

Although not without danger, the patient now is much better and his chances of survival are good. In fact, he continues to improve:

> In the spring of 1824 he had perfectly recovered his natural health and strength; the aperture [of the stomach] remained; and the surrounding wound was firmly cicatrized to its edges.[70]

Alexis St. Martin eventually married, fathered many children, and died in 1880 at the ripe age of eighty-three. His survival, to be considered almost miraculous, was due to luck and Mother Nature more than to the science of the physician—not because Doctor Beaumont, according to the state of the art at the time, made any mistake but because, as we mentioned before, medicine did not have much to offer until later.

For millennia, soldiers knew that most probably they would die if hit. The wounds of the battlefield were always dirty and infection would rage unchecked. Not only were antibacterial drugs unavailable, the existence of bacteria and infections was not even suspected. Extraction of foreign bodies from wounds was an ordeal that often produced more harm than good, and wounds with foreign bodies were very frequent because of the low speed of the missiles. The primitive surgery of the time was easily defeated by foreign bodies that could not be extracted—as, for example, on sailing ships, where the "cannon balls scattered jagged splinters which were much more feared as wounding agents than the shot itself."[71]

World War I was the first war in history in which soldiers, if lucky enough to be brought soon to medical care facilities, had a fairly good chance of surviving even quite serious wounds. Sulfa drugs and antibiotics were not yet available, but antiseptics helped to control infections and anesthetics allowed surgical practices not possible before, sparing millions from horrible suffering.

The capacity to relieve pain is probably the greatest achievement of medicine, and although civilian victims of disease and accidents have benefited from pain-relieving medications and anesthesia, the soldier, of course, has been the greatest beneficiary. It is difficult for us to appreciate now what it must have been to be wounded when analgesics and anesthetics were nonexistent or else not administered appropriately. The following is a description of a column moving wounded soldiers during the American Civil War:

> The column moved rapidly, considering the rough roads and the darkness, and from almost every wagon for many miles issued heart-rending wails of agony....Many of the wounded in the wagons had been without food for thirty-six hours....Very

few of the wagons had even a layer of straw in them, and all were without springs....The jolting was enough to have killed strong men, if long exposed to it. From nearly every wagon as the teams trotted on, urged by whip and shout, came such cries and shrieks as these: "O God! Why can't I die?" "My God! Will no one have mercy and kill me?" "Stop! Oh! For God's sake, stop just for one minute; take me out and leave me to die on the roadside." "I am dying! I am dying! My poor wife, my dear children, what will become of you?"[72]

Although the smallest wound could easily result in death, for much of history the most likely cause of death for the soldier was not enemy action but disease. The First World War was also the first war in which battle deaths exceeded those from non-military causes; as late as the Boer War of 1899-1902, diseases were the main killers. The army of Leclerc, for example, sent to put down the rebellion of Toussaint l'Overture in Haiti in 1801, was reduced from 25,000 men to 3,000 by yellow fever. In 1632 the armies of Wallenstein and Gustavus Adolphus faced each other outside Nuremberg; they were decimated by typhus and scurvy and were forced to withdraw without engagement.[73]

The number of soldiers killed by disease in the Middle Ages was even more staggering. Not until the twentieth century could medicine control those additional causes of suffering and death for the soldier.

Our attitude toward the value of human life has changed greatly through history. Although during the Christian era human life has always been considered sacred without distinction of rank, this laudable attitude was, for many centuries, only a philosophical abstraction. In practice human life was cheap. One of the manifestations of this attitude was that, after the battle, the soldiers, dead and wounded, conscious and unconscious, suffering and beyond suffering, were left on the battlefield, prey and victims of the robbers of the dead (who did not hesitate to murder the wounded) for a day or two or more, until some form of always inadequate succor could be organized. Even this late and inadequate help was usually limited to the wounded of the victor, who was in control of the battlefield.

After the Battle of Waterloo, for example, by nightfall forty thousand bodies lay in two square miles of land. Many were still alive and suffering horribly. Who could help? The French had fled, the Prussians were pursuing them, and the British who were left in control of the field had to take care of the many less seriously wounded men who were still with the ranks. In addition, they had no transportation to evacuate those who could not walk, and finally, there was very little that could be done to relieve their suffering. Therefore nothing was done until next morning:[74]

> From the plateau of Mont-Saint-Jean to the height of Rossomme, from Hougoumont to Plancenoit, and even as far as Mohain, the ground was covered with dead bodies and slain horses. More than 25,000 French, and 20,000 English, Belgians, and Prussians lay upon the ground, in some places scattered about like fallen trees, in others lying in long files like rows of wheat cut down by the reapers' sickles. The moon had risen and lit up distinctly their ghastly, blood-stained faces and their mud-stained uniforms smeared with red stains, the weapons that had dropped from their hands gleaming in the moonlight. Now and again thick, dark clouds, spreading over the sky, veiled this vision, from which the least sensitive among the old warriors turned away their eyes. But soon the vision reappeared in the cold light of the moon. Amidst the agonized moans of the dying and the groans of the wounded, at short intervals, a hoarse cry went up, stifled as it were with horror and dread. It was some officer whom a vile robber of the dead was finishing with the butt end of a gun in order to rob him of his purse or his cross of honor.[75]

This happened in 1815; this had happened, after each battle, for millennia. There have been rare, short-lived exceptions. For example, during the late Enlightenment it was common, in European wars, for field commanders to agree on "cartels" or conventions, which, before the battle, established

44 MAN AND WAR

rules concerning the location of field hospitals and regulations for their security. The medical personnel engaged in the care of the wounded were immune from attack and from liability to capture as prisoners of war.[76] Much of this civility ceased after the French Revolution (see Chapter 9). We must wait until the middle of the nineteenth century before substantial progress is made.

The first field hospitals were created by Queen Isabella during the war for the conquest of Granada: six hospital tents were used at the siege of Alora in 1484 and four at the siege of Baza in 1489; wagons with beds were used at the siege of Otrera in 1477.[77] These measures were forgotten after the war. Sully, minister of Henry IV, ordered the establishment of field hospitals in 1597, during the siege of Amiens. There were two kinds, the movable (*hôpitaux ambulants*—from which came the term "ambulance") and non-movable ones (*hôpitaux fixes*). They were forgotten after the siege.[78] Temporary military hospitals were also organized, later, by Richelieu, and permanent ones by Louis XIV.[79] The care of the wounded remained, however, insufficient.

Toward the middle of the nineteenth century, public opinion was alerted to the inadequate arrangements for the wounded by the work of Florence Nightingale during the Crimean War, and later by Dunant, the founder of the Red Cross. In 1864 the Geneva Convention specified that sick and wounded soldiers should be humanely treated and cared for, whatever their nationality. The important underlying principle was that a wounded soldier was no longer an enemy with all the negative traits attributed to him as such, but an unfortunate human being.[80] By reaffirming this principle, the first Geneva Convention underlined the necessity of avoiding the attribution of guilt among the belligerents if progress in humanitarian legislation was to be achieved (see Chapter 5).

Another principle that was put forward, and which was to cause a considerable amount of controversy later on, was the "neutralization" of all involved in helping the wounded:

>...enough rays from the Napoleonic sunset remained to put

upon the French a continuing appearance of military mastery, and while the Prussian and other German armies had commendably adopted the Geneva Convention and taken it very seriously, the French had in fact taken it very lightly and made difficulties about its enlargement. The French got their come-uppance in 1870. Roles suddenly reversed. The French, who on the whole had known little about the Convention, and whose practice had considerably misused or abused it and its emblem, now became prominent in recommending its strengthening, while the Prussians and Germans, who had suffered (or at any rate felt they had suffered) a great deal both from French slackness and from outsiders' casual misunderstandings, became loud in demanding that it be put on a better footing before it was next needed. The current vogue for humanitarian good works, they complained, coupled with the lax language of the Convention (i.e., its repeated invocation of that risky word "neutrality") had fathered all kinds of bothersome problems for the high command: principally, the cool assumption by cosmopolitan do-gooders that they only needed a Red Cross label to get them the freedom of the battle zone; the prevalence of the notion that neutral "Red Cross" organizations were invited to relieve the wounded more or less where and when they chose; and the idea, which the French took to enthusiastically once they heard of it, that a minimal show of looking after some wounded and a Red Cross flag in front of the house were guaranteed to protect house owners from invaders' importunities. French and German alike had observed, with equal nausea, that advantage had been taken of the Genevan emblem by those who still pursued the immemorial occupation of robbing the wounded and dead after battle. It was understandable that the Germans should feel especially affronted by all this slackness and nastiness. The Convention needed to be tightened up, and the authority of the military unmistakably restored.[81]

Since then further progress has been made, but the concept of the "neutralization" of all involved in helping the wounded has been abandoned.

Once the armies started to make a serious effort to care for the wounded the soldier's lot improved immeasurably, but he still faced grim possibilities. Until recently, the capacity of logistic and sanitary services was such that often—for example, during the First World War—the large number of casualties coming from the battlefield to a facility immediately behind the front forced the surgeons to a brutal selectivity that was called "triage" (division in three parts), which was first instituted in the French army. The military surgeons would divide the casualties in three groups: the first consisted of the less seriously wounded who could be evacuated to the rear, the second of those who needed emergency treatment and had a chance to survive, the third of those so seriously wounded that no time would be wasted in attempting to treat them. They were put in a special tent where they were left to die.[82]

Today, death and suffering are still close to the soldier in time of war, but the agony caused by lacerated flesh is greatly reduced, epidemics have been eliminated, and, for the wounded, the chances of survival have increased very significantly.

Even though medicine was able more and more to increase his chances of survival and to moderate his suffering, the fear of annihilation was, and is, the soldier's constant companion in combat. This fear is such that man cannot tolerate it without some support, usually found in rituals that may be used only in the hour of danger:

> Do you know the old expression "There are no atheists in the foxholes"? Generally speaking, that's true. It may be a formal type of God you are praying to, or it may be a rabbit's foot, but you are praying to something. And if you are faced with a heavy mortar attack, you are praying like a madman.[83]

Organized religion, especially in the past, contributed to the relief of the soldier's anxiety concerning death and killing by assuring him that all was part of his duty and that, provided he died in a state of grace, his eternal happiness was assured. The knight made confession and took communion before combat. When individual attention became impractical because of the increased numbers, chaplains would grant collective absolutions after Mass. Among the Protestants, benediction services were held for the troops. Collective absolutions were valid only for a certain time and the soldier was expected to attend those ceremonies regularly. Military elements were interwoven with liturgy (for example, the presentation of arms at the consecration of bread and wine, the fanfare at elevation) and the religious ceremonies in the field assumed a somewhat martial aspect. Funeral services also had martial rituals some of which, like marching past with reversed arms, had been reintroduced during the Renaissance from Roman antiquity. The practice of firing volleys as a last salute came from Italy.[84]

Religious rituals still play an important role in relieving suffering and anxiety, especially when the soldier is subject to the heavy stresses of battle.

(c) Hero and Beast

Cowardice, valor, heroism, bravery, etc., are words that indicate behavioral patterns in combat. Although we can conceive of a soldier who is neither brave nor a coward, in practice we consider absence of bravery the equivalent of cowardice. When we refer to our soldiers and we want to express a positive feeling toward them we say "our brave soldiers," implying that bravery is one of their normal attributes. If we were to say "those soldiers, some of whom are brave," the utterance would be construed as meaning that those who are not brave are cowards.

The absence of bravery has a derogatory connotation because, for millennia, bravery was expected from every male of the group (or at least from every male member of the elite) and the absence of it was considered despicable. *The Iliad*, the oldest major poem of Western Civilization, is a hymn to valor in which the importance of the "heroes" is proportional to their prowess in war. *The Odyssey* has a different tone that makes it more "modern" in that, although Ulysses is a great warrior, he is especially "the man for wisdom's various arts renown'd." Combat prowess, however, remained the main virtue of the "heroes" of the Western world's epic poems, from *Beowulf* to the *Chansons de Geste*, from the *Nibelungenlied* to the Arthurian legends, until the Renaissance, when, with the *Orlando Furioso* and the *Gerusalemme Liberata*, this central and all-pervading martial spirit became less dominant.

So, for centuries, a man was a man because, if young, he was brave in combat, if old, he could recall his valorous exploits. If bravery was expected, however, heroism was not. In spite of all the blunders, the follies, the absurdities that man has committed in his long history, he seems to have been able to maintain, most of the time if not always, a certain sense of measure concerning the limits of virtue. For example, although the Roman of the Republic was expected to be honest and temperate, there was no pressure to make all citizens Catos. Similarly, during the Middle Ages religiosity was expected but not sainthood, and now we usually expect our children to be high achievers but not geniuses.

Saints, heroes, and geniuses are at the very end of the normal distribution curve that encompasses humanity, and are able to achieve what the vast majority of mortals are not only incapable but very often also unwilling to achieve. Unlike the genius, who may obtain immediate universal fame, the soldier-hero and the saint must settle for a recognition that is usually less than universal because they are, most often, considered fanatics by "the other side." Everybody agrees that Newton was a genius, but some may believe that Saint Maria Goretti held rather fanatic views about sex and morals.[85] Similarly, the kamikazes were not particularly revered and respected among the Allies during the Second World War. Even today they are considered, by many, fanatic suicides. Yet they were not.

This is a letter of one of them, Ensign Susumu Kaijitsu:

> Dear Father, Mother, brothers Hiroshi and Takeshi, and sister Eiko:
> I trust that this spring finds you all in fine health. I have never felt better and am now standing by, ready for action.

The other day I flew over our home and bade a last farewell to our neighbors and to you. Thanks to Mr. Yamakawa I had a chance recently to have a last drink with Father, and there now remains nothing but to await our call to duty.

My daily activities are quite ordinary. My greatest concern is not about death, but rather of how I can be sure of sinking an enemy carrier. Ensigns Miyazaki, Tanaka, and Kimura, who will sortie as my wingmen, are calm and composed. Their behavior gives no indication that they are momentarily awaiting orders for their final crash-dive sortie. We spend our time writing letters, playing cards, and reading.

I am confident that my comrades will lead our divine Japan to victory.

Words cannot express my gratitude to the loving parents who reared and tended me to manhood that I might in some small manner reciprocate the grace which His Imperial Majesty has bestowed upon us.

Please watch for the results of my meager effort. If they prove good, think kindly of me and consider it my good fortune to have done something that may be praiseworthy. Most important of all, do not weep for me. Though my body departs, I will return home in spirit and remain with you forever. My thoughts and best regards are with you, our friends, and neighbors. In concluding this letter, I pray for the well-being of my dear family.[86]

This is not a letter of a fanatic suicide. There is a dignity and a grandeur incompatible with mental pathology.

The following letter of Flying Petty Officer First Class Isao Matsuo of the 701st Air Group was written just before he left for a kamikaze attack. His home was in Nagasaki Prefecture:

Dear Parents:

Please congratulate me. I have been given a splendid opportunity to die. This is my last day. The destiny of our homeland hinges on the decisive battle in the seas to the south where I shall fall like a blossom from a radiant cherry tree.

I shall be a shield for His Majesty and die cleanly along with my squadron leader and other friends. I wish I could be born seven times, each time to smite the enemy.

50 MAN AND WAR

How I appreciate this chance to die like a man! I am grateful from the depth of my heart to the parents who have reared me with their constant prayers and tender love. And I am grateful as well to my squadron leader and superior officers who have looked after me as if I were their own son and given me such careful training.

Thank you, my parents, for the twenty-three years during which you have cared for me and inspired me. I hope that my present deed will in some small way repay what you have done for me. Think well of me and know that your Isao died for our country. This is my last wish, and there is nothing else that I desire.

I shall return in spirit and look forward to your visit at the Yasukuni Shrine. Please take good care of yourselves.

How glorious is the Special Attack Corps' Giretsu Unit whose "Suisei" bombers will attack the enemy. Our goal is to dive against the aircraft carriers of the enemy. Movie cameramen have been here to take our pictures. It is possible that you may see us in newsreels at the theater.

We are sixteen warriors manning the bombers. May our death be as sudden as the shattering of crystal.[87]

Again, this is not a letter of a mentally unbalanced person. Survival is perhaps the strongest of human instincts, and those who, because of their beliefs, sacrifice their life after a decision that is a result of calm deliberation indeed deserve our most profound respect, no matter if guerillas, political activists, soldiers, saints, or kamikazes.

There is a qualitative difference between heroism and bravery; in other words, great bravery does not amount to heroism. We define heroism as the sacrificing (or the endangering) of one's own life for altruistic beliefs, after calm deliberation. The crucial part of the definition is "after calm deliberation," because this is what distinguishes heroism from bravery. The soldier who throws himself on a grenade, in the heat of the battle, to save the lives of his comrades, is undoubtedly a very brave man, but is not a hero if he did not decide on his course of action calmly and deliberately. Bravery (or valor), on the other hand, is the impulse that makes the individual sacrifice or endanger his own life, on the spur of the moment, for the protection or the advantage of another individual or a group, or, in a burst of bellicosity, to inflict damage on the enemy; in heroism, the bellicose element is often less evident and the will to protect an individual or a group more prominent.

Conditio sine qua non for heroism and bravery is, of course, courage. Clausewitz distinguishes two kinds of courage in face of personal danger: one is the result of "a permanent 'condition,' " the other "is a feeling, an emotion, not a permanent state." He then states: "The first leaves the mind calmer; the second tends to stimulate, but it can also blind."[88] It is interesting to speculate that the first kind may be responsible for heroism and the second for bravery.

Clearcut examples of heroism are the typical kamikazes, while an instance of bravery is the case of the officer who, leading a company of Marines against an enemy position at Belleau Wood, is reputed to have shouted: "Come on, you sons of bitches, do you want to live forever?"[89] As is the case with all definitions, borderline instances can be found which are difficult to place in one or the other category:

> We'd returned about halfway when the Japs hit us. We all jumped for cover, but several of the men were hit. You couldn't see the Nips, so we began firing in the direction from which their fire had come.
> Then this runner of mine named Wesley Simmons started to yell:
> "Christ, there's Bernie Fetchko, lying out in the open. He is still alive!"
> It would have been suicidal to go after him, but he was a good buddy of Wes's and that's all there was to it.
> He said, "I can't leave him out there to die. The hell wth those bastards!" And with that, he took off. We gave him all the covering fire we could. He got to Fetchko, threw him over his shoulder, and started back.
> It all looked like a picture out of a Civil War book I'd had when I was a kid. This picture showed a big Union soldier carrying a wounded buddy in. The caption read, "Saving a Buddy under Fire."

Anyway, I'm sorry to say that Wes got about halfway back when he went down.

After a while the fire stopped. I guess the Japanese just took off. We went over to where Simmons and Fetchko were lying. Fetchko was dead, but Wes was still alive. He'd been badly hit, but it looked like he would make it. We got him back to our area as soon as possible...one of our hospital ships had pulled in to pick up our sick and wounded. We immediately rushed Wes out to the ship.

Then they did a baffling thing. They put Simmons in an upper rack and didn't strap him in. That night he started to thrash around and finally fell out of his sack onto the deck. We heard he was killed instantly.[90]

Either as a hero or as a very brave man, Wes was surely welcomed in the Great Hall of Valhalla even if he smote no foe and was killed by a fall from his bed.

In some cases, we cannot decide, not only between heroism and bravery, but even between heroism and fanaticism. Some time ago, for example, a man driving a truck full of explosives against the gate of an American Marine compound in Beirut blew himself up and in so doing killed 240 Marines. If the driver of the truck had decided in cold blood to sacrifice his life for the cause in which he believed, he was a hero; if, on the other hand, drunk or under the influence of drugs, or, eager to improve his lot, he gave his life with the view of procuring for himself pleasures, eternal or otherwise, he could indeed be considered a fanatic. In this case a decision cannot be reached because we do not have enough evidence.

Bravery and heroism in war are manifestations of that tendency that contributes to the unity of the group and that we call Centripetal Force, as opposed to the one that tends to cause its disintegration, the Centrifugal Force (see Chapter 8). It is therefore to be expected that episodes of heroism and bravery would be more frequent in groups with high cohesion and less frequent in others. The cumulative effect of individual acts of heroism and bravery will finally determine the martial effectiveness of the army of a given group or nation.

In the Second World War, among the major powers, we find Italy and Japan at the two ends of the scale.

As will be discussed in Chapter 8, a decrease of the Centripetal Force (and therefore an increase of the Centrifugal) is a sign of decline for a group. If bravery and heroism are manifestations of the Centripetal Force, they must decrease during periods of decline, when instances of cowardice must be more frequent and also reported and declared with little fear of disapproval. In addition, during the group's decline, bravery and martial prowess are often derided.

We have already mentioned that, in Homeric times, bravery was considered an indispensable quality for any honorable man. In the *Iliad*, the only character who is described as deserving contempt is the coward Thersites. After being beaten by Ulysses,

> Trembling he sat, and shrunk in abject fears,
> From his vile visage wiped the scalding tears.[91]

Later, when Greece was still flowering but the seeds of decadence were being sown, poets—as for example Archilochus, Alcaeus, and Anacreon—report without fear or shame, in fact with a certain complacency, their own inglorious souvenirs of war.[92] Archilochus, for example, writes: "Surely somebody now is flaunting my shield that I reluctantly abandoned behind a bush. However, I then avoided death; damned the shield, I will buy another not worse than that one."[93]

At the time of Caesar—when Rome had not yet reached the peak of her power but when, again, the seeds of decay were starting to germinate—Catullus, an avant-garde poet, had only contempt for the conqueror of Gaul and for Mamurra, his *praefectum fabrum* (that is, his commander of the Corps of Engineers), and describes them in terms so scurrilous as to be unprintable even in our era of unbounded "artistic freedom."[94]

Under Augustus, when Rome was a step closer to the end, Horace could write without restraint:

> Tecum Philippos et celerem fugam
> sensi, relicta non bene parmula.[95]

Still later, at the end of this process of decadence, Roman youths cut off their fingers to avoid military service, as mentioned previously.

Then the barbarian invasions destroyed the old world.

Civilization was laboriously rebuilt during the Middle Ages, when the valor and heroism of the knights was held in the highest honor and flight from the enemy in the deepest contempt. The Western world has now reached its zenith, and may be in the process of repeating the old pattern of decline. In Europe the spirit of bravery seems to be dead or dying, and many shields were abandoned in the fields of Vietnam, not by the American soldiers, but, more ominously, by American leaders and intellectuals.

War propaganda tries to make it easier to kill the enemy by depicting him as a monster of iniquity who, in addition, is crazy, especially when performing acts of bravery that would be considered magnificent if done by one's own side:

> The Nips...most of the time they'd blow themselves up before surrendering.
> It was this type of action that used to really concern the tankers. We knew all about the kamikaze satchel-chargers long before they had the suicide pilots. We had to be constantly on the lookout for them. They'd load themselves with dynamite and wait in some kind of spider hole. When the tanks would appear, these nuts would jump out of the ground and run against the tanks. Someone had to plug them before they reached the tanks or the Sherman and everything in it would blow sky high.[96]

At best the enemy may possess some kind of inferior cunning:

> However, don't think everything those Nips did was as stupid as that charge. They were really clever as hell. They had most of the American habits down cold and they tried to make the most of 'em.
> For instance, if you spent the night in a hole up on the lines,

you'd probably have to go to the head in the early morning. The Nips knew the Americans didn't like to crap, or even take a leak, in the same hole they were staying in. So their snipers would all be on the lookout when dawn started. It was the most dangerous goddamn time of the day.[97]

Rarely, and only in very particular circumstances, does the enemy soldier elicit admiration:

> In the Netherlands, the Dutch tell of a German soldier who was a member of an execution squad ordered to shoot innocent hostages. Suddenly he stepped out of rank and refused to participate in the execution. On the spot he was charged with treason by the officer in charge and was placed with the hostages, where he was promptly executed by his comrades.[98]

The mechanism that, in war, makes man kill and destroy so readily has been a matter of much speculation. One of the elements responsible for this phenomenon is what we call bellicosity. The dictionary defines the word as the inclination to war or fighting. Inclination, in turn, is defined as "natural disposition"; in other words, the language seems to recognize that bellicosity is one of the traits that we have inherited from our primeval ancestors. This is supported by the observation that often primitive people were extremely warlike. For example, "the Norse vision of paradise was a battlefield on which warriors struck down by the enemy were instantly restored to life so that—so great was the Vikings' enjoyment of fighting—they may at once return to the fray."[99] Although more marked among primitive barbarians (the Huns and the warriors of Genghis Khan come immediately to mind), bellicosity is still with us. Ernst Jeunger, in his diary of World War I, describing an attack, wrote:

> The great moment had come. The curtain of fire lifted from the front trenches. We stood up.
> With a mixture of feelings, evoked by bloodthirstiness, rage, and intoxication, we moved in steps, ponderously but irresistibly toward the enemy lines. I was well ahead of the company,

followed by Vinke and a one-year veteran named Haake. My right hand embraced the shaft of my pistol, my left a riding stick of bamboo cane. I was boiling with a mad rage, which had taken hold of me and all the others in an incomprehensible fashion. The overwhelming wish to kill gave wings to my feet. Rage pressed bitter tears from my eyes.

The monstrous desire for annihilation, which hovered over the battlefield, thickened the brains of the men and submerged them in a red fog. We called to each other in sobs and stammered disconnected sentences. A neutral observer might have perhaps believed that we were seized by an excess of happiness.[100]

This "monstrous desire of annihilation" brings to mind the "frenzy" that sometimes takes hold of certain animals (e.g, sharks) and makes them attack and bite, in a blind rage, everything that is moving. In war, this desire to kill is sometimes called by the officers "the will to close with the enemy":

This innocent-sounding phrase conceals the very substance of the delight in destruction slumbering in most of us. When soldiers step over the line that separates self-defense from fighting for its own sake, as it is easy for them to do, they experience something that stirs deep chords in their being. The soldier-killer is learning to serve a different deity, and his concern is with death and not life, destruction and not construction.[101]

And one of the most troubling reasons men love war is the love of destruction, the thrill of killing....As anyone who has fired a bazooka or an M-60 machine gun knows, there is something to that power in your finger, the soft, seductive touch of the trigger. It's like the magic sword, a grunt's Excalibur: all you do is move that finger so imperceptibly, just a wish flashing across your mind like a shadow, not even a full brain synapse, and "poof!" in a blast of sound and energy and light a truck or a house or even people disappear, everything flying and settling back into dust.[102]

Some have rejected the assumption that this *furor necandi* is a remnant of our ferine ancestry. Gray says:

> When man is at his destructive work, he is on a different plane from the animal altogether. And destructive urges are as capable of being found in highly cultivated natures as in the simpler ones, if not more so. The satisfaction of destroying seems to be peculiarly human, or, more exactly put, devilish in a way animals can never be. We sense in it always the Mephistophelean cry that all created things deserve to be destroyed.[103]

The argument that a given human perversity cannot be of animal origin because it is never seen in animals has the same flaw as the reasoning that carbon monoxide cannot be poisonous because it is made of carbon and oxygen, two rather innocuous substances. When we say that human capacity to torture, for example, has its roots in our animal ancestry, we mean that (disregarding possible sadistic elements) it is the result of the combination of the disregard for suffering, typical of the animal (probably due to its incapacity to identify with the victim), and intelligence, typical of man. The fact that animals do not practice torture does not prove that this perverse capability has nothing to do with our animal ancestry; it simply means that animals do not have the intelligence necessary to conceive such an atrocity. As in the case of carbon monoxide, in other words, it takes the properties of two ingredients to make the final product which may have characteristics that were not evident in the original ones.

Without implying that bellicosity necessarily means primitiveness, it would appear that, in the Western world at least, there is a rough proportionality between lack of bellicosity and the "age" of a country (see Chapter 8). By age is meant the length of time in which a country has been civilized. For example, Italy, as mentioned before, showed, during the Second World War especially, a marked lack of bellicosity. Although bellicosity is, obviously, not equivalent to bravery, it is *conditio sine qua non* for it. This has, of course, only a

58 MAN AND WAR

statistical value because episodes of bravery among Italian soldiers were not lacking, as, for example, over Malta in 1940:

> I watched them twisting and diving and trying to get on each other's tail....In a desperate effort to elude him, Keeble came down to ground level and flew under the wireless aerials to Pinella, hoping his pursuer would hit one of the cables. But the trap failed. As Keeble dipped under the aerials the Italian followed and shot him down; but he himself was so close to the ground that he hadn't time to pull out of his firing dive. The two aircraft crashed in the same field and exploded within a few yards of each other. Both men were brave pilots, and very young.[104]

As different groups seem to be endowed with various degrees of bellicosity, so are individuals. Lack of bellicosity in the individual manifests itself in various ways, sometimes by making him a conscientious objector or, if he is compelled to go to war, a soldier who may become paralyzed by fear:

> There was one young Marine who was lying flat right there on the beach. I could see he wasn't hit so I went over to see what was wrong.
> "I can't move, gunny; I just can't move," he said, "I am just too scared."
> I could see him shaking all over, almost as if he were having convulsions.
> "Come on, Marine," I said, "the fire isn't that bad. Besides, you are just as apt to get hit lying here as you are if you keep moving."
> "I know, I know, but I just can't move."
> I tried everything I could think of but he just wasn't going to budge. He wasn't necessarily a bad kid, just paralyzed with fear. It happens.[105]

During war, killing and destruction are often accompanied by cruelty. A cruelty that is sometimes so mindless that the perpetrators are reduced to the level of beasts.

Examples are not difficult to find:

Often cited is the instance of Russian soldiers who, two days after the capture of Otchakof in 1788, amused themselves by tossing children from the ramparts, while their comrades caught them below on the points of their bayonets.[106]

After the occupation of Memel in 1757, the inhabitants were tortured, hanged, and mutilated.[107] The forces that occupied Memel were also Russian, but it must be underlined that mindless cruelty is not limited to any particular nationality:

> On the evening of the Battle of Waterloo, for example, Jackson, one of Wellington's staff officers, came across some Prussians busy bayoneting French wounded near Rossomme and saved a British Light Dragoon, over whose unfamiliar uniform they were hesitating, by calling out, "Er ist eine Englander." Earlier in the day, French lancers had been seen sticking British wounded lying on the ground in front of La Haye Sante, and on another part of the battlefield British Dragoons had sabered some young and unresisting French transport drivers sitting inert on their draft-horses.[108]

And in the Second World War:

> A young German soldier lay sprawled just inside a sagging doorway, his hobnailed boots sticking into the street. Two American soldiers were resting and smoking cigarettes a few feet away, paying the body no attention. "Oh, him?" one of them said in response to a question. "Son of a bitch kept lagging behind the others when we brought them in. We got tired of hurrying him up all the time." Thus casually was deliberate murder announced by boys who a year before had taken no lives but those of squirrel or pheasant. I found that I was not shocked nor indignant; I was merely a little surprised. As weeks went by *and this experience was repeated many times* [our emphasis], I ceased even to be surprised—only, I could never again bring myself to write or speak with indignation of the Germans' violations of the "rules of warfare."[109]

The killing of a prisoner who has ceased to be a combatant, and therefore a danger to the safety of the soldier, is particu-

60 MAN AND WAR

larly repulsive—as is the killing of a civilian who also represents no threat; yet civilians and prisoners are often the victims of war. So many are the reported cases that it must be concluded that it is a common occurrence:

"...Look here, we took a lot of prisoners in those trenches yesterday morning. Just as we got into their line, an officer came out of a dugout. He'd got one hand above his head, and a pair of fieldglasses in the other. He held the glasses out to S____, ...and said, 'Here you are, sergeant, I surrender.' S____ said, 'Thank you, sir,' and took the glasses with his left hand. At the same moment, he tucked the butt of his rifle under his arm and shot the officer straight through his head. What the hell ought I to do?"

"I don't see that you can do anything," I answered slowly. "What can you do? Besides I don't see that S____'s really to blame. He must have been half mad with excitement by the time we got into that trench. I don't suppose he ever thought what he was doing. If you start a man killing, you can't turn him off like an engine. After all, he is a good man. He was probably half off his head."

"It wasn't only him. Another did exactly the same thing."

"Anyhow, it's too late to do anything now. I suppose you ought to have shot both on the spot. The best thing now is to forget it."[110]

Sometimes the deed is dictated by the necessity of war:

Still, patrolling had its peculiar risks. If a German patrol found a wounded man, they were as likely as not to cut his throat. The bowie knife was a favorite German patrol weapon because of its silence. (We inclined more to the "cosh," a loaded stick.) The most important information that a patrol could bring back was to what regiment and division the troop opposite belonged. So if it proved impossible to get a wounded enemy back without danger to oneself, he had to be stripped of his badges. To do that quickly and silently, it might be necessary first to cut his throat or beat in his skull.[111]

In his novel *The Thin Red Line*, one of the best accounts of jungle fighting in World War II, James Jones tells of another incident of "extra" killing. He describes a new army unit, its members unbloodied and without confidence in their ability to fight. After a hard march through the jungle, they came upon a Japanese position from the rear. There is a brief and savage fight. At a certain point, Japanese soldiers start trying to surrender, but some of the Americans cannot or will not stop the killing. Even after the firefight is definitely over, those Japanese who have succeeded in surrendering are brutally treated—by men, so Jones wants to suggest, who are caught up in a kind of intoxication, their inhibitions suddenly gone. The commanding officer watches all this and does nothing. "He did not want to jeopardize the new toughness of spirit that had come over the men after achieving success here. That spirit was more important than whether or not a few Jap soldiers got kicked around or killed."[112]

How are we to explain cruelty that often is not even partially justified by "necessity"? How can it be that normal, law-abiding citizens, our boys even, our good boys whom we saluted when they left for the war and of whom we were so proud, can become incredibly cruel fiends capable of killing inoffensive civilians and men who have surrendered? The question has been asked many times. Christopher Herold, concerning the storming of Jaffa by Napoleon in 1799, writes:

> Men, women, and children, Christians and Moslems, "anybody with a human face fell victim of their fury," declcares Malus, whose pages describing the sickening scene still vibrate with shock and shame.
> The behavior of victorious troops in a town taken by storm is a phenomenon to be investigated by psychiatric medicine rather than by historians. A description of the scene is unnecessary—everybody has read several such accounts, and they are all alike. One cannot help asking what transforms a group of fundamentally good-natured people—kind husbands, dutiful sons, sentimental lovers, and fathers of families—into ferocious, screaming beasts, sinking their bayonets into old men, young girls, and babies, raping daughters still locked in the arms of their dead mothers, redoubling their fury at the sound of cries of mercy....[113]

62 MAN AND WAR

Because episodes like this were very frequent, soldiers were most often judged worthy of contempt. Voltaire called them hired murderers and the scum of the nation, and Rousseau said that armies were the pest that ravaged Europe, made to oppress the neighbors or their own people.[114]

One century before, Grimmelshausen wrote of soldiers:

> For gluttony and drunkenness, hunger and thirst, wenching and dicing and playing, riot and roaring, murdering and being murdered, slaying and being slain, torturing and being tortured, harrying and being harried, robbing and being robbed, frighting and being frighted, causing trouble and suffering trouble, beating and being beaten: in a word, hurting and harming, and in turn being hurt and harmed—this was their whole life.[115]

The question of soldiers' cruelty remains, and the answer is bound to be unsatisfactory as long as we know so little about the human mind.

One of the many traits that distinguish man from animals is his capacity for identification. When we help the little old lady across the street, we are performing an act that is probably determined by many causes, but one of them is identification. We "identify" with the little old lady and her problem in crossing the street even if we are male, thirty years old, and weigh 200 pounds. In the same way, the act of killing includes an identification component. No matter how toughened by the smoke and gore of a hundred battles, even the most rugged veteran cannot avoid, to a certain extent, identifying with the enemy soldier being killed. As civilization progresses, and as man increases his distance from his pre-human ancestors, this process of identification becomes more and more pronounced, and therefore man finds it more and more difficult to kill in war. To compensate for this, because wars are still fought and therefore soldiers have to be found who are ready to kill, propaganda becomes necessary. Propaganda is in fact an attempt to destroy the process of identification and replace it with a reverse mechanism by which the enemy is identified as a subhuman monster. In other words, an attempt is made to make the soldier feel that the killing of the enemy is not the annihilation of a human being, with whom he could identify, but the elimination of a monster, an act similar to the killing of vermin. As a rule, this attempt is only partially successful and some resistance to killing remains deep in the subconscious of the soldier.

The dehumanization of the enemy encourages killing, but the conflict with the identification process remains and this, together with the continuous feeling of imminent annihilation, produces such a stress that the normal psychological pattern is likely to be disrupted, at least temporarily. In addition, if one considers that our ferine ancestors are still very near and lurking deep inside us, it is not difficult to understand how, in certain war situations, normal, law-abiding, usually peaceful citizens can become bloodthirsty fiends. If we also consider those who in civilian life were not law-abiding citizens but criminals who find in the situations produced by war an excellent opportunity to let their perversions guide their actions and, in so doing, stimulate others to act in a similar way, it becomes easier to understand some of the horrors of war. Constant contact with gore and death, a normal occurrence in the battlefield, also contributes to reducing the value of life and facilitates cruelty and slaughter.

Although the atrocities described above are, obviously, to be condemned, and propaganda must be considered an element that contributes to their perpetration, it would be simplistic to urge the elimination of this powerful war tool as a first step toward the abolition of atrocities. Cruelty and propaganda are simply parts of a whole and cannot be eliminated without abolishing the whole itself, namely war. Furthermore, if we assume that propaganda is essential in transforming a peaceful citizen into an effective fighting soldier, its elimination in a given group would simply cause subjugation of the group, which would itself then become a victim of cruelty and propaganda. In other words, the problem would not be solved but only shifted in time and space. It is evident that, as long as war continues to torment mankind, the solution does not lie in such simplistic approaches.

64 MAN AND WAR

If it is easy to find examples of cruel behavior on the part of soldiers, it is equally easy to find instances of nobility and humanity. Several such instances have been mentioned in this book. It is also interesting to note that, occasionally, the soldier has been exalted with the most absurd hyperbole—sometimes by professionals who should have known better. General MacArthur, confirming the death sentence imposed on General Yamashita (see Chapter 6), wrote:

> The soldier, be he friend or foe, is charged with the protection of the weak and unarmed. It is the very essence and reason for his being. When he violates this sacred trust, he not only profanes his entire cult but threatens the very fabric of international society.[116]

At the end of this rapid sketch of the soldier, we may attempt to answer the question "who is the soldier?" It would appear that the answer is not dramatic or unexpected; it is in fact rather banal: the soldier is man. If he is man, he is not a monster, or a moron full of lust to kill, or a being with a limited, criminal mind, or, as General MacArthur so naively thought, a knight in shining armor dedicated to the protection of the weak and the oppressed, or a liberator, or an oppressor, or a hero, or a coward, or a killer, or a patriot. Being man he is all that.

Albrecht Dürer — *The Four Riders of the Apocalypse*

Chapter 3

> ...guerra...una arte mediante la quale gli uomini d'ogni tempo non possono vivere onestamente...[1]
>
> Machiavelli,
> *Dell' Arte della Guerra*, I

> A peste fame et bello libera nos Domine.[2]
>
> *Litany of the Saints*

WAR, FAMINE, AND PESTILENCE

(a) *A peste...*

Pestilence, famine, and war, three of the Horsemen of the Apocalypse, have tormented humanity for millennia. They have caused deaths innumerable, they have changed the course of history, they have been responsible for social disruptions the magnitude of which we cannot assess. To get an idea of the ravages they have wrought, lacking other data, we must rely on the writings of ancient authors who were often not very rigorous.

Some of the epidemics of antiquity are reported in the Bible. In Exodus is mentioned the plague of Egypt of 1500 B.C., and in Samuel I we find another account of the plague that followed the capture of the Ark by the Philistines. In the classical world, several major pestilences were recorded. Athens was stricken, in the 5th century B.C., by the great epidemic described by Thucydides, in which Pericles died. The disruption of the social fabric of the city became profound when fear of punishment, the old keeper of discipline and order, seemed to have disappeared:

> Athenian life was completely demoralized, and a spirit of extreme lawlessness resulted....As Thucydides expresses it: "They saw how sudden was the change of fortune in the case both of those who were prosperous and suddenly died, and those who had nothing but, in a moment, were in possession of the property of others." There was no fear of the laws of God or man.[3]

Shortly after, in 396 B.C., another epidemic attacked the Carthaginians besieging Syracuse and the mortality was so high that the siege had to be raised. Pestilences of varying intensity continued to occur. Some were localized, like the one that attacked the Roman and Carthaginian armies again at Syracuse in 212 B.C., the severe disease—possibly malaria—that appeared in the agricultural district around Rome in the first century B.C., and the epidemics in the reign of Nero and in the year 79 A.D. shortly after the eruption of Vesuvius. Others were more widespread and devastating, like the "Plague of Antoninus" (or of Galen), which started in the East among the soldiers of Varus in 165 A.D. and spread to the whole Empire. Marcus Aurelius contracted the disease while campaigning against the Marcomanni, and it is said that, recognizing the contagiousness of it, he refused to see his son before his death in Vienna in 180 A.D.[4,5] The plague of Cyprian in 250 A.D. (so called because it was described among others, by Saint Cyprian, Bishop of Carthage) spread over the entire known world; Hieronimus wrote that the human race was almost destroyed and that the earth was returning to a state of desert and forests.[6] The great plague of Justinian started about 540 A.D., and was perhaps the most devastating epidemic of the ancient world; it has been reported that at one time there were 10,000 deaths per day in Constantinople alone.[7] A considerable part of the known world was devastated.

In the Middle Ages, epidemics of various kinds affected the Crusaders, but the disease, or diseases, seemed, for a while, to be confined to the Middle East; then, from 1346 to 1361, the Black Death swept Europe and killed an estimated 24 million people—about a quarter of the European population.

> The devastation was terrible...crews were entirely wiped out, so that many ships drifted unmanned and helpless about the Mediterranean and North Seas. In southern France mortality was so great that the Pope consecrated the River Rhone at Avignon, so that corpses flung into the river might be considered to have received Christian burial.[8]

The last great pestilence that ravaged Europe was in the wake of the Thirty Years War and its horrors are described in Manzoni's *I Promessi Sposi* (The Betrothed). Epidemics have not, however, abandoned man, smaller ones having been reported up to our own time, but antibiotics and a better knowledge of their pathogenesis make it unlikely that the great ones of the past will occur again. Figures concerning total casualties are unreliable, but they were probably of the same order of magnitude as those caused by war.

The role of war in the development of pestilence was of primary importance. The devastations of warfare caused famine and, consequently, epidemics due to the unchecked spreading of diseases in starving bodies devoid of resistance; in addition, by moving and mixing large numbers of men over large areas, war caused primitive self-contained communities to come in contact with new pathogens for which they lacked acquired resistance. In the absence of war, therefore, epidemics would have been rarer and possibly less violent.

(b) ...*fame*...

Famines have been chronicled since antiquity, but many remain unknown to us. A large number were unrecorded because they took place in remote areas or because the evidence of their occurrence was lost; in addition, the number of those accounted for is imprecise and unreliable because available lists do not include all those that have been known to occur. For example, a list of world famines up to 1940, considered fairly complete, mentions a total of 370, but it was found that 62, none of them included in the list, took place in the Hupei Province in China between 1644 and 1911. In addition, a study made at the University of Nanking reported 1,828 famines in China between 108 B.C. and 1911.[9]

The first written record of mass starvation (circa 3500 B.C.) was found carved on the "stele of famine" in the tomb of an early Pharaoh on the island of Sahal near the first cataract of the Nile. The text is a poignant document of suffering and sorrow:

> I am mourning on my high throne for the vast misfortune, because the Nile flood in my time has not come for seven years. Light is the grain; there is a lack of crops and of all kinds of food. Each man has become a thief to his neighbor. They desire to hasten and cannot walk. The child cries, the youth creeps along, and the old man; their souls are bowed down, their legs are bent together and drag along the ground, and their hands rest in their bosoms. The counsel of the great ones in the court is but emptiness. Torn open are the chests of provisions, but instead of contents there is air. Everything is exhausted.[10]

Since then, famines have been recorded at relatively short intervals all over the world. Natural factors were commonly responsible, although often war produced the devastation that caused the famine.

The Bible mentions ten famines, and famines are recorded in the writings and legends of most of the other major world religions. In more recent times, many have been reported. The most serious were: 1333-37 in China, 4,000,000 died; 1600 in Russia, 500,000 died; 1769 in France, 5 per cent of the population said to have died; 1769-70 in India, estimates of deaths range from 3,000,000 to 10,000,000; 1770 in Eastern Europe, about 200,000 died; 1876-79 in China, cannibalism reported, estimated deaths 9,000,000 to 13,000,000; 1932-34 in Russia, 5,000,000 died.[11]

In our days, man's folly has caused one of the most devastating famines. The Government of China has conceded that in the period between 1959 and 1962, during the famine that followed Mao Tse-Tung's "Great Leap Forward," more than 10 million people died. Some experts estimate that the number of victims may have been much higher, between 27 and 30 million.[12]

It must be underlined that even the famines that are not the direct result of military conflict are often caused by efforts to acquire the economic and military strength needed in case of war. The famine resulting from the "Great Leap Forward" is a case in point. Another example is the famine of 1257-1259 in England, when the kingdom had been exhausted by the taxes levied by the king (Henry III) to pay German troops to support his brother, who was a candidate for the imperial crown of the Holy Roman Empire.[13]

It would appear that, although the figures are far from precise, we may assume that the number of casualties resulting from mass starvation throughout history are of the same order of magnitude as those caused by pestilence and war. Man, however, has overcome plague and famine. As antibiotics and medical progress now offer the possibility of avoiding great epidemics, modern communications and large-scale international assistance may avoid the repetition of the great famines of the past. India, for example, avoided widespread starvation of its people in 1966-67 by importing large quantities of grain. The Second and the Third Horsemen may have been tamed by civilization; the First is still raging.

(c) ...*et bello*...

By necessity, little is known about the incidence and characteristics of war in prehistoric times. We may assume that violent conflict was common from the beginning, since we know that it has been a more or less constant activity of man since history began to be recorded.

If, in modern times, war means an act of violence intended to compel our opponent to fulfill our will,[14] in antiquity it simply meant slaughter and destruction:

> The Assyrians, the Phoenicians, and the Egyptians were given to treachery, inhuman passion, destruction of every thing and every living being in their way, whether or not the victims took part in the wars against them. Ptolemy Lathyrus [as reported by Josephus], for example, overran the territory of Judea, strangled Jewish women and children, and boiled them in cauldrons, thus securing for his country a reputation for cannibalism.
> Among the Hebrews there was a time of similar practice of indiscriminate slaughter, and seizure of land, which were considered to be by divine decree destined for the favored conquerors. Their deeds of blood were conceived to be a religious duty toward God, a fulfillment of the divine judgement....But from time to time they manifested conspicuous moderation and even remarkable generosity....Similarly in ancient China extreme cruelty and brutality obtained; but occasionally there were likewise prominent instances of mercy and generosity....As to the Hindus, the code of Manu established striking relaxations. The Hindu warrior was forbidden to use poisoned arrows, to put to death the suppliant, the enemy who surrenders as a prisoner, disarmed or defenseless persons, laborers in the field, or to devastate plantation and land under cultivation. These rules, however, were—to judge from the native epics and narratives of warlike operations—frequently violated. Besides, they were held to apply only to kindred races, and not to the "barbar-

ian" aliens....Persia is an example of constant devotion to pillage, destruction, and massacre. Herodotus relates that when Darius took Babylon he not only demolished the walls, and bore away all the gates, but he impaled some three thousand of the most distinguished inhabitants....After the defeat of the Emporer Valerian at Edessa, A.D. 260, Sapor overran Syria, Cilicia, and Cappadocia, and ordered a general massacre at Caesarea. Roman prisoners were subjected to every form of relentless cruelty. "We are told," writes Gibbon, "that Valerian, in chains, but invested with the imperial purple, was exposed to the multitude, a constant spectacle of fallen greatness; and that whenever the Persian monarch mounted on horseback, he placed his foot on the neck of a Roman emperor.... When Valerian sunk under the weight of shame and grief, his skin, stuffed with straw, and formed into the likeness of a human figure, was preserved for ages in the most celebrated temple in Persia." Probably this report, as Gibbon points out, is based on fictitious stories; though the act in question was certainly in keeping with the general war practices of the Persians. Still later, in A.D. 359, a Persian monarch crucified Roman captives, treacherously seized Arsaces, the Armenian king, blinded and tortured him.

The Macedonians were no exception to the rule. Alexander's wars form a narrative of pillage and conflagration, putting to death prisoners, women, and children, and the sick. As Plutarch says, he considered war a distraction or pastime....The Carthaginians' war practices were likewise characterized by unremitting ferocity and inhumanity. The *crudelitas* of Hannibal was a byword with the Romans. Livy says (no doubt with some exaggeration) that his soldiers, who were savage and ferocious by nature, were made still more so by their general's orders to form bridges and works with heaps of human bodies, and by his teaching them to live on human flesh....[In Homeric times] hostilities for the most part assumed the form of indiscriminate brigandage, and were but rarely conducted with a view to achieving regular conquests, and extending the territory of the victorious community. Extermination, rather than subjection of the enemy, was the usual practice. After Troy was taken, the Greeks did not think of taking possession of Priam's kingdom; the town was simply destroyed, the inhabitants enslaved or put to death, and an imprecation pronounced on the

74 MAN AND WAR

very soil that had belonged to the victims. Sometimes prisoners were sacrificed to the gods, corpses mutilated, and mercy refused to children, and to the old and sickly.[15]

Not that cruelty and destruction in war was limited to the ancient world, of course:

A contemporary wrote in 1741, after Frederick's passage through Moravia: "Never since the Goths has war been waged in such a fashion as this." In 1744 the Austrians advanced to the frontiers of Lorraine and called on the inhabitants to submit; those who resisted, they proclaimed, would be hanged, "after being forced to cut off their own noses and ears." The Seven Years War surpassed all previous wars in atrocity. The Count of St. Germain wrote in 1757: "The countryside for thirty leagues around is sacked and ruined as though a fire had raged through it." "We are surrounded by hanging corpses," wrote another witness, "and the soldiers do not hesitate to massacre women and children as well if they resist the ransacking of their houses." Frederick sometimes enrolled prisoners in his own army, and if this was their lot they were lucky—for at other times, as at Crefeld, all who laid down their arms were massacred. The ferocity of Russians and Prussians towards each other was terrible. The Russians occupied Memel in 1757, enrolled all the garrison and deported the townspeople. "Nothing like it has been seen since the invasion of the Huns. Inhabitants were hanged after their noses and ears had been cut off, their legs torn off, their hearts and entrails cut out." In the following year at Kustrin the Prussians took their revenge. "The Russians," Frederick relates, "lost two thousand prisoners and at least fifteen thousand men they had left there, for the soldiers gave no quarter." In 1788 Prince Potemkin laid siege to the Turkish town of Otchakof for six months. He was a courtier and a man of highest refinement. He prided himself on his literary tastes and feeling. "The cruelties of the Spaniards in the New World and of the English in the Indies," wrote a Russian, "are nothing in comparison with our military philosopher, who is busy translating Rousseau's *Héloise* and in putting to death all those who have valuables to tempt his greed." On December 16th the assault was launched. Of twenty thousand Turks who defended the place ten thousand were killed. The town was put to the sack, the pillage went on for three days and more than six thousand inhabitants were slaughtered. "The fury of the Russian soldiers was such," says Segur, "that two days after the assault, when they found Turkish children hidden in forts and underground refuges, they seized them, threw them in the air, caught them on the points of their bayonets, and cried, 'These anyhow will never do harm to Christians!' "[16]

We have already mentioned other examples of war atrocities in modern times (Chapter 2).

Besides atrocities, another characteristic of war is the progress of its techniques. Man, in contrast to animals, has "the gleam of heavenly light which...he calls reason...."[17] Therefore, he also has the capacity of devising better ways of killing and destroying. For this reason, the way war is fought undergoes periodic changes. The Hyksos introduced the war horse into Egypt and overran it, and the Roman legion, a formation more flexible than the Greek phalanx, conquered the world. In the Middle Ages the art of war continued to be refined:

> About the eighth century...important technical innovations entered the European style of making war....The most important one was the introduction of the stirrup. Simple though it is, it invests the rider with vastly improved control over his mount, allowing him to charge in armor against the enemy, bearing a lance which the horse's speed endows with great shock force. Hitherto cavalry had never played more than an ancillary role in warfare; thereafter it became for eight hundred years the dominant arm, to be opposed only by infantry either foolhardy—like Harold's axemen at Hastings—or with a remarkable mastery of their weapons and belief in each other. The English archers at Agincourt possessed that mastery over a weapon which local art had brought to the highest possible level of its development.
>
> But Agincourt was an isolated check to the unbroken run of cavalry superiority which was to be ended only by a genuine technological revolution ushered in by gunpowder. Its influ-

ence was slow to make itself felt. Primitive cannons appeared on the battlefield as early as the fourteenth century; Edward III of England had some at Crécy in 1346. But, though developed by the end of the fifteenth century to the point where they nullified the value of traditional fortifications, it would be another century before reliable small arms would break the tactical dominance of the horseman....[18]

Man's capacity for killing continued to increase with gunpowder, with mechanized war, and finally—a jump of many orders of magnitude—with nuclear weapons. It is interesting to note, however, that in the past the number of deaths in the battlefield did not seem to increase with the evolution of new weapons and techniques:

Hannibal started across the Alps in 218 B.C. with 100,000 infantry and 12,000 cavalry and had only 20,000 infantry and 6,000 cavalry when he reached Italy. In his victory at Lake Thrasymene (217 B.C.), 13,000 Romans were destroyed and 10,000 taken prisoner....At Cannae (216 B.C.) the Romans suffered the staggering loss of 60,000 killed and 10,000 taken prisoner, out of an army of 85,000. Hasdrubal lost 56,000 out of 60,000 at Metaurus (207 B.C.) and Hannibal 20,000 killed and 20,000 prisoners out of 50,000 at Zama (202 B.C.).... In 102, Marius destroyed 200,000 Teutons at Aquae Sextiae and took 80,000 prisoners; in 101, 130,000 out of 150,000 Cimbri were killed.[19]

Josephus reports that at the destruction of Jerusalem, in 70 A.D., 1,100,000 were slain. The losses among the northern barbarians invading the Roman Empire were very large; Attila, for example, is said to have lost 160,000 to 300,000 out of a horde of 700,000 when defeated by Aetius in 451.[20]

At Fontenay (841) 100,000 Franks were killed. The Hungarians, defeated by Henry I at Merseburg in 933, lost 80,000. When Rudolf of Hapsburg defeated the Bohemian King Ottokar in 1278, some 14,000 were slain....At Crécy (1346) the losses were 2,500 nobles, 4,000 horsemen, and 30,000 soldiers....[21]

In the Middle Ages, figures of battle casualties were usually exaggerated and the numbers reported must be considered approximations in excess. Later figures start to be more reliable and are often smaller—in part, no doubt, because of the more modest size of the armies involved.

At St. Jakob de Birs (1444) 1,300...Swiss Confederates were killed and 200 wounded, while the Armagnacs lost 2,200 killed and 400 wounded. At Grandson (1476) 14,000 Burgundians were killed, while the Swiss lost 500 and many wounded. At Frastenz (1499) 3,000 Swabians were killed and 1,300 drowned....In the Italian campaign of 1500-29 1,500 Swiss were killed and 1,500 wounded at Novara (1513) out of an army of 5,000, while 8,000 of the enemy were slain; at Marignano (1515) the Swiss army of 24,000 lost 6-7,000 killed, and 1,500 wounded, the French about the same number. At Pavia (1524) the Swiss lost 6,000.[22]

The figures mentioned above (chosen at random among those of innumerable battles) indeed suggest that the battles of our time may not be as bloody as those of the past in spite of the increased efficiency of weapons; the point, however, is emphasized if we express casualties in percentage of the total number of soldiers in a given battle: at Cannes (216 B.C.) about 70% of the Roman army was wiped out; Hasdrubal, at Metaurus (207 B.C.), lost 93% of his soldiers; at Zama (202 B.C.) Hannibal lost 40%; Attila, on the Catalaunian plains (451 A.D.), lost about 35%; the Swiss, at Novara (1513), lost 30% and at Marignano (1515) 27%; at Waterloo (1815) the English lost 22%; at Gettysburg (1863) 8.5% of the Union Army was destroyed in three days—that is to say, about 3% for each day of battle. In 1918 in the battle of the Meuse-Argonne, the American Army lost 2.5% in forty-seven days, that is to say, about 0.05% per day.[23]

At the decisive battle of Qadisiyya, A.D. 636, in which the Persians suffered a great setback, the victorious Moslems lost seven thousand five hundred dead, although the battle lasted four days only. The number of Moslem participants was thirty-eight thousand. This means that one out of every five Moslem soldiers was killed in that particular battle in which they emerged victorious. To understand how great a loss this twenty per cent was, it is helpful to remember that American losses in the Second World War were about ten per thousand or one-twentieth the amount per thousand which the Moslems lost at Qadisiyya...

...On July 22, 1954, the United States Department of Defense announced that the number of Korean losses in American lives was 23,345 dead, or just slightly above the losses in the battle of the Camel [between Ali and the party disputing his election to the Caliphate] thirteen centuries ago, which lasted one day. On July 6, 1946, Prime Minister Attlee informed Parliament that 357,116 British were killed in the Second World War. This is just five times the number of those killed at the minor battle of Siffin which lasted for ten days.[24]

The casualty figures considered above refer to battles. However, to get an idea of the extent of the carnage caused by warfare, we must consider the number of deaths caused by some of the main wars.

When Carthage was destroyed in 146 B.C., the city of 700,000 inhabitants had been reduced to 50,000 by the Punic Wars.[25] It has been estimated that Caesar's campaigns caused the death of 3,000,000.[26] According to Procopius the wars between the Ostrogoths and Byzantines caused the destruction of over 15,000,000 men.[27] The Crusades caused the death of 3,000,000 (2,000,000 Europeans) in 194 years.[28] In more recent times, the Thirty Years War accounted for about 7,000,000 dead,[29] while Napoleon's campaigns between 1801 and 1805 caused the death of about 6,000,000 French and Allied soldiers.[30]

In the Franco-German War of 1870-71, more than 20,000 Germans were killed and 89,000 French lost their lives.[31] The First World War caused 12,000,000 deaths directly related to the conflict and another 12,000,000 died of "indirect" causes.[32] The Second World War caused 15,000,000 deaths among the soldiers alone.[33]

Although the nineteenth century was a relatively peaceful

one for Europeans and, in that period, only 15 million died in war,[34] it has been estimated that in the last few centuries, in Europe, there has been an average of 40 million deaths per century due to warfare.[35] An awesome figure that, however, indicates a decline in the percentage of war deaths in view of the steady increase in population.

It is of interest that the number of soldiers engaged in battle, in relation to the total population, has increased in Europe since the Middle Ages. In France, for example, the great battles of the Hundred Years War were fought by a few thousand soldiers while the population of the country was a little less than 20 million. At the time of Louis XIV, while the population had reached about 23 million, the French Army had 300 thousand soldiers. The French Revolution and Napoleon brought an army of more than a million out of a population of 25 million, and during the First World War, the French army was almost 4 million while the population of France was 40 million.[36]

Even if we consider the previously mentioned casualty figures approximated in excess, it is evident that, over the centuries, war has caused death and suffering of a staggering magnitude. We do not know which one of the Three Horsemen (pestilence, famine, and war) can claim the largest number of victims but, considering that pestilence often followed famine and that famine often resulted from the devastation of war, we may give the palm to war. In the last two centuries, pestilence and famine seem to have lost some of their violence, but until now we have continued to kill each other with unabated fury. However, the decline of war deaths as a percentage of the number of combatants and population may perhaps suggest that, over the centuries, man is slowly getting ready to satisfy his need for survival by means other than war.

Goya — *Bitter Presence* (From Los Desastres De La Guerra)

Chapter 4

> Perché, intra le altre cagioni che ti
> arreca di male lo essere disarmato, ti fa
> contennendo.[1]
>
> Machiavelli,
> *Il Principe*, 14.

PRISONERS AND MILITARY OCCUPATION

(a) The Prisoner

The prisoner of war is a disarmed soldier in the hands of the enemy. A disarmed soldier is not a civilian, is not a neutral, and is not a belligerent; he is an entity that was previously a source of danger, is still potentially dangerous, and, being the property of the victor, is to be either eliminated or changed into something innocuous and useful such as a work animal. This was how the prisoner was perceived from antiquity until

82 MAN AND WAR

relatively recent times. Usually, therefore, the defeated soldier was killed or sold as a slave. As a slave, he was sometimes branded like cattle: the Samians marked the foreheads of Athenian prisoners with the figure of an owl while the Athenians branded the Samians with the figure of a vessel; the Syracusans stamped Athenian prisoners with the image of a horse, while Ptolemy IV Philopator used the brand of an ivy on Alexandrian Jews and Theban prisoners were branded by the Persians with the royal mark.[2]

Examples of killing or selling prisoners are abundant among the ancient Greeks. In 476 B.C., the Athenians took Eion and sold the inhabitants into slavery; in 427 B.C., after taking Notium, they killed all the Arcadians they found there; and a similar fate befell the people of Melos in 416 B.C. The Spartans put to death all the male prisoners taken after the surrender of Platea and all the women were reduced to slavery.[3]

The Roman penchant for legalism distinguished two categories of prisoners, those who surrendered voluntarily and those who were vanquished in battle. Enemies who surrendered at discretion and delivered to their conquerors their persons, their territories, and all other possessions were designated *dediticii*, or *peregrini dediticii*. They were assigned to the class of freemen (*libertini*), but although enjoying a certain degree of civic freedom, they could not acquire Roman citizenship. They were prohibited from residing in Rome or within a hundred miles of Rome and those who disobeyed this provision were sold, together with their goods, and were to be held in servitude beyond the hundred milestone without possibility of emancipation.[4] Horace[5] advised against killing a prisoner if he could be sold—"vendere cum possis captivum, occidere noli"—although this may reflect convenience rather than a moral principle.

As for the vanquished enemy, Flavius Josephus so describes the capture of Jotapata:

> ...the Romans...spared none, nor pitied any, but drove the people down the precipice from the citadel, and slew them as

they drove them down....And on this day it was that the Romans slew all the multitude that appeared openly; but on the following days they searched the hiding places and fell upon these that were underground, and in the caverns, and went thus through every age, excepting the infants and the women....And thus was Jotapata taken....[6]

If the prisoner was treated ruthlessly by the enemy, he was not treated much better by his own side. As far as his country was concerned, a disarmed soldier was a contradiction in terms, something that was not intended to be, something to be forgotten as dishonorable and almost monstrous.

This attitude is illustrated in Horace's ode about Regulus, the 5th of Book III. In 53 B.C., the army of Crassus had been defeated by the Parthians at Carrhae and about ten thousand Romans were taken prisoners. At the time of Augustus, about thirty years later, when the ode was written, the shame of the defeat was still felt so keenly that the prince was planning an expedition to avenge it—which, however, never materialized. In the meantime, in Rome, many had been pressing for negotiations for the release of those prisoners. Augustus was opposed to the idea and probably encouraged Horace to write against it. The poet chose an episode that had taken place more than two hundred years earlier, during the First Punic War (264-241 B.C.), when Atilius Regulus, the commander of the Roman army in Africa, was defeated and captured by the Carthaginians. Later, as the war turned in favor of the Romans, he was sent to Rome to present the Senate with proposals for peace and a prisoner exchange. He was made to promise that he would return to Carthage as a prisoner if unable to convince his compatriots to accept the proposals. Regulus exhorted the Roman government to reject the Carthaginian proposal, and, in spite of the knowledge of what would happen to him, returned to Carthage, where he was tortured to death. The episode, although of dubious historical veracity, has been used as an example of Roman fortitude through the centuries.

Of interest are the arguments used against the exchange of prisoners:

Hoc caverat mens provida Reguli
dissentientis conditionibus
   foedis et exemplo trahentis
      pernicem veniens in aevum,

si non periret immiserabilis
captiva pubes. "Signa ego Punicis
   adfixa delubris et arma
      militibus sine caede" dixit,

"derepta vidi; vidi ego civium
retorta tergo bracchia libero
   portasque non clausas et arva
      Marte coli populata nostro

Auro repenso scilicet acrior
miles redibit! Flagitio additis
   damnum: neque amissos colores
      lana refert medicata fuco,

nec vera virtus, cum semel excidit
curat reponi deterioribus.
   ....
      ....erit ille fortis

qui perfidis se credidit hostibus,
et Marte Poenos proteret altero,
   qui lora restrictis lacertis
      sensit iners timuitque mortem.

Hic, unde vitam sumeret inscius,
pacem duello miscuit....[7]

The return of Regulus to Carthage after his mission, although an example of moral fortitude, was expected from all Roman citizens in similar circumstances. Aulus Gellius reports that, after the battle of Cannes, Hannibal sent ten prisoners to Rome to arrange an exchange. Before they departed, they took an oath to return to the Carthaginian camp if the exchange were not to take place. When the senate rejected the offer, the parents, relatives, and friends of the ten messengers tried to convince them not to return to captivity. Eight, faithful to their oath, went back; the other two, however, remained in Rome, asserting they had already fulfilled their obligation. After they had left the enemy's camp, they said, they had returned on the same day on the pretext that they had forgotten something, but in reality to satisfy the terms of their engagement in that manner. This, however, was considered so base that they were despised by all and branded by the censors. Finally, their lives became so unbearable that they committed suicide.[8] This respect for an oath extracted by the enemy under duress was probably due not only to the respect that the Romans had for oaths in general but also to the contempt felt for the soldier who chose to surrender instead of fighting to the end.

If the drive for war is one side's longing for survival (obviously at the expense of the other), one can easily understand why the lot of the prisoner, as a conquered member of the other group, was so grim. On the other hand, another force in the subconscious of man was working in favor of the prisoner: identification with the victim. The thought that among those young men waiting to be killed or sold there could one day be a brother, a son, or oneself must often have presented itself to the mind of those involved. For this reason, and also because on occasion mercy proved expedient, exceptions were not uncommon.

Sometimes prisoners taken in war could be ransomed, and the practice was already frequent in Homeric times: at the beginning of the *Iliad*, Chryses, a priest of Apollo, succeeds in ransoming his daughter from Agamemnon; in the sixth book, in the famous episode of Hector and Andromache at the Scaean Gate, Andromache mentions that her mother was admitted to ransom by Achilles.

Cases are not wanting where captives were dismissed on parole, to give them an opportunity of finding ransomers. In Athens there was a law that the ransomed prisoner should reimburse his ransomer or become his slave; similar provisions existed in Crete and in Rome. Sometimes prisoners were exchanged: after the Athenians defeated the Peloponnesian fleet, in 429 B.C., they exchanged prisoners man for man; in 422 B.C. Cleon conquered Torone and exchanged prisoners with the Olynthians.[9] When Scipio conquered Carthagena in 209 B.C., he made all the inhabitants of the city prisoners of war but liberated the free-born citizens, and even promised freedom to the skilled slaves at the end of the war.[10] On several occasions Caesar liberated his prisoners on the condition that they not take up arms again. A humane attitude toward captives is also expressed by Seneca in the dialogue between Pyrrhus and Agamemnon in *Troades*; Pyrrhus says: "Lex nulla capto parcit aut poenam impedit,"[11] and Agamemnon replies: "Quod non vetat lex, hoc vetat fieri pudor."[12] There are numerous examples of prisoners of war being admitted to ransom by their Roman captors, and after the great Carthaginian victory at Cannes Hannibal permitted the Roman prisoners to ransom themselves.[13]

These were exceptions. The fate of war captives, in remote antiquity, was usually death or worse. Eventually the exceptions, however, became more and more frequent, to the point that toward the end of the Middle Ages, at least in Europe, the custom of allowing prisoners who could afford to pay the ransom to return home was quite common. In the seventeenth century, officers of equal rank were exchanged and allowed to live freely on parole while negotiations were completed. Sometimes whole captured armies might be released for repatriation.[14] Instances of inhuman treatment of prisoners, however, continued to abound. Some acts of cruelty were committed to extort information. During the Thirty Years War, one of the most horrible and usually fatal tortures employed for this purpose was the "Swedish drink"—the forcible filling of mouth and stomach with waste products of human and animal origin.[15] Other occurrences were undoubtedly the result of sadism. Ambroise Paré reports the following episode:

> Afterward the Spanish soldiers entered by the breach without any resistance, our men thinking that they would hold their

Prisoners and Military Occupation 87

faith and agreement, that they should have their lives saved. They entered in a great fury to kill all, to plunder and to sack. They retained some men, hoping to have ransom from them; they tied them by their genitalia with their arquebus cords, which were thrown over a pike that two held on their shoulders; then they would pull the cord, with great violence and derision, as if they had wished to sound a chime, telling them that they must put themselves to ransom, and to tell to what houses (family) they were; and if they saw they would have no profit from them, they killed them cruelly in their hands, or soon after their genitalia would have fallen into a gangrene and total mortification. But they killed them all with their daggers and cut their throats.[16]

As late as the seventeenth century, some commanders were reluctant to keep prisoners alive if they "threatened to become a burden or even a danger to the rearguard troops, above all when supplies were low."[17]

By the eighteenth century, prisoners were not usually killed, although examples of massacres can still be found. Here is what Citizen Peyrusse wrote concerning the killing of the prisoners at Jaffa by Napoleon (1799):

> That, in a city taken by storm, the infuriated troops should loot, burn, and kill whatever comes their way is something demanded by the laws of war, and humanity covers these horrors with a veil. But that, two or three days after the attack, when passions have calmed down, one should order, in cold-blooded savagery, the murder of 3,000 men who have surrendered to us in good faith! Posterity no doubt will pass judgment on this atrocity, and those who ordered it will find their place among the butchers of humanity.
>
> About 3,000 men put down their arms and were instantly led to our camp. By order of the commander-in-chief, the Egyptians, Moroccans, and Turks were separated.
>
> The next morning, all the Moroccans were taken to the seashore, and two battalions began to shoot them down. Their only hope of saving their lives was to throw themselves into the sea; they did not hesitate, and all tried to escape by swimming. They were shot at leisure, and in an instant the sea was red

with blood and covered with corpses. A few were lucky enough to reach some rocks. Soldiers were ordered to follow them in boats and to finish them off....Once this execution was over, we fondly hoped that this would not be repeated and that the other prisoners would be spared...Our hopes were soon disappointed, when, the next day, 1,200 Turkish artillerymen, who for two days had been kept without food in front of General Bonaparte's tent, were taken to be executed. The soldiers had been carefully instructed not to waste ammunition, and they were ferocious enough to stab them with their bayonets. Among the victims, we found many children who, in the act of death, had clung to their fathers....[18]

Often, especially in antiquity, when the fate of prisoners was known, many soldiers (and civilians) preferred death to capture:

And David said unto the young man that told him, How knowest thou that Saul and Jonathan his son is dead? And the young man that told him said, As I happened by chance upon Mount Gilboa, behold, Saul leaned upon his spear; and lo, the chariots and horsemen followed hard after him. And then he looked behind him, he saw me, and called unto me. And I answered, Here am I. And he said unto me, Who art thou? And I answered him, I am an Amalekite. He said unto me again, Stand, I pray thee, upon me, and slay me: for anguish is come upon me, because my life is yet whole in me. So I stood upon him, and slew him, because I was sure that he could not live after that he was fallen....[19]

Flavius Josephus described the famous mass suicide at Masada:

Nor was there at length any one of these men found that scrupled to act their part in this terrible execution, but every one of them dispatched his dearest relations. Miserable men, indeed, were they! whose distress forced them to slay their own wives and children with their own hands, as the lightest of those evils that were before them....They then chose ten men by lot out of them, to slay all the rest; every one of whom laid himself down by his wife and children on the ground, and threw his arms about them, and they offered their necks to the stroke of those who by lot executed that melancholy office; and when these ten had, without fear, slain them all, they made the same rule for casting lots for themselves, that he whose lot it was should first kill the other nine, and after all should kill himself. Accordingly, all these had courage sufficient to be no way behind one another in doing or suffering; so, for a conclusion, the nine offered their necks to the executioner, and he who was the last of all took a view of all other bodies, lest perchance some or other among so many that were slain should want his assistance to be quite dispatched, and when he perceived that they were all slain, he set fire to the palace, and with the great force of his hand ran his sword entirely through himself, and fell down dead near to his own relations. So these people died with this intention, that they would leave not so much as one soul among them all alive to be subject to the Romans.[20]

Examples can be found in the Middle Ages. In February 1220, Bukhara surrendered to Genghis Khan. An orgy in the great mosque, where he and the chiefs had assembled, ensued; in the meantime

> ...the civil population had been ordered to assemble outside the walls to enable the conquerors to plunder the city unhindered. Orders were then given for the distribution of the people as slaves to various Mongol units. Most of the women were raped but a number of Muslims succeeded in killing their wives and daughters and themselves to escape such fate. The city was then set on fire. Tens of thousands of people were massacred and their bodies left unburied.[21]

Examples are also easy to find in modern times. The following refers to episodes of the First Opium War of 1839-42. It occurs after British forces have attacked and conquered the city of Chin-kiang-foo:

> All the work inside the city seemed over for the day, when a heavy volley, followed by considerable popping of musketry, was heard, which turned out to be the last volley of the unfortu-

nate Garrison of Chin-kiang-foo, who meant to die in defense of their houses and country. It seems they had been driven from the walls and gates, had assembled in the public buildings and barracks in the center of the city, where their general had harangued them, and exhorted them to die for their country rather than submit to the hated barbarians. They had first rushed into their homes and slaughtered their wives and children, then joined the general to fight to the last man....

Frightful scenes were witnessed among the houses; whole families were slaughtered in their own homes by their own people in the streets occupied by the Tartar troops and mandarins—little children, some still breathing and writhing in agony with a broken spine or a stab. In one house seven dead or dying persons were found in one room. In another house an old man, probably an old retainer endeavoring to tend two dying children, both with their spines broken. The poor old fellow was weeping bitterly but would not say who committed the shocking barbarity. On a bed near lay the body of a beautiful young woman, quite cold and dead, her neck covered by a silk scarf to hide a terrible gash in her throat, and near her the body of an older woman stretched on a silk coverlet, with her features distorted as if she had died of strangulation. A dead child, stabbed through the neck, lay near her, and in the veranda were the corpses of two more women suspended from the rafters by twisted clothes, both young, one quite a girl who was said to be quite lovely notwithstanding her distorted features. These were only a sample of the horrors to be witnessed in the devoted city.[22]

During the Great Mutiny in India:

[A group of civilians, trying to escape by river from Fatehpur, were being pursued by the mutineers, who were in the process of reaching them]....the women and children were urged to jump into the water "rather than fall into the hands of their inhuman enemies." Most of them did so. Some were shot there by sepoys or by rebel villagers on the banks; others were borne away by the stream and drowned....[When the British regained control of Delhi many Indians were afraid of the inevitable reprisals.] Some came out of their houses along with their children and killed themselves by jumping into the wells. Others were killed by their husbands or fathers. "We found fourteen women with their throats cut from ear to ear by their own husbands, and laid out on shawls," one officer recorded. "We caught a man there who said he saw them killed, for fear they should fall into our hands; and showed us their husbands who had done the best they could afterwards and killed themselves." [In another case]...Captain Gordon [Deputy Superintendent of Jhansi], after making a most gallant resistance, finding the place was no longer defensible and preferring death to surrender, shot himself through the head....[23]

The Japanese suicides at the end of the Second World War are well known:

Tales of mass suicide make one sceptical. But there seems to be no doubt that acts of mass suicide have been occurring among the Japs; and at times the behavior of German troops, especially on the Russian front, seems definitely to come under the same heading.

Most interesting is the account which Robert Sherrol has given of the taking of Saipan, the first area with a large body of Jap civilians to be conquered. He describes an officer cutting off the heads of his kneeling men with a samurai sword, crowds of civilians and soldiers walking off cliffs, wading into the ocean, blowing themselves up ceremoniously with grenades—even playing ring games with them first.

Three women sat on the rocks leisurely, deliberately combing their long black hair. Finally they joined hands and walked out into the sea. A hundred Japs on the rocks of Marpi Point bowed to the Marines on the clifftops, stripped and bathed in the sea, spread a large Jap flag on the rocks, and then pulled the pins out of the grenades that the leader handed out.[24]

While the certitude of suffering and death made many kill themselves, in other situations, when hope was not lost, prisoners killed each other to survive:

After the ship was loaded, tugs pulled us away from the dock and moored us to a buoy in the harbor. Tropical sun on a steel deck. Body heat from 500 men packed together. All around men began passing out. They just slid down out of sight, where men stepped or stood on them. Wearing heavy clothes on the dock got us warm and we drank our water. Somehow it never crossed our minds what was going to happen to us.

As a guy goes crazy he starts to scream—not like a woman, more like a howl of a dog. We were locked in a hold together, 500 of us. We are in there solid, wall to wall. Tight so you couldn't put your feet between people when you tried to walk. I don't know how to describe heat, there was no way we measured temperature. We were all practically naked by that time, because we had taken off everything in order to cut down on the heat. It must have been 120 or 125 degrees in that hold. The Japs' favorite trick was to cut off our water...there, in this oven, when they cut it off, guys started going crazy. People running, people screaming. An American colonel was on deck...The Japs told the colonel to tell us to be quiet. He shouted down, "Be quiet or the Japs will completely cover over the hatch with canvas"....The screaming and running got worse. The colonel topside hollered down, "They are going to do it. They're going to cover you with canvas!" With the temperature we were in, if they'd close off the little air we got, I don't know how many of us would have been alive by morning. I had picked up the habit of wearing a small sweat towel around my forehead like the off-duty Japs did....The next guy that went by screaming they caught and killed....He was strangled with my little towel. ...Several others were also killed.... If they howled, they died. The screaming stopped. The running stopped. Men realized that if they ran one more time, they were going to be killed. Just one man near us questioned what was done. When he was invited to come a little closer to discuss it, he stopped talking and turned his head the other way. The Japs didn't cover the hatch.[25]

In other cases, when despair was tempered by hope and forethought, some preferred captivity to death. Flavius Josephus, commander of a garrison besieged by the Romans, decided to surrender in the hope of saving his life and the lives of a few soldiers who were with him. They, however, preferred death to servitude and threatened to kill him if he were to surrender. Writing in the third person, he continues:

> However, in this extreme distress, he was not destitute of his usual sagacity; but, trusting himself to the providence of God, he put his life into hazard [in the following manner]. "And now," said he, "since it is resolved among you that you will die, come on, let us commit our mutual deaths to determination by lot. He whom the lot falls to first, let him be killed by him that hath the second lot, and thus fortune shall make its progress through us all; nor shall any of us perish by his own right hand, for it would be unfair if, when the rest are gone, somebody should repent and save himself." This proposal appeared to them to be very just; and when he had prevailed with them to determine this matter by lots, he drew one of the lots for himself also. He who had the first lot laid his neck bare to him that had the next, as supposing that the general would die among them immediately;...yet was he with another left to the last, whether we must say it happened so by chance, or whether by the providence of God. And as he was very desirous neither to be condemned by the lot, nor, if he had been left to the last, to imbue his right hand in the blood of his countryman, he persuaded him to trust his fidelity to him and to live as well as himself.[26]

When the general repulsion toward atrocities committed against war prisoners reached a sufficiently high level, formal international agreements followed. The suffering of Union prisoners in the Andersonville camp during the American Civil War aroused sufficient indignation that on April 24, 1863 the Adjutant General Office in Washington issued the U.S. Army General Order Number 100, which came to be known as the "Lieber Code." The document was the work of the German-American jurist Francis Lieber, and became the model on which all subsequent rules and agreements on the treatment of prisoners were based. Article 56 states, "A prisoner of war is subject to no punishment for being a public enemy, nor is any revenge wrecked upon him by the intentional infliction of any suffering, or disgrace, by cruel imprisonment, want of food, by mutilation, death, or any barbarity." Article 76 orders that he is to be "fed upon plain and wholesome food whenever practicable, and treated with humanity." Although the humane treatment of prisoners was its main contribution, it is interesting that the code (Article 59) also states, "All prisoners of war are liable to the infliction of retaliatory measures."[27]

In spite of the "Lieber Code" and of the moderation in the treatment of prisoners that took place in the eighteenth century, of the five million Russians who fell into German hands during Second World War, four million died of starvation and disease.[28] The horrible mistreatment of German prisoners by the Russians is well known, and the Japanese, who followed a warrior code that held men who offered their surrender contemptible, worked thousands of their European prisoners to death. The cruelty with which American prisoners were treated during the Korean and Vietnam wars adds to what appears to be a twentieth-century step backward. On the whole, however, in spite of these exceptions, there has been a moderation in the treatment of war captives in the last three centuries. Man is slowly emerging from his primeval ferality.

Cruelty in battle, detestable as it may be, is at least in part the result of fear and fury. Cruelty toward the prisoner is more abject because it is often committed in cold blood on helpless men. This is to be attributed to the bestial nature of man, not because animals are prone to cruelty, a human evil, but because animals have no capacity for identifying themselves with their victims. Cruelty against the defenseless becomes possible when the perpetrator, like an animal, lacks this capacity, if only while he is committing the act.

(b) Military Occupation

An occupied country is a disarmed power in the hands of the enemy. In antiquity, this meant that the country became the property of the victor, who therefore gave his own interests priority and substituted his convenience for all previously existing rules. The lot of the inhabitants depended on his will.

Prisoners and Military Occupation 95

This attitude was the result of the proposition, then considered self-evident, that the victor was the absolute arbiter of the fate of the vanquished. When Caesar asked Ariovistus to return the Aedui hostages and to desist collecting tribute, the German chief righteously answered:

> Ius esse belli, ut qui vicissent eis, quos vicissent, quem ad modum vellent imperarent...stipendium capere iure belli, quod victores victis imponere consuerint...omnes Galliae civitates ad se oppugnandum venisse ac contra se castra habuisse; eas omnes copias a se uno proelio pulsas ac superatas esse. Si iterum experiri velint, se iterum paratum esse decertare; si pace uti velint, iniquum esse de stipendio recusare....[29]

Ariovistus obviously felt that Caesar's requests were unusual and that justice, tradition, and reason were on his side. To the primitive mind the tenet that the capacity to impose one's own will by force is sufficient justification to do so is self-evident, and to go beyond this simplistic belief is a significant step in the progress of civilization. The result of this belief is the brutality, so common in history, with which the strong behave while in a territory that is at mercy. Here is an example from the Middle Ages.

In preparation for the First Crusade, various petty lords started to collect bands of soldiers. One of them was Count Emich of Leisingen, who, from the Rhineland, started to march with his troops toward the Holy Land.

> On 25 May [1096] Emich arrived before the great city of Mainz. He found the gates closed against him by order of Archbishop Rothard. But the news of his coming provoked anti-Jewish riots within the city, in the course of which a Christian was killed. So on 26 May friends within the city opened the gates to him. The Jews, who had assembled in the synagogue, sent gifts of two hundred marks of silver to the archbishop and to the chief lay lord of the city, asking to be taken to their respective palaces. At the same time a Jewish emissary went to Emich and for seven gold pounds bought from him a promise that he would spare the community. The money was wasted.

Next day he attacked the archbishop's palace. Rothard, alarmed by the temper of the assailants, hastened to flee with all his staff. On his departure Emich's men broke into the building. The Jews attempted to resist but were soon overcome and slain. The lay protector, whose name has not survived, may have been more courageous. But Emich succeeded in setting fire to his palace and forced its inmates to evacuate it. Several Jews saved their lives by abjuring their faith. The remainder were killed. The massacre lasted for two more days, while refugees were rounded up.[30]

Until the eighteenth century the behavior of occupying troops remained about the same: the invaders would kill, rape, take all that could be taken, and destroy most of the rest. The loot was used not only to sustain the army but to build up a treasure to provide for future wars.[31]

In the eighteenth century, under the influence of the Enlightenment, a significant change took place: it became necessary to justify the ravages perpetrated in occupied territories. In other words, the conquered land could no longer be pillaged just because it was the obvious thing to do; the deed had to be justified by proving that it was necessary. It was felt that a belligerent could lay waste a country to prevent the enemy from subsisting there, but devastation motivated by "hatred and passion" was considered wrong.[32] Gérard de Rayneval, a French diplomat who wrote the treatise *Institutions du Droit de la Nature et des Gens*, concluded that devastation of enemy territory could sometimes be justified when retreating before superior forces but that it is likely to be more dangerous than it is worth: "It is sure to exasperate the enemy; it makes him thirst for revenge, and leads him to make reprisals if he gets onto your own territory. Therefore, only the most extreme necessity can make a general take upon himself the responsibility of ordering it."[33]

The dramatic changes that took place in the conduct of warfare during the Enlightenment shall be discussed elsewhere (see Chapter 5). Here it will be noted that, if moderation then prevailed, everything returned to the *status quo ante* with the French Revolution. The French revolutionary armies were characterized by large numbers, much enthusiasm, small baggage-trains, lack of professionalism, great mobility, and by the necessity of being supplied from the resources of the occupied country.[34] The results for the civilian populations of the "liberated" territories was disastrous.[35]

In addition, old-fashioned greed masquerading as revolutionary fervor replaced the more civilized attitude brought by the Enlightenment:

> [In October 1792] Lebrun had written to [General] Custine: "You must sweep up everything before and beside you the length of the Rhine, while treating the people with fraternity.... I believe it would be very nice if you profited by the circumstances to enrich the Bibliothèque Nationale with several great and costly works found in the libraries of the places you have conquered for liberty...." In the autumn of 1792...the Committee of Public Safety instructed the generals of the republic that, beyond "taking hostages from among the most notable inhabitants," raising massive financial contributions, and collecting everything materially necessary for their forces, they were to "seize and take safely to the rear of their armies the victuals, forage, cattle, horses, ropes, iron ware, hemp, linen, leather, fabrics, woollens, and everything else which, while not being immediately necessary, may be for use later...." The avowed theory was still that the liberating and unjustly attacked French were only collecting what was due to them from the liberated populations and their former oppressors. The practice was one of efficient financial and economic leeching.... Its most spectacular achievement was Napoleon's "enrichment" of the Bibliothèque Nationale and the Louvre (and his own family palaces) with art treasures from everywhere his victories had taken him.[36]

Until the nineteenth century, for an invading army to get its means of subsistence from the occupied country was a necessity because the network of roads needed to resupply large amounts of men did not exist. The railroad, of course, made the biggest difference in this respect.[37]

The change for the worse in the conduct of war following the

French Revolution was due mostly to the fact that, at that time, people became active participants in international politics. As wars became conflicts between people and not between kings, the perverse logic of propaganda dictated that each war be labeled what it was not; a fight against a given ruler, a ruling clique, an ideology (held by few, of course), or the other side's military machine, but *not* against the people. For this reason William I declared in 1870: "I am making war against the soldiers and not the citizens of France." At the beginning of the nineteenth century the struggle was held to be against Napoleon. In World War I it was against the Kaiser and his clique of war criminals (to make the world safe for democracy), and still later, of course, against Fascism. Now the struggle is against Imperialistic Capitalism or Communism, depending upon the side one is on. In reality the struggle is (and was) for predominance among groups.

The advent of the "people's war" brought two important phenomena to the fore: the all-out economic war and the guerrilla war. Although an economic component had always existed in war and guerrilla-like actions were occasionally undertaken in the past (e.g., peasant bands in the Middle Ages, the actions of Francis Marion—the Swamp Fox—during the American Revolution), we find the clearest examples of these new kinds of conflict during the Napoleonic wars. France attempted the closure of the continent to British trade, and the British responded by attempting to close it to neutral trade. The object was not only to weaken the enemy's war effort by cutting essential supplies, but also to lower the bourgeoisie's standard of living and produce unemployment and hunger in the lower classes so that national morale and war-weariness would be exacerbated.[38] As for guerrilla warfare:

> Spain, 1808—partisans snipe at the French column as it slowly advances up the valley of the Sil—non-combatant camp-followers injured as well as troops—so, as soon as it can be done, "the French Almanazor, General Loison" leads a punitive column into the snipers' hinterland—villages on fire everywhere—"Never before can so terrible a storm have hit

this previously peaceful valley. Its people got out and watched its destruction from afar; those we were able to find, we killed."[39]

Since then, the economic component has played an increasingly important role and guerrilla warfare has been employed extensively: against the British in India, the French and Spanish in Morocco, the Americans in the Philippines, the British in the South African War, etc. During the First World War, significant guerrilla operations were carried out in the Middle East (by Lawrence) and in German East Africa (by Lettow-Vorbeck). During the Second World War, guerrilla warfare was common in many occupied countries, and after the war became particularly important as a means of subversion against government troops during peacetime instead of against occupying soldiers.

The problem of resistance to occupation is complicated by the decreasing distinction between armed forces and civilian populations. In antiquity and, even more, in the sixteenth and seventeenth centuries, when wars were fought by mercenaries, such a distinction was obvious. Soldiers conducted the war and civilians supported the army with work, money, and, sometimes, soldiers. Although the army and the civilians formed a sort of partnership in the conduct of hostilities, civilian participation was indirect and passive. When nationalism and ideology generated the people's war, the civilians started to participate more actively in the effort; in fact the idea that soldiers and civilians were struggling for the same goal became an essential tenet of modern war. The phrase "the home front" indicates this unity of the soldier and the civilian in the common effort. This is not just empty rhetoric. In modern times, industrialized warfare needs indeed the direct effort of the workers at the "home front." For this reason, especially in authoritarian societies, there is a ceaseless effort to prepare the population for the war effort: the Fascists by presenting war as the magnificent expression of people's vitality and the Communists by presenting "the world as an arena of class struggle unceasing, turning now and then into wars...in which whole classes are necessarily involved whether they know or like it or not."[40]

However, if unity of civilians and soldiers is useful or even indispensable for war, it has deleterious effects on the relations between the armed forces of the occupying power and the civilian population: if civilians are essential participants in the conflict, they cannot expect to be treated as peaceful non-combatants, especially if they continue to fight by means of guerilla warfare and sabotage. By the same token, the occupying army cannot be expected to show restraint when it is the object of hostile attacks and cannot easily distinguish the guilty from the innocent. In addition, the members of an occupying army are particularly prone to being influenced by two strong determinants of human behavior: necessity (or what is interpreted as such) and revenge (often mixed with cruelty and sadism). The following is an example of necessity (or what was interpreted as such) in Burma in 1944:

> Four villagers from Ngusharawng came to my headquarters—the headman and three more, one with his hands bound behind his back, all wizened and starved. An Intelligence officer and two men of the Burma Rifles led them. I stared at them. Civilians, by God. Now what? Have they got any food for us?
> "This man betrayed us to the Japanese, because we helped your soldiers a week ago [provided guides for the Cameronians]. The Japanese came, crucified my wife, and bayoneted my eldest son and five others whom they caught in the village. We escaped."
> Terrible. But what the hell has it got to do with me?
> "The government, " the old man said and waited.
> The government was back. Me. They could not themselves kill a murderer. That was against the law. So it was. Rule of law, first principle of British justice.
> I held a court-martial. It took about half an hour. The Intelligence officer had seen the bodies. The accused said he hadn't told the Japanese. The others said he had. Why should they bring him to me if they were trying to work off a private

grudge? A knife in the back, in the jungle, and no one would ever have known.

Guilty. Under no circumstances could we afford to let anyone in Burma help the Japanese now, and get away with it. I sentenced him to death. The Intelligence officer took him away with two Burma Riflemen. I tried to write a message, listening, until two shots exploded very close down the hill and the Burma Riflemen came back.[41]

And the following is an example of revenge, indeed mixed with cruelty and sadism, which followed the assassination of Kléber, a French general, on June 14, 1800, during Napoleon's Egyptian campaign:

A drum roll gave the alarm from Esbekiya Square. Within a few minutes, all drums in Cairo called the soldiers to their stations. The news of Kléber's murder spread with incredible speed. Terrified of the consequences, the population sought safety in their houses, while the soldiers, seized by fury (and, perhaps, mistaking the murder for the beginning of another rebellion), ran amuck in the streets. "We cut down with our sabres and daggers all men and children we came across," reminisces Sergeant François, apparently without shame. Fortunately, the disorder stopped as soon as the murderer was apprehended....as for Soliman [the apprehended murderer], the court chose to apply the penalty permitted by local custom but scarcely in keeping with the enlightened principles of the French Republic. To order a man to have his right hand burned off and to be impaled alive may strike some as too zealous a gesture of respect for indigenous traditions.

...In the life of Barthelmy the Greek [the executioner], this must have been the supreme day. He began by hacking off the heads of the three sheiks [alleged accomplices]. In the meantime coals had been heating in a brazier. Soliman made no complaint while his hand was being roasted, but when a lump of red-hot coal rolled to his elbow, he drew Barthelmy's attention to the fact that his sentence did not mention the elbow—only the hand. Barthelmy expressed the opinion that Soliman was quibbling. Soliman called Barthelmy a Christian dog and insisted on his rights until the coal was removed. The surgical details of Soliman's impaling, which followed, have been recorded by Sergeant François, who claims to have observed them from a distance of five paces: amateurs of such matters are free to look them up in his memoirs....When Barthelmy had completed the preliminary part of the operation, the pole with Soliman on it was set upright and planted in the ground. Soliman begged a French soldier who stood nearby for water. The soldier was about to hand him his canteen when Barthelmy prevented him: the least bit of water, he pointed out, would cause instantaneous death and thus frustrate the due course of justice.[42]

The occupying army is often provoked into taking retaliatory measures by partisans who strive to acquire more popular support. This was the case in Russia during the Second World War:

Several German or other Axis soldiers would be captured, mutilated, and killed. Their bodies would then be left in a place where the Germans would surely find them, often next to villages sympathetic to the invaders or neutral in their political sympathies. When the bodies were found, German [or other] security troops would take revenge on all the villages in the area by killing everyone they saw, by confiscating all cattle and crops, and by devastating entire sections of land. The survivors fled to the forests, where they would be met by the partisans who would sympathize with them and offer help.[43]

German forces had captured partisan manuals of instruction telling the units that any means were justified against the invaders, and the evidence the Army saw before them made it plain enough that the instructions were being followed. Partisans had missions to infiltrate the German lines and to use women agents to put poison in the Germans' food. German soldiers found the bodies of comrades with eyes gouged out and of others who had been crucified, and they reacted with fire and sword. Villages from which the partisans operated were burned down, the male inhabitants slaughtered, the women sent to work. The decision as to the extent of the reprisals was made not by a military court or by higher authority but by the troop leader of the action. No holds were barred in the East on either side.[44]

If excesses were sometimes deplored by members of the side committing the atrocities, the disapproval was based on the ineffectiveness of the measures taken:

> It is utter insanity to murder babies, children, women, and old men because heavily armed red bandits [i.e. guerrillas] billeted themselves overnight, by force, in their house, and because they killed two German soldiers near the village. The political effect of this senseless bloodbath is disastrous for us; while—to compound the folly of the event—the military effect is negligible; the partisans continue to live and they will again find quarters by use of submachine guns in completely defenseless villages....[45]

In spite of the fact that reprisals are often useless or even counterproductive, all armies of occupation tend to behave in the same way because the need for revenge seems to be irresistible, the possibility of limiting losses with the deterrence of terror real, the soldiers become more cruel and remorseless as they are subjected to elusive attacks and ambushes,[46] and, finally, because war propaganda has depicted the enemy (including the civilian enemy) as subhuman and unworthy of pity. Although in the Second World War the Germans were notorious for the killing of hostages in reprisal for attacks against their soldiers, the Allies were not innocent:

> As for the killing of hostages, it is an old and deplorable practice, but it is one of the few ways of preventing the killing of one's own troops by partisans or other staunch patriots on the home front....After the close of World War II, the French commander at Stuttgart threatened to kill Germans at the rate of twenty-five to one, a figure that was upped to two hundred to one by the Americans in the Harz region of Germany. At Reutlingen the French shot four German hostages for the killing of a French soldier. In September 1944, forty German prisoners of war were shot by the French because a Russian battalion in

German service had allegedly committed atrocities, and on the same day forty more Germans were executed apparently for the same reason. Eight German prisoners were shot by an American detachment in the spring of 1945 after an American had been killed by someone shooting from a house.[47]

It must be noted, however, that during the Second World War, if military occupation was associated with bloody and cruel reprisals, it was also characterized, at least in Western Europe, by remarkable restraint when the occupying troops were not the object of guerrilla attacks or sabotage. During the occupation of France, for example, off-duty German soldiers often behaved more like tourists than members of an invading army.[48]

Ideology and nationalism injected into war another phenomenon that became particularly evident with the Second World War: collaborationism. This crime is defined as the act of "collaborating with an enemy or an opposed group rather than struggling or resisting."[49] After the war, in the countries of Europe occupied by the Germans, those who collaborated with the invaders were persecuted by those who sided with the winner. Hundred of thousands of Frenchmen and Italians were killed or imprisoned by their compatriots in a desolate orgy of blood and revenge. Concerning France:

> ...statistics about summary executions...cannot be reliably established. Robert Aron, who assembled probably as much evidence as remained, calculated that after the liberation there had been between 30 and 40,000 summary executions in France. Adrien Tixier, postwar Minister of Justice, offered the higher figure of 105,000 summary executions between June 1944 and February 1945. "National indignity" was a newly invented crime for which many thousands of former collaborators were imprisoned. Between August 21 and October 1, 1944, according to the specialist publication *Historia*, in its issue Number 41 entitled "La justice sommaire de l'été 1944," "There were apparently 1 million arrests, 100,000 of them in the Paris region...." What the French did to themselves after the occupa-

tion was in some ways more painful than what the Germans had done to them during it. For the number of Frenchmen killed by other Frenchmen, whether through summary execution or rigged tribunals akin to lynch mobs or court-martials and High Court trials, equalled or even exceeded the number of those sent to their death by the Germans as hostages, deportees, and slave laborers. So liberation did not begin where occupation ended, but completed a cycle of violence and bloodshed.[50]

In Italy, the fratricidal fury took the same form and resulted in comparable brutalities. The number of victims of summary executions, lynchings, and kangaroo courts is, again, difficult to establish. Reported totals vary from 1,732 to 300,000.[51] It would appear that tens of thousands (possibly as many as 70,000) were slaughtered.

It is interesting to note that during the persecution of the collaborators, the Allies sometimes intervened to protect them from the hate of their compatriots. This brings to mind similar events that followed the Third Macedonian War (168 B.C.). Although Greece itself had played a rather secondary role in the war between Perseus, king of Macedonia, and Rome, there was in each Greek city both a Macedonian party and a party favorable to the Romans. After the Macedonian defeat:

> ...trials for high treason began in all parts of Greece. Whoever had served in Perseus' army, was immediately executed; whoever was compromised by the papers of the king or the statements of political opponents who flocked to lodge information, was dispatched to Rome....To the Achaeans...the senate, wearied by constant requests for the commencement of the investigation, at length roundly declared that till further orders the persons concerned were to remain in Italy...they were...tolerably well treated...and the enraged Greeks of the Roman party were far from content with the paucity of the executions.[52]

Ancient Greece had ceased to play a significant role in history.

Resistance to occupation is a noble or despicable endeavor depending on the side of the observer. Active resistance to occupation in the modern sense (with guerrillas, hit-and-run raids, propaganda, etc.) is a relatively recent phenomenon that had its beginning in the nineteenth century and became fully developed in the twentieth. To wage a successful struggle, the guerrilla must have the widespread support of the civilian population; in other words, the occupying force (or the unpopular regime, for that matter) is faced with a struggle that usually involves direct armed conflict with only a small portion of the population but that indirectly is a confrontation with a much larger one.

Is it legal or justified for the population of the invaded country to resist occupation? In case of resistance, how severe should repression on the part of the occupying forces be? How justified are nationals of the occupied country in collaborating with the victor (for example, by maintaining the civilian infrastructure)?

The first question would be better asked in this form: how much is the population of an occupied country prepared to pay for resistance? It is in the interest of the invading army to have peace and order in the invaded territories, but it is to be expected that guerrilla attacks will be met with violent repression. Propaganda aside, therefore, the problem becomes a question of comparing the price to be paid with the advantages to be gained by resisting occupation.

As for the second question, it is evident that if the only concern were a purely military one, it would often be in the interest of the occupying forces to eliminate the local population. This was sometimes done in antiquity, as mentioned. There are other concerns, however. First of all, there is the revulsion that, in modern times, such an act would cause both in the invading country and in the rest of the world. Then there is the old principle that the enemy of today may be the friend of tomorrow. And, finally, the possibility exists that, at least in certain cases, the population, made desperate by the threat of liquidation, may put up a serious resistance. The problem facing the occupying army is, again, a mathematical one: the advantages of a given degree of repression must be measured against the disadvantages of the reaction to reprisals.

As for the problem of the "collaborators" of the Second World War, it is evident that, had Germany won, Pétain and Quisling would have been considered not traitors but patriots who tried to limit the damages of military defeat.

Albrecht Dürer — *Astronomer*

Chapter 5

> Dovete, adunque, sapere come sono dua generazioni di combattere: l'uno con le leggi, l'altro con la forza: quel primo é proprio dello uomo, quel secondo é delle bestie.[1]
>
> Machiavelli,
> *Il Principe*, XVIII

LAWS OF WAR AND PEACE

(a) Rules of War

As William Tecumseh Sherman succinctly described it, "War is hell." When man recognized this, he started to classify armed conflicts as just and unjust (see Chapter 7) and to identify the culprits (those who started the unjust wars). The idea was that once the culprits were identified (and punished), the example would discourage others from fighting unjust wars. Because wars that were just for both sides were considered rare indeed, the abolition of the unjust ones would have virtually eliminated armed conflict. Soon it became evident, however, that, for this purpose, the distinction between the two kinds of war was not very effective: the victor invariably declared that he had been on the just side, the defeated had no way of arguing, few paid any attention to the distinction, and wars continued to be fought with the usual ardor.

Incapable of stopping the bloodshed, man then tried to find a way of at least moderating its horrors. The success of these endeavors has been limited but not negligible. Early attempts at regulating war were specific in time and circumstances, but, later, general international laws began to be formulated.

It is interesting to note that an important concept of the international law of war is that the doctrine of just and unjust war should be ignored:

> While clearly some belligerents have a just cause and some do not, and therefore, according to classical just war theory, are differently placed vis-à-vis their legal obligations, in practice, argues Vattel, if the law of war is to be enabled to do its softening work, the causes of belligerents must be counted as equally just (or unjust) *for that purpose alone*. This was a giant stride forward in the development of the law of war.[2]

The necessity for considering the causes of all belligerents equally just is evident. A system of international law of war establishes rules and regulations to be followed by all in various circumstances during the conduct of warfare. For example, civilians are protected by regulating the use of weapons in non-military areas and prisoners of war by guidelines dealing with their life in captivity. These rules and regulations are not enforced by a superior authority with power to punish, but simply encouraged not only by the fear of retaliation but also by the fear of loss of credibility in the international community. It is, therefore, essential that all countries recognize the right of all to be protected by international law; if, on the other hand, one of the belligerents is deemed to be fighting an unjust war, he may come to be considered a sort of outlaw not worthy of the benefits of the rules and regulations that were made for members in good standing of the international community. The branding of one of the belligerents as an international outlaw does not need to be universal; even if only the other side takes that position, this could start a chain of retaliations difficult to control.

Only with the assumption that all belligerents are morally equal can the international law of war be applied with a fair chance of success. Hence, judgments concerning ethics and righteousness, far from being valuable in the conduct of international affairs, may, at least in war, hinder the application of the very laws that are designed to advance as much as possible the humanity of man toward man. This point is particularly interesting because it identifies one of the causes of the unhappy and not unusual failures of pious resolves (e.g., pacifism; see Chapter 7).

When the foundations of international law were laid, many recognized the difficulty that the distinction between just and unjust wars and right and wrong sides would cause. Vitoria (1480-1564), for example, held that a war could be just on both sides.[3] However, not being able to free himself from the prejudices of the time, he also held that Moslem prisoners of war could be killed and their wives and children sold as slaves. Suarez (1548-1617) concluded that soldiers of a prince who wages an unjust war, if taken prisoners, could not be protected by law and could be killed. If the logic of the just war doctrine forced him to reach such a conclusion, his piety (he was called *doctor eximius et pius*) made him try to find ways to render the harsh verdict void:

> ...through various distinctions, exceptions and presumptions, he tries to save most of them. For example, in his opinion mercenary soldiers, when doubtful about the justness of their cause, are protected by the law if their doubt is "negative," that is, if they do not know of "probable reasons" favorable to the other side; in the case of a "positive doubt" they would have to start a search of their own and follow the "more probable" opinion, lest they be at the mercy of their captors![4]

112 MAN AND WAR

Pietro Belli (1502-1575) used the just war doctrine in trying to set forth the principle of compulsory arbitration. He stated that if a prince shows willingness to arbitrate, the war should be suspended lest it becomes "unjust."[5] The principle was ignored.

Balthasar Ayala (1548-1584) realized that there was some difficulty with the just war doctrine in the context of international law and declared that a war between legitimate sovereigns, lawfully conducted, might be called just on both sides. He also introduced into the doctrine of the law of war the principle that good faith must be kept with the enemy, except with those waging an unjust war or with rebels.[6]

Alberico Gentili (1552-1608), an Italian teaching at Oxford, recognized, as Vitoria had, that a war can be just on both sides and, perhaps more important, that the rules of war regarding prisoners, booty, etc., are independent of the justness of the cause.[7] Grotius (1583-1645) stated that if a war is declared by the proper authority, each side is to be considered as fighting a just and legal war.[8] He also insisted on moderation during the conduct of hostilities, on the necessity for treating prisoners fairly, on sparing the lives of hostages except in extreme circumstances, etc. With regard to diplomatic exchanges he advocated the extra-territoriality of the ambassadors (*quasi extra territorium*).[9] On the other hand, the belligerent fighting the just war had, according to Grotius, the right of passing through neutral territory and the right of taking possession of places situated in that territory.[10] However, this "infusion of the just war doctrine into the law of neutrality was later repudiated in state practice as well as in legal doctrine...."[11]

The idea of a set of rules, freely agreed upon, that would regulate the conduct of war and the relations between countries evolved slowly. Montesquieu asserted that there is in mankind an innate idea of international law.[12] This is a fantasy similar to the myth of the noble savage. In reality

> ...not even the distinction between war and peace is always known to primitive tribes. Some have not yet developed the notion of collective and organized fighting such as is charac-

teristic of warfare, while others are living in a permanent state of open or latent hostility toward their neighboring tribes. The idea that the foreigner as such is an enemy has left traces in early civilized thought; among the primitives he is sometimes not even considered a human being....[13]

The first examples of formal treaties between groups date from the fourth millennium B.C.: around 3100 B.C., for example, an agreement was concluded between two Mesopotamian city-states, Lagash and Umma.[14] However, it was only in the classical world that such agreements became common.

Greek concepts of war and international relations were dominated and deformed by their fundamental racism. "Barbarians"—that is, non-Greeks—were naturally inferior men who existed to be slaves of the Greeks. Aristotle based his definition of a just war (one of the earliest) on this very concept:

> ... the art of war is a natural art of acquisition, for it includes hunting, an art which we ought to practice against wild beasts, and against men who, though intended by nature to be governed, will not submit. For war of such kind is naturally just.[15]

Socrates, according to Plato, proposed that the concept of war should be limited only to fights against barbarians because fights among Greeks were "disease and discord" and should be waged with moderation.[16] This was the reason for the establishment of the noble custom which forbade the erection of stone or bronze trophies on the battlefields so that the wooden ones, the only kind allowed, would not last for long as a symbol of enmity.

Although non-Greeks were considered almost sub-human, a few treaties between Greek and non-Greek communities were concluded. It is, however, among Greek city-states that relations were regulated by principles that resembled those of our "law of nations."[17] Truces and compacts during war were already negotiated at the remote times of the Homeric epics. In the *Iliad*, for example, are described the truces between

114 MAN AND WAR

Achaeans and Trojans for the single combats of Menelaus and Paris (Book III) and of Hector and Ajax (Book VII), and also the eleven-day suspension of combat granted by Achilles to Priam for Hector's funeral ceremonies (Book XXIV).

If the Greeks were able, as Vergil says, to "better work bronze and better bring life out of marble,"[18] the Romans introduced into the civilized world a system of law that remains one of the greatest cultural achievements. As early as the sixth century B.C., the *Fetiales*, a special group of priests organized in the *Collegium Fetialium*, was entrusted with the religious ceremonies concerning relations with foreigners. At this time the concept of the "just war" began to evolve (see Chapter 7). It is of interest that even a people as bellicose as the Romans felt the need to justify war and to go through rituals to assure the approval of the gods. In fact, the delegates of the *Fetiales*, when asking a foreign nation to give satisfaction for a wrong committed against the Roman people, would be under oath as to the justice of his assertions. The oath culminated in condemnation of the whole Roman people, should the delegate's assertion be wrong. If all the rituals were properly observed, the war, if declared, would be just and pious (*Bellum iustum et pium*).[19]

Contributions of the Romans to the international laws of war were, of course, not limited to the "just war." For example, various forms of vassalage treaties and a highly characteristic type of treaty of surrender (*deditio*) were also developed.[20] Roman concern with the law took aspects that we may find at times disconcerting. Tacitus reports the following episode which, in its brutality, well underlines such a concern. During the rebellion of Mithridates of Bosporus in 45 A.D., the legions invested Uspe, in Pontus, and almost conquered it on the first day of siege. As the besieged realized that they had no chances:

> Postero misere legatos, veniam liberis corporibus orantes: servitii decem milia offerebant. Quod aspernati sunt victores, quia trucidare deditos saevum, tantam multitudinem custodia

cingere arduum: belli potius iure caderent, datumque militibus, qui scalis evaserant, signum caedis.[21]

The Romans could have accepted the terms, chosen the few that they wanted to keep as slaves, and killed the rest. It would have been an act of cruelty not worse than many others so common in war. They chose instead to pay with some inevitable losses for what they could have obtained but for the price of breaking the Roman rule of war that forbade the killing, without valid reason, of men who had surrendered.

Foreigners were considered to be outside the pale of the law, but the Romans did not automatically consider them enemies as the Greeks tended to do. The *ius gentium* (law of nations) is one of the great contributions to international law although it is not the law of nations in the modern sense (governing relations between independent states) but a law concerned with the relationship between Roman citizens and foreigners.[22]

While Rome was conquering the Western World, the Code of Manu (*Manava Dharma Shastra*) was developed in India between the second century B.C. and the second century A.D. Manu (cognate with the Indo-European "man") was the first man in the mythology of India and the author of the Code, which displays an astonishing degree of humaneness in matters of warfare. For example, the honorable warrior is not supposed to strike the enemy who is running away, who is sleeping, who is naked, who has lost his arms, etc.[23] These precepts are so unlike the practices of warfare of the time, even in the Orient, that the hypothesis has been advanced that their significance was, in practice, very limited, especially because they were not accompanied by legal sanctions.[24] On the other hand, there is historical evidence of an Indian custom to spare, during war, crops and farmers (another of the commands of Manu).[25] It is of interest that these ignored precepts are similar to those of the Christian message, also largely ignored. Usually, in the Orient as in the West, armed conflict was pursued in antiquity with the cruelty and disregard for age and sex that are characteristic of the primitives and which have continued with various degrees of intensity until recent times.

For centuries, in the West, the law of Rome was the only law. Then barbarian ignorance swept the world and the Church kept civilization alive in the dark of the early Middle Ages until the revival that culminated in the Renaissance. During the Middle Ages, Canon law was "supranational" in the sense that it exacted obedience all over the Christian World. Several acts of Church legislation were related to war. In 1139 the Second Lateran Council forbade the use of the crossbow because it was considered too dangerous a weapon, and in 1179 the Third Lateran Council prohibited the enslavement of Christian prisoners of war, although the interdiction did not extend to non-Christians. The Third Lateran Council also condemned piracy, but again, only if it was practiced against Christians.[26]

This distinction between Christians and non-Christians does not satisfy our modern principles concerning the protection of the rights and dignity of man regardless of religion or race. These modern concepts, developed from Roman law, had to wait until the Western World could further emerge from the darkness of barbarism in which it had been thrown by the great invasions of the fifth century. The Church helped the slow process of "recivilization" and, in so doing, often used practices that may now seem objectionable but that were the result in part of necessity, in part of the spirit of the age:

> ...The use of poisoned weapons, widespread in the period, was not prohibited....Church law developed a refined and perilous doctrine regarding the invalidity of oaths and promises. Not only were various "tacit conditions" admitted, the deficiency of which would invalidate the oath, but generally oaths and promises running counter [to] the interest of the Church—and this was extended to agreements with heretic and schismatic princes—were declared null and void. The promisor might even be duty-bound to act contrary to his illicit promise. Moreover, validity of the oath would not make it inviolable. The Church could intervene by way of dispensation, for which the Pope had supreme and unlimited power, while other Church dignitaries

possessed that power either by papal delegation or, to a limited extent, ex officio. The frequency of such dispensations finally led to a reaction on the part of the princes....[27]

The most important contribution of the Middle Ages toward doctrines related to international relations was the doctrine of "just war" (see Chapter 7). Created by the Romans, it was resuscitated and modified by St. Augustin (354-430) and formalized by St. Thomas Aquinas (1225-1274).

While the Western half of the Roman Empire finally succumbed to the barbarians in 476, the Eastern half survived for another thousand years until the fall of Constantinople to Mohammed II in 1453. The division of the Empire in two was decreed by the last will of Theodosius (d. 395), although the center of gravity of the Roman world had shifted to the East after Constantinople became the capital in 330. Since Constantine, the Empire had been Christian. In 1054 the Roman Catholic and the Greek Orthodox Church split formally. In the Eastern Empire, although still Roman in theory, the official language was Greek, the emperor was for all intents and purposes an Oriental monarch, Roman culture was considered crude, and the Latin language ignored. Even in questions of religion, there was enmity (Pope Leo IX, for example, excommunicated the Patriarch of Constantinople and his followers). Because there was really little left that was Roman, we refer to the Eastern Roman Empire, more appropriately, as the Byzantine Empire. From the point of view of international law, the most interesting examples of Byzantine treaties are the sixth century peace conventions with Persia, particularly the one contracted in 562 by Emperor Justinian with Chosroes I. This treaty provided protection for religious minorities, a subject that was to assume great importance in later periods.[28]

Even if the long history of the Byzantine Empire consisted mainly of decay rather than glory, the recollection of Rome's greatness still exerted a powerful influence on the minds of men. In 1472 Ivan III, Grand Prince of Moscow, who considered himself the successor to the Emperor of the recently

118 MAN AND WAR

defunct Byzantine Empire, married the niece of the last Emperor, Constantine Paleologus (who had died in the last battle for Constantinople), introduced Byzantine ceremonials at his court, and adopted the coat of arms of the last Byzantine dynasty, the double-headed eagle of the Paleologi. He was crowned Czar (the slavic version of the word "Caesar"), and Moscow was to become the "third Rome" (the second having been Constantinople). The influence of Roman law on Russian law is still evident today.

During the slow decline of the Byzantine Empire, Islam appeared on the scene of history, and for a time it seemed as if its extraordinary vitality and energy were going to submerge the West. Islamic culture and law became of primary importance.

> The Islamic law on international relations is scanty and vague, except for some aspects of war. Islamic law is based on the Koran, compiled shortly after Mohammed's death (632 A.D.). The Koran is considered all-comprehensive and is, therefore, closed to amending legislation. The actual Islamic law is largely the result of interpretation and implementation by the scribes (muftis and other religious and legal authorities). These authorities differ widely, particularly according to country and periods. With a disparity between theory and practice which is no peculiarity of Islam, they failed to develop an approximate uniformity such as that attained by the centralized system of the Catholic Church. The subject of war is central in Islamic doctrine on international relations. While the Moslem countries are conceived as a political unit (*dar-al-Islam*), there exists a latent state of war between the Moslems and the infidels. The actual war against the infidels is a holy war (*jihad*), but opinion seems to differ as to whether it is so in itself or only after the issuance of a formal declaration by the competent authorities. Every able-bodied Moslem has to join such war; and death in battle will open the gates of paradise, the pleasures of which (by no means spiritual only) are depicted in the most elaborate manner....On the other hand, Moslem ideas on warfare are in some respects superior to Christian conceptions of the same period. A proclamation of Caliph Abu Bekr (died 634), Mohammed's first successor, is significant. He warns his victor-

ious soldiers to spare women, children, and old men; he exhorts them not to destroy palms and orchards, or to burn homes, or to take from the provisions of the enemy more than needed; and he demands that prisoners of war be treated with pity. Ransoming and the exchanging of prisoners were far more practiced in the East than in the West, and in a number of cases prisoners received their freedom in a large scale by acts of generosity. Booty had to be delivered to the authorities for distribution, the treasury keeping one-fifth of it—a rule adopted, surprisingly enough, by the Siete Partidas of Alfonso X of Castile. The hostility of Islam toward infidels was tempered by remarkable exceptions. The Koran, despite the paramountcy of Mohammed's teachings, embodied the Old and New Testaments in the Islamic creed, and Christians and Jews received preferential treatment. As "people of the book" (*dhimmi*)—namely, of the Bible—they were permitted to stay in Moslem countries and to live there according to their own religions and under their own laws, provided they paid poll taxes and submitted to restrictions regarding their conduct and their garments. Perhaps the most impressive application of the doctrine occurred after the fall of Constantinople, when the conqueror Mohammed II convoked representatives of the Greek Orthodox Church, of the Armenian Church, and of the Jews, to tell them that they might stay in Constantinople under their own laws and the leadership of their religious superiors. Because the Orthodox Patriarch had died before the conquest, the Sultan caused the Greeks in Constantinople to elect a new Patriarch, whom he treated with high honors....Both doctrine and actual practice held more tolerance in the Islamic than in the Western world....Any Moslem originally had the power to grant any foreigner protection by a one-sided act (*amân*) which was binding upon the whole community. The foreigner became thereby a *mustamîn*. This extraordinary privilege, which gradually came to be a prerogative of the competent authorities, was a residue of an Arab tribal custom of hospitality: a foreigner who entered a tent with the owner's consent was protected...the record of Islam is definitely good on this score. The Crusaders, although aggressors, proceeded on the principle that no faith need be kept with infidels. Says the noted historian Lane-Poole, with an eye to the Crusaders, "The virtues of civilization were all on the side of the Saracens."[29]

The Islamic invasion of Europe was halted by Charles Martel at Poitiers (732 A.D.), and the last Arabs were expelled from Spain with the conquest of Granada in 1492. The modern era begins and modern international law starts to be forged.

One of the signs of the new interest in international law, in the sixteenth century, was the frequent exchange of permanent representatives between countries. In 1520 ambassadors were exchanged between Emperor Charles V and King Henry VIII of England, and soon the concept of diplomatic immunity was put to a severe test. In 1584, Mendoza, the Spanish ambassador to the English court, was found to be one of the principals in a plot to dethrone and kill Queen Elizabeth and to liberate Queen Mary of Scotland. One can easily imagine the situation: a foreigner was involved in a plot to kill the Queen, the concept of the immunity of ambassadors was not familiar, religious prejudice was widespread (a Catholic foreigner was plotting in favor of the Catholic Mary of Scotland), and, finally, the legal process of the time was less concerned with particular rights than it is today. Public opinion demanded that the Spaniard be brought to trial in an English court. England, on that occasion, wrote an important page in the history of international law by following the advice of Gentili and other scholars versed in Roman law, who held that Mendoza was protected by diplomatic immunity. The Spanish ambassador was simply expelled.

Not long ago, another episode involving diplomatic immunity took place in London. During a demonstration against the Libyan regime in front of the Libyan embassy, shots were fired from the building, an English policeman was killed, and several demonstrators were wounded. In spite of the public outcry, it is evident that the English Government had no choice: the culprit had diplomatic immunity and had to be expelled without trial in an English court.

As the progress of the laws of war acquired momentum, the elaboration of written rules for the maintenance of strict military discipline was bound to have a beneficial effect. After the fall of the Roman world, the first traces of such military ordinances can be found in the last centuries of the Middle Ages, but greater advancement was achieved later. Imperial ordinances issued in 1570 prohibited pillaging without permission and afforded some protection for women and old people. However, the idea that a soldier was to seek his own profit in warfare still prevailed.[30]

The Peace of Westphalia (1648), at the end of the Thirty Years War, was a landmark in the history of international law: it had a provision that is the first attempt at the maintenance of peace through an international organization. It was agreed that any violation of the treaty was to be submitted for discussion and amicable settlement and that, if the efforts were to prove vain, all parties to the treaty would take up arms to subdue the offender. No joint action ever took place, of course, but it is interesting that the principle was accepted. The Peace of Westphalia also marked the end of Latin as the international diplomatic language. From then on, French became predominant and maintained its supremacy for almost three centuries. The Peace also brought forth the first international recognition of freedom of conscience (*conscientia libera*) regarding religious worship, in spite of the opposition of the Pope (Innocent X), who

> ...by the bull *Zelo domus Dei*, declared the tolerance and other religious clauses, core of the peace, "null, void, invalid, inequitable, unjust, condemned, reprobated, frivolous, of no force or effect"—a nullification extended to oaths taken under the treaty; but the treaty was carried out in all its parts.[31]

The treaty's lack of validity and effect, according to the same bull, was to be "for past, present, and future,"[32] but the words of the Pope, not being backed by power, were ignored by both sides. In addition, Innocent X, under the influence of his sister-in-law and chief counselor, Olimpia Maidalchini, did not have much prestige in the international community.

Slowly, after the Thirty Years War, an astonishing change for the better that reached its peak in the following century started to develop concerning warfare. It is not that conflicts became less frequent or that they were conducted with much less destruction of lives and goods, but that attitudes toward war changed. For a century or more, under the influence of the humane ideas of the Enlightenment, man seemed to have acquired some degree of sanity and war seemed to have become somewhat less cruel and more civilized. Toward the end of the eighteenth century one could have thought that warfare was going to be eliminated in the foreseeable future.

The American-Prussian Treaty of 1785 stipulated, for instance, that in case of war between the two powers not only were women and children to be provided for, but "scholars of every faculty, cultivators of the earth, artisans, manufacturers, fishermen, and all others whose occupations are concerned with the common subsistence and benefit of mankind, shall be allowed to continue their respective employment and shall not be molested." Merchants were to be allowed nine months to collect their debts and for settling their affairs before freely departing for their homes "with their effects." Merchant vessels "rendering the necessaries, conveniences, and comforts of human life more easy to be obtained" were to be permitted to pass free and unmolested. Elaborate provisions, foreshadowing the Red Cross Convention, pledged humane treatment of prisoners of war. Though these rules were in part adopted by the Jay Treaty and other conventions of the period, they were on the whole too unrealistic for survival.

Perhaps the most amazing feature of warfare in those days was the ease with which private persons traveled from one belligerent country to the other. Laurence Sterne, who went to France in 1763, comments casually, "I had left London with so much precipitation that it never enter'd my mind that we were at war with France"; he reached Paris without having a passport and had friendly contacts with French "people of culture," including army officers....during the seventeenth and the eighteenth centuries this trend was reflected in military agreements which, in the case of the capitulation of a fortress, city, or military unit, provided for a certain protection of the sick and wounded. Similar though more limited provisions are found at the end of the seventeenth century and throughout the eighteenth as incidents of military *cartels*, that is, in arrangements between military commanders for the exchange and ransom of prisoners of war; in a few cases the cartels took the form of conventions between the warring rulers themselves. A main concern of the cartels was to secure refund of expenses to the army, which, as a result of military events, had taken care of wounded and sick enemies. The provisions of the cartels varied greatly. Ordinarily, wounded and sick enemies had to be sent back to their army as conveniently as possible; until then they were accorded the right to be cared for by surgeons of their army and by their own servants, a regulation apparently meant for higher officers. Hospitals were sometimes exempted from confiscation by the enemy. Particular praise for humaneness has been bestowed on a cartel of 1743 between the English General Count Stairs and the French General Duc de Noailles. Its main merit was that it guaranteed the inviolability of military hospitals.[33]

The change in attitude described above is astonishing. It was as if man had made a quantum jump in his evolutionary road, but unfortunately it was only temporary (see Chapter 9). With the Revolution of 1789, the most enthusiastic principles of brotherhood and international justice were proclaimed by the French Government, which was bent on insuring that *"liberté, égalité, fraternité"* would reign supreme with all peoples. In practice, however, the armies of Revolutionary France did not uphold those principles and it is with the French Revolution that a new era of disregard for international law was initiated. During the Napoleonic wars, its most brazen violation was the abduction, by Napoleon, of the Duke of Enghien from neutral territory to France, where he was executed after a summary trial in 1804. The episode produced the famous comment (variously attributed to Talleyrand, to Fouché, and to Boulay de la Meurthe), "C'est plus q'un crime, c'est une faute."[34]

As usual, violations of international law were not made by one side only. In 1806 the English Government tried to establish a blockade of the European continent from the sea, and Napoleon, with the "Continental Blockade" to be carried out from the land, attempted to stop British commerce. Both violated accepted rules of international law concerning neutral powers. Perhaps an even more notorious deed was the English bombardment of Copenhagen in 1807, which resulted in the surrender of the Danish fleet. The English action was dictated by the information, received by the Government, that in the Franco-Russian Peace Treaty of Tilsit there was a secret clause which stipulated that Denmark would be compelled by Russia and France to close her ports to English ships and join the war against Great Britain.[35] The Danes had, of course, nothing to do with those machinations.

The Napoleonic era ended with the Congress of Vienna in 1815. The peace document was signed by Austria, France, Great Britain, Portugal, Prussia, Russia and Sweden. It marked the end of the more extreme dreams of the French Revolution and, as all historical acts, was to be judged by some as a positive, by others as a negative, accomplishment. One of its most positive results was undoubtedly the suppression of the still-flourishing international slave trade. It is of interest that, in the one hundred years following the Congress of Vienna, about sixteen thousand treaties were concluded. In 1917, it was estimated, about ten thousand treaties were in existence.[36]

A definite improvement in warfare was brought about by Jean Henri Dunant of Geneva. He was an eyewitness of the Battle of Solferino (1859), in which forty thousand French and Austrian soldiers were killed or wounded. The horrible sufferings of the wounded, buried alive or left to die almost unattended on the battlefield, were described by Dunant in the famous "Un Souvenir de Solferino." The book stirred public opinion and greatly helped his proposals to found an international association for the care of wounded and sick soldiers. As a result, the Red Cross eventually came to be.

Another milestone was the first Hague Peace Conference (1899), which resulted in various international agreements, including some providing for the protection of prisoners of war, limitations on the exercise of military power in occupied territory, and the prohibition of the use of poisons and the bombardment of hospitals, inhabited places, and buildings dedicated to worship, art, science, and charity.[37] In the twentieth century, additional treaties have contributed to the creation of a body of international law (see list beginning on p.128).

A sign of progress in the evolution of international law is the respect for neutrality. The essential point of neutrality is that, following the signing of a certain treaty, the powerful, even if stronger, may not harm the neutral. It is understandable that many centuries have to pass before man can be induced to honor such commitments with consistency. Not to take advantage of one's superiority when vital interests are at stake—as is often the case in war—requires a high degree of civilization. Although there has been undeniable progress in this respect in the last few centuries, we are still far from the goal.

In the Middle Ages, the terms *neuter* and *neutralitas* were used simply to state a condition of non-participation in a war. A treaty of neutrality having legal significance was concluded in 1492 between the principality of Liège and the Netherlands, then at war with France. Liège declared that it would not participate in the conflict and it was guaranteed against invasion or other acts of war.[38] At the time, the neutrality of a country was generally a matter of agreement between a powerful belligerent and the country in question. In the absence of such an accord, any belligerent felt entitled to pass through any neutral country with troops and supplies, and even to levy mercenaries there. The situation was not better in maritime warfare. In the fifteenth century, English law decreed that neutral cargo would be seized or destroyed if in an enemy ship ("enemy ship, enemy goods"). In 1543 a French ordinance decreed that the same principle applied also in the opposite situation ("enemy goods, enemy ship"), and the rule was accepted by England, although not by Spain.[39]

The question of trade greatly interfered with progress in international agreements concerning neutrality. It was easier for a neutral country not to take sides in the war than to renounce trading with the belligerents, and this, of course, created problems. In fact, in the eighteenth century, practically all maritime countries had difficulties with neutrality and trade with belligerents. Usually the problem was that, when a given country was not involved in a given war, it wanted to take advantage of its neutrality and have the liberty of trading with all. On the other hand, when the same country was a belligerent, it wanted to be able to enforce blockades against the other side and tended to see any merchandise that was sold to it as contraband. Holland, Sweden, the United States, England, and France were all involved in controversies of this type.

The neutrality of Switzerland was recognized by most European countries in 1815, while most of the laws concerning neutrality are contained in the Declaration of Paris of 1856 and the Hague Conventions V and XIII of 1907. Other agreements were reached from time to time and modified when needed; others have not been modified yet, although the need exists. For example, under the Hague Rules of Air Warfare (1923), neutrals have the right to defend their air space from the passage of belligerent aircraft. The question of how to deal with ballistic missiles and artificial satellites, however, has not yet been addressed.

Events of the First and Second World Wars have confirmed that, even among the most "advanced" nations, respect for the acknowledged rights of neutral states and for international law is far from being perfect. The First World War began with the violation of Belgian neutrality by Germany. England then violated international law by mining the North Sea so that the navigation of neutral ships, coming and going from German ports, was interfered with. The Germans retaliated by declaring the waters around England, Scotland, and Ireland precluded to neutrals, and England responded by barring all neutral vessels from entering or leaving Germany. Germany, as a reprisal, declared that all vessels, enemy and neutral, found in certain areas would be torpedoed by her submarines without warning (because such warning would endanger the security of the submarine). As a result, the British ship Lusitania was sunk on May 7, 1915 with the loss of more than eleven hundred lives, many American civilians. During the war, air attacks were carried out against areas inhabited by civilians and confiscation of enemy private property was practiced on a large scale. Unfortunately this trend was repeated and accentuated during the Second World War. The German invasion of Belgium, the Italian invasion of Greece, the English occupation of Iceland, the United States Lend-Lease Act of 1941, and the Russian declaration of war on Japan in 1945 are cases in point. If, during the Second World War, any of the belligerents had judged it to be in its interest, Switzerland would have been invaded.

The laws of war, slowly and painfully agreed upon in the last couple of centuries, have not solved the main problem, nor does their observance stand as a monument to human coherence and respect for promises and oaths.

A committee of the International Red Cross in 1951 found that many of the provisions of the Hague Conventions were no longer applicable, and a committee of the American Society of International Law in 1952 declared the laws of war to be in a "chaotic state."[40] Since then, progress has been slow and painful. Nevertheless, those laws, with some exceptions (e.g. the "laws" of the International Military Tribunals of Nuremberg and Tokyo; see Chapter 6), represent genuine progress toward a more civilized society and are the basis on which, one day, a world free of the scourge of warfare will be built. The international agreements concerning prisoners of war, treatment of the wounded, and protection of captured civilians have been particularly successful. In spite of frequent, shocking exceptions, modern wars have been, in general, much less cruel toward the helpless than the wars of the past. Unfortunately, concerning abolition of war, international laws have been singularly ineffective. This will be discussed later in this chapter.

Here is a chronological table of the milestones in the history of the law of war from 1758 to 1979.[41]

128 MAN AND WAR

1758	Emmerich de Vattel's "Le droit des gens: ou principes de la loi naturelle appliqués à la conduite et aux affairs des nations et des souverains."
1777-80	Johann Jacob Moser's "Versuch des neuesten Völkerrechts in Friedenszeiten und Kriegszeiten..."
1789	Georg Friedrich von Marten's "Précis du droit des gens modernes de l'Europe fondé sur les traités et l'usage."
1836	Henry Wheaton's "Elements of International Law."
1856	The Declaration of Paris on Maritime Commercial Warfare.
1862	Henri Dunant's "Souvenir de Solferino."
1863	United States Army General Order No. 100: "Instructions for the Government of Armies of the United States in the Field" (Francis Lieber's Code).
1863	Foundation of the Red Cross.
1864	The first Geneva Convention, for Wounded and Sick on Land.
1868	The St. Petersburg Declaration of Prohibited Weapons.
1868	Johann Kaspar Bluntschli's "Moderne Völkerrecht als Rechtsbuch dargestellt."
1874	The Brussels Conference on the Rules of Military Warfare, and its Draft Code.
1880	The Institute of International Law's Manual of the Laws of War on Land, 1880 ("The Oxford Manual").
1899	The (first) Hague Conference on Peace and Disarmament, and its Conventions, Land War Regulations, and Declarations.
1906-7	Second generation of Geneva Conven-

	tions: Wounded and Sick on Land and at Sea.
1907	The (second) Hague Peace Conference, and its Conventions and Land War Regulations.
1909	The London Conference, and its Declaration on the Rules of Naval Warfare.
1923	The Hague Rules for Aerial Warfare.
1925	The Geneva Gas Warfare Protocol.
1929	Third generation of Geneva Conventions: Wounded and Sick on Land and at Sea; Prisoners.
1944-45	International Military Tribunal, Nuremberg.
1946-48	International Military Tribunal, Tokyo.
1949	The fourth generation of Geneva Conventions: Wounded and Sick on Land and at Sea; Prisoners; Civilians.
1956	International Committee of the Red Cross's Draft Rules for Protection of Civilians.
1968	"International Year of Human Rights"; United Nations' Secretary-General begins inquiry into "Human Rights in Armed Conflicts."
1974-77	Geneva Diplomatic Conference for the Reaffirmation and Development of The Law of Armed Conflict.
1977	Additional Protocols I and II.
1979	Diplomatic Conference at Geneva on Prohibited Weapons.

(b) Dreams of Perpetual Peace

Man's efforts to achieve lasting peace have historically taken two forms, one rational, the other irrational. The latter, which we call pacifism, will be discussed in Chapter 7. The former, the striving to achieve perpetual peace through legislation and changes in political structure, will be discussed here. We call pacifism irrational because, as we will see, it springs from certain subconscious needs that are not easily controlled by our will. Efforts to achieve perpetual peace (based on supranational structures and laws designed to abolish war) are, on the other hand, rational attempts to overcome man's drive for war.

Peace is a central element in many of the world's great religions. The *Wu-Wei* (non-action) of Taoism and the *ahisma* (non-injury) of Jainism and Buddhism are cases in point.[42] Isaiah prophesized that "...they shall beat their swords into plowshares, and their spears into pruning hooks: nation shall not lift up sword against nation, neither shall they learn war any more,"[43] and Christian teaching rests on the idea of peace through brotherhood and love. In the classical world the peace proclamations of Ptolemaic Egypt (the *philantropa*) and the Roman concept of *pax* were examples of the desire for peace expressed in public policy.[44] In spite of this yearning, however, it was only in the thirteenth century that the first project to achieve perpetual peace was proposed.

To our modern mind, perpetual peace is synonymous with universal peace. It was not so in the past. For example, for Pierre Dubois, one of the earliest proponents of perpetual peace, who lived between 1250 and 1312, the idea of universal peace would have been unacceptable because it would have meant peace with the infidels and therefore renunciation of the Holy Land that they were occupying. What Pierre Dubois meant was perpetual peace among the Christian princes so that, united, they could better fight the infidels. The fall of Acre, captured by the Mameluk in 1291, marked the abandonment of the last Crusader strongholds and caused consternation in Christendom. A flood of projects for the recovery of the Holy Land ("De recuperatione Terrae Sanctae") poured into the pontifical curia.[45] The pamphlet of Dubois, titled in fact *De Recuperatione Terrae Sanctae*, was one of them. It differed from the others, however, in its elaboration of the concept of peace among Christian princes and the ways to enforce it. He proposed a council, composed of prelates and princes, presided over by the Pope, which would settle disputes. War would be outlawed and peace enforced by the joint armies of the other members of the council.

The proposal was ignored, as were similar plans presented later. The main problem is that such plans do or do not involve a recognition of the supremacy of the country that happens to be the strongest at the time: if they do, the other countries will not accept this fact; if they do not, the strongest country will not agree to participate. In either case failure is the result. In 1462, for example, the king of Bohemia proposed to Louis XI of France the formation of an alliance against the Turks that would have involved the other Christian princes. The scheme, prepared by the French adventurer Marini, included provisions for a council, a tribunal, compulsory arbitration, etc.; it meant a prominent position for France and little regard for papal and imperial prerogatives.[46] Naturally, it failed. A similar plan for peace among the Christian princes, prepared by Cardinal Wolsey, was actually incorporated in a treaty between Henry VIII of England and Francis I of France. It was a diplomatic game. When a similar idea was proposed by Pope Leo X, Wolsey himself opposed it.[47] The whole scheme was soon abandoned. Emeric Crucé, in 1623, proposed a permanent international assembly in Venice to decide disputes between princes. France was to be the dominant power in the scheme, which was not taken very seriously even in his time.

The Duke of Sully, a minister of Henry IV of France, proposed a "Grand Design" that showed some interesting traits:

> ...a European federation on the basis of a redistribution of European territory. There should be fifteen states; namely, six hereditary monarchies (France, Spain, Great Britain, Denmark, Sweden, and Lombardy), six elective monarchs (the Pope, the Emperor, the Duke of Venice, the kings of Hungary, Bohemia, and Poland), and the three republics of Switzerland, the Low Countries, and a proposed Italian republican state. The federation would operate through a General Council with supreme political and judicial functions, and through six pro-

vincial councils. The crucial point of the scheme was a weakening of Austria and Spain, then both under the Hapsburgs, and both France's adversaries. They would not only forgo their prominent position through the egalitarian structure of the federation, but also lose important territories; for instance, Spanish Belgium would fall to the United Provinces of the Netherlands, the Tyrol to Switzerland, and so on. A Europe so reconstructed would be able to expel the Turks from its territories; Sully even gives details of the contingents to be furnished by the various states for the Turkish war.

It is difficult to understand how Sully himself could have considered all this as anything but a wishful dream, a playing with thoughts.[48]

We have already mentioned that the Peace of Westphalia (1648) contained a provision for the maintenance of peace through an international organization. In 1693, William Penn, in his *Essay Toward the Present and Future Peace of Europe*, proposed, in contrast with his predecessors, a plan that would have included the Turks in a federation the Supreme Council of which would have had the function of arbitrating disputes among the members. In 1713, the Abbé de Saint-Pierre envisaged a federation that, through a Senate, would mediate international disputes. The arbitration would be compulsory, and those who would not conform with the judgment of the Senate would be coerced to do so by war. In the Senate, only the strongest states would have a vote, the smaller would vote in groups with a vote for each group. Concerning the inclusion of non-Christian states in the federation, the Abbé proposed different ideas at various times.[49] He had a distinguished position at the French court and therefore his plan was received with polite respect and indifference; also with irony, which he did not always perceive.

Since the end of the eighteenth century, a new coryphaeus of perpetual peace has repeatedly appeared on the scene of history: revolution. Every revolution is supposed to open a new chapter in the history of mankind, and each revolutionary is convinced of being able to pinpoint the ills of society and the means to cure them. War is usually one of the first ills singled out for immediate elimination. The first of the modern populist revolutions, the French Revolution, was, in fact, supposed to inaugurate a golden age of peace. The 1791 Constitution states that "the French nation renounces the undertaking of any war with a view to making conquests, and will never employ its forces against the liberty of any people."[50] The idea, of course, was that war was a perifidious machination of kings and that the people, freed from their bonds of servitude, would never engage in such a thing. Except, of course, when forced to defend country and liberty from aggression. This happened in 1792 when the French declaration of war affirmed:

> ...[this] war...is not a war of nation against nation, but the just defense of a free people against the unjust aggression of a king. That the French will never confound their brothers [i.e., the people of Austria] with their real enemies....[51]

Naturally, when the enemy becomes really obnoxious, one can easily forget the most noble intentions; so the Paris department member Lullier proposed that, to teach the British a lesson:

> One hundred thousand men should be landed on the shores of England and left there after burning their boats, so that, forced to live by despoiling the inhabitants, they would avenge the many wrongs that these perverse neighbors have inflicted on us....[52]

In spite of this, the Convention did not have the slightest intention of abandoning the lofty principles that made the French superior to the perfidious British led by the no less perfidious Pitt. In the words of representative Couppé:

> ...the Convention did not mean that our country should renounce all ideas of humanity, nor set itself on the road toward emulating its atrocious enemies....[53]

In the words of Barère:

> We do not wish to conduct ourselves barbarously, not make war like cannibals; we wish simply to give up those principles of universal philanthropy which get in the way of our military operations, and of which our enemies take advantage.[54]

From this point of view, the French Revolution is the prototype of all those that have followed, up to our time: great proclamations of peace and prosperity followed by war, suffering, and, often, famine, and declarations of social justice followed by the substitution of one privileged class with another. Revolution, in fact, seems most often to be a convulsive disorder that does not accelerate, but rather retards, the normal progress of mankind.

As man persisted in his intermittent attempts to solve social ills (including war) with revolutions, the quest for perpetual peace continued. Immanuel Kant's essay *Toward Perpetual Peace* (1795) is usually included among the plans to abolish war.

> Kant is there concerned with a critical evaluation of the conception of perpetual peace, which he thinks is not a chimera but a goal attainable by a long process of gradual approximation under certain conditions defined by him, conditions that are all within human power....He wisely refrains from any attempt to expatiate upon the structure of the future confederation (if any); he merely points out that a confederation of free states would be a prerequisite of perpetual peace. In a measure, his superior reasoning amounts to a confutation of what one might call the "dreamer" school of international political planning.[55]

Kant's essay is not a dream about easily attainable peace but a profound view of the bloody road that humanity must travel so that peace may perhaps be achieved one day.[56]

Later, the hope for peace was based on free trade. It was felt that man, being a rational animal, would realize the immense advantages of peace in a world where the links of free trade made all men partners and where war would be so obviously damaging for all. Norman Angell, a free-trade pacifist, argued in 1910 that the internationalism of finance and commerce had made war impossible.[57] Comte, founder of the Positivist school and father of modern sociology, was also convinced that the rise of industry would eventually eliminate war and bring perpetual peace. He states:

> In antiquity the greatest industrial efforts were related primarily to war, which gave rise to prodigious inventions, especially in connection with sieges. In modern times, on the contrary, the system of armaments is relatively less perfected than in Greek and Roman times, when we take into consideration the great industrial development.[58]

He could not foresee that leaders of industry like Krupp and Armstrong were going to make a fortune in armaments and that Nobel and Maxim would become rich and famous by discovering new tools for war.[59]

New hope for perpetual peace arose after the creation of the League of Nations. Another dramatic effort to achieve peace among states was the Pact of Paris, better known as the Kellogg Pact. The main sponsors were Aristide Briant, French Minister of Foreign Affairs, and Frank B. Kellogg, U.S. Secretary of State. The treaty was formally proclaimed on July 24, 1929 and was subsequently ratified by sixty-three nations. The signatory powers renounced war as an instrument of national policy and pledged themselves to seek the solution to controversies by pacific means only. Japan, one of the signatories, invaded Manchuria in 1931, and Italy invaded Ethiopia in 1935. The Second World War followed soon after. The United Nations, established after the Second World War, has not been more successful in eliminating war.

It is evident that all the plans for the achievement of perpetual peace by the creation of supranational organizations have one or more of the following faults depending on the historical period in which they were conceived:

a) Provincialism. The peace sought is only among the Christian states and is only a means with which a more effective war can be waged against the infidels.

b) Prevarication. The frequently advocated supranational organization is so structured as to provide advantage to a state or group of states at the expense of others.

c) Paralysis. The more powerful members are given, by necessity, veto power, which, especially when discussing important issues, is used to paralyze the organization. This happens because important issues almost always involve the global interests of the most powerful members and a decision in favor of one side is bound to damage the other.

d) Perpetuation of the *status quo*. This is probably the most serious and the most difficult to eliminate. The fluid and dynamic state of the international scene is the result of struggle and conflict. Any plan to maintain perpetual peace will tend to favor the "freezing" of international society as it is at the time the scheme goes into effect. Because the *status quo* is never satisfactory for all and forever, efforts to alter it will be inevitable. Any future plan will have to take this problem into account.

Although designs for perpetual peace appeal to man's intellect, they do not have the capacity to control the drives that impel groups to fight. The elimination of war, therefore, will not be the result of efforts to create organizations, laws, and supranational bodies capable of enforcing peace, but of the irresistible action of some agent capable of controlling the drive toward war. This point shall be discussed in Chapter 9.

As wars follow each other in a seemingly unending succession, in recent times disarmament has often been proposed in an attempt to find a formula for peace.

In 1816 the Czar of Russia proposed to the British Government a simultaneous reduction of the armed forces of both countries. The English replied by suggesting an international conference to determine the respective strength of each power. Everybody agreed that it was a magnificent idea worth pursuing, and the matter was dropped. The French Government made a similar proposal in 1831; it was favorably received, and nothing more was heard about it. Napoleon III, who must have been a believer in the iterative approach, made similar proposals in 1863, 1867, and 1869, with the same results. In 1870 Great Britain proposed disarmament to Prussia and was rebuffed. In 1877 Italy approached Germany with the same result.[60] The First Hague Peace Conference of 1899 had as one of its main purposes the limitation of armaments, and concluded with the affirmation of the desirability of such limitations; the Second Hague Peace Conference of 1907 confirmed the resolution adopted in the first conference concerning reduction of armaments and, noting that military expenditures had in the meantime increased in almost all countries, declared that all governments should seriously consider the matter.[61] At the Treaty of Versailles, another approach was taken: instead of trying to disarm all, it was decided to disarm only the loser—who, of course, was the guilty party and the troublemaker. The success of the attempt is well known. The idea of general disarmament was, however, not dropped. The League of Nations established a Preparatory Commission for a Disarmament Conference, which led to the World Disarmament Conference that convened in Geneva in 1932. Its general commission met for the last time in 1934, and the whole effort was an "unmitigated failure, unable to reach formal agreements of any kind."[62]

After the Second World War, in 1946, the General Assembly of the United Nations created an Atomic Energy Commission for, among other things, "the elimination...of atomic weapons and of all other weapons adaptable to mass destruction."[63] In the "Principles Governing the General Regulation and Reduction of Armaments" the General Assembly also recognized the necessity for the reduction of conventional armaments and instructed the Security Council to consider all practical means to achieve this end. Consequently, in 1947, the Security Council passed a resolution establishing a Commission for Conventional Armaments, with the purpose of preparing proposals for disarmament. So far, almost forty years later, the results of all those efforts have been nil.

Efforts to reduce armaments have not been uniformly unsuccessful. The most notable success was achieved by the Rush-Bagot Agreement of 1817 between the United States and Canada, limiting the strength of naval forces of each nation on the Great Lakes to three vessels of equal tonnage and armament. Revised during the Second World War, the treaty is still in force. The Washington Treaty of 1922 for the Limitations of Naval Armaments achieved some success in limiting the number of capital ships of the United States, Britain, Japan, France, and Italy. The conference failed to produce agreement on craft other than capital ships, such as cruisers, destroyers, and submarines. Some limited successes were also achieved by other naval conferences in 1927, 1930, 1935, and 1937, but their effectiveness in securing peace was practically zero. The Second World War began shortly after the last such conference.

The successes of these naval agreements were either of very local and limited importance (e.g., the Rush-Bagot Agreement), or were the result, not of any genuine belief in their effectiveness in the search for peace, but of their usefulness as subterfuges to obtain temporary advantages. For example, the Washington Treaty limiting capital ships was signed when, according to many experts, such ships were becoming obsolete and it was thought that future sea battles would be fought and won mainly by smaller and faster craft. Japan accepted a smaller number because it felt that it was to its advantage to temporarily stop the battleship-building race and come out of the isolation caused by the understanding between the United States and England. When the conditions that made the treaty useful no longer existed, Japan terminated it.[64]

Other attempts to achieve disarmament have ended in failure mainly because all nations strive to attain superiority over the others. Therefore, any agreement is considered a temporary maneuver or a tool to achieve this goal, to be discarded when no longer useful. In addition, as mentioned before, if the agreement tends to confirm the superiority of the stronger, it will not be accepted by the weaker; if it does not, it will be rejected by the stronger.

The difficulties of reaching meaningful agreements in the field of disarmament are universally recognized. It is, however, often assumed that, if such agreements were reached, great benefits would result and a new era of peace would dawn on mankind. The idea of disarmament is based on the concept that man fights because he has weapons. Once the weapons are eliminated, so the argument goes, war becomes either impossible or at least less destructive, because sticks and stones are less lethal than advanced weapons.

The argument is not valid. Men do not fight because they have weapons, they have weapons because they fight. As discussed in Chapter 1, primates are known to kill each other and even to engage in conflicts resembling a primitive form of warfare. It is difficult to believe that primitive man got the idea of killing his neighbor only after discovering the lethality of a heavy stick. War, as we have seen (Chapter 1), is the result of subconscious drives and not of the availability of weapons; it is, therefore, to be expected that disarmament would not have an effect on the achievement of perpetual peace.

The question remains whether disarmament would at least reduce the likelihood of war. If by disarmament we mean a reduction in the number and availability of the most lethal weapons, and if, as such, it were to reduce the likelihood of war, we should be able to discern an historical pattern of increased frequency of conflicts as weapons became more lethal and more commonly available. No such pattern has been detected. If by disarmament we mean the total abolition of weapons, we return to the point discussed above concerning the relation between weapons and war. We must therefore come to the conclusion that disarmament would not reduce the incidence of war, let alone result in perpetual peace.

At this point the second part of the argument in favor of disarmament is to be examined. Even if it does not reduce the incidence of conflict, could a general weapons reduction be expected to reduce the amount of death and devastation in case of war? The answer is: yes in theory, no in practice. The reason is clear. Obviously bows and arrows, as weapons of mass destruction, are not in the same category as nuclear bombs. Therefore, if the former were the only arms used, death and devastation would be limited. In practice, however, even if a complete ban on nuclear weapons were agreed upon, by necessity the agreement would be valid only as long as the signatories were at peace. Once war started, even if fought with bows and arrows, every country would start to build nuclear weapons if for no other reason than the belief that the other side would do so. Treaties can eliminate weapons but not the capacity to build them; as a rule, a nation will use all the weapons that can be made available to avoid a catastrophic defeat.

The fact that poison gases were not used in the Second World War is usually brought up as encouraging evidence and as an example of the usefulness of disarmament treaties. The point is not valid:

> The observance of the prohibition of the use of poison gas in the Second World War is but an apparent exception. All the major belligerents manufactured poison gas; they trained troops in its use and in defense against it and were prepared to use it if such use would seem to be advantageous. Only considerations of military expediency deterred all belligerents from making use of a weapon of which they had all availed themselves with the intention of using it if necessary.[65]

Sometimes attempts to achieve arms limitations may even result in more effectively waged war. As mentioned above, the Treaty of Versailles imposed disarmament on the loser. The limitations were so strict that for Germany it would have been impossible to wage a war similar to the First World War. For this reason, Germany waged a different kind of war that took her opponents by surprise and brought her to the brink of victory. It is also conceivable that, once the more sophisticated weapons are abolished by treaty, war may become more likely because, although all the conditions for its starting remain, the fear generated by the most lethal weapons is removed.

From the above we must conclude that disarmament:
a) as a bona fide step toward peace, is impossible to achieve;
b) if achieved would not abolish war;
c) would limit death and devastation only in the very beginning of a war and simply postpone for a short period the use of more lethal weapons; and
d) in certain situations, could encourage war by eliminating the deterrence of the more lethal weapons.

Does this mean that disarmament is useless, dangerous, and to be avoided? Does this also mean that we should allow the arms race to continue unchecked?

It has been pointed out that the arms race "which generates, and feeds on, fear and imposes ever-increasing financial burdens, may lead to so intolerable a situation that all or some parties to the race will prefer its termination by whatever means, even at the risk of war, to its indefinite continuation."[66] The problem of the nuclear arms race and nuclear disarmament will be discussed in Chapter 9. We must remember, however, that, in general, disarmament, although an ideal goal as part of a permanent settlement of international conflict, cannot and must not be considered the first step in that direction. Disarmament can only be a consequence, not a cause, of the reduction of tension. If we were to consider international tension as an infectious disease, we could say that disarmament represents the decrease in the fever, not the antibiotic. This means that it may make the international community feel better but that it has no therapeutic effect on the underlying disease.

Goya — *The Way Is Hard* (From Los Desastres De La Guerra)

Chapter 6

> Sanno rarissime volte gli uomini essere al tutto cattivi o al tutto buoni.[1]
>
> Machiavelli, *Discorsi*, I, 27.
>
> You have to be good good or bad bad to be remembered.
>
> Simone Rodia[2]

ETHICS AND WAR CRIMES

(a) Ethics and War

As a general rule, each group will expand at the expense of others unless checked by external forces. In other words, each group exerts, and is the object of, expansive pressure as a member of the world community.

The word "expansion" is to be understood in terms of economic or political dominance or even territorial conquest resulting from military operations. In recent times, especially in the twentieth century, politico-economic dominance has largely replaced territorial conquest as the manifestation of the expansive thrust. The pressures exerted by groups tend to result in a state of equilibrium that readily adjusts to the dynamics of international politics. It is easy to imagine, for example, that even as peaceful a country as Switzerland, if suddenly surrounded by nations that, for whatever reasons, had fallen to the military-economic level of, let us say, Nepal, could not avoid filling the vacuum and assuming all the attributes, attitudes, interests, behaviors, and duties of a dominant power in the area.

The intensity of the expansive pressure is modified by many factors—as, for example, distance. The pressure is, in fact, inversely proportional to the distance between the groups considered, although in modern times the importance of distance has decreased. The impetus toward expansion is also modified by internal forces. However, revolutions and internal problems capable of interfering with the group's capacity to generate pressure are usually temporary phenomena.

A country's expanding force is similar to the individual's drive for the acquisition of power, but in the international arena it can be observed in a clearer form without interference from the innumerable factors that tend to modify the behavior of the individual. Without attempting to analyze the mechanisms of the subconscious, one can assume, with Adler, that it is in the nature of man to strive for power. Gibbon says: "Of all our passions and appetites, the love for power is of the most imperious...nature,"[3] and Bertrand Russell repeats: "Of the infinite desires of man, the chief are the desires for power and glory."[4] The nature of this drive can be better understood if one assumes that it is an expression of the basic instinct of survival. In other words, power, like war (see Chapter 1), is used as a means to attain immortality. Man seeks power and glory to leave something behind after his death. The general and the politician want to leave their mark on history, the businessman on the company, the writer on literature, the scientist on science, and so on. Each man strives to build his own monument. The real purpose of the acquisition of power and glory is not enjoyment of their possession but survival. The ways and means to acquire power vary greatly from individual to individual according to ethical, religious, cultural, and psychological factors. The modifying influence of these factors is such that it is not unusual to encounter individuals who seem to lack the drive for the acquisition of power. It is to be assumed, however, that even in such cases, given a modification of external conditions or different circumstances, such a drive would become manifest.

In the case of groups, the need for power could be considered as the expression of the sum of individual components without most of the ethical, cultural, and religious *impedimenta*. In fact the ways and means used by groups to acquire power, in any given historical period, are stereotyped as opposed to the great variability observed in the case of individuals.

The power of a country (the most common form that the group assumes in the international scene) is composed of three main elements (see Chapter 8): military, economic, and psychological. Power is the springboard of the expansive force; in fact, the latter is directly proportional to the former. As a consequence, in view of the obvious variations that exist among countries in terms of total power, the intensity of the expanding force will vary greatly. However, at any given historical period, countries of equal power exert equal pressure, except for temporary modifications produced by internal or external circumstances.

The expanding force of each country is opposed by those exerted by the others, and an equilibrium is maintained until a new one is established, usually by war. The expanding force exerts a continuous pressure with its military and economic components. The proportion of these two elements varies according to circumstances and country considered. It is understood that "military pressure" in this context means military capability and not actual application of military force. Many factors, as stated before, can modify the pressure exerted by the expanding force; some of them are very effective, others are less so. Among the least effective are the ethical ones. In fact, relations among states seem to be governed by rules that are essentially amoral. This statement means that, to the observer, it looks as if the conduct of foreign policy were governed by amoral rules. It will be discussed later (Chapter 7) whether such acts as killing civilian enemies, stealing other countries' military secrets (espionage), willful dissemination of lies (propaganda), unilateral abrogation of treaties, etc., are really amoral acts or if we only react to them as if they were.

The fact that relations between groups are governed by rules that are amoral was perceived in antiquity, as shown by the famous dialogue of Melos.

During the Peloponnesian war, as Thucydides reports,[5] the Athenians landed an army on the island of Melos, a colony of Sparta. The Melians had declared themselves neutral and the Athenians, before attacking, sent envoys to negotiate the surrender. They started the discussion by encouraging the islanders to consider the situation in the most realistic terms; they recognized that the Melians were neutral and that Athens had suffered no injury from them; however, they said, "we both alike know that into the discussion of human affairs the question of justice only enters where there is equal power to enforce it, and that the powerful exact what they can, and the weak grant what they must." The Melians started by pointing out that it was in the interest of both sides to avoid a conflict. The envoys responded that, for the Athenians, it was necessary that the Melians be subjugated because, they said, "the real danger is from our many subject states, who may of their own motion rise up and overcome their masters. If we were to withdraw our forces from Melos," they continued, these subject states would "think that states like yours are left free because they are able to defend themselves, and that we do not attack them because we dare not. So your subjection will give us an increase of security, as well as an extension of empire." The Melians mentioned the dishonor that surrender would bring, and the Athenians retorted that "the question is not of honor but of prudence." Then the Melians advanced the argument of ethics and protection by the gods: "We do not despair of fortune; for we hope to stand as high as you in the favor of heaven, because we are righteous and you...are unrighteous."

At this point, the Athenian envoys explained man's use of power in terms valid not only for that particular time and place, but for all times and for all places. They said: "For of the gods we believe, and of men we know, that by a law of their nature wherever they can rule they will. This law was not made by us, and we are not the first who have acted upon it; we did but inherit it, and shall bequeath it to all time, and we know that you and all mankind, if you were as strong as we are, would do as we do." The Melians refused to surrender; the Athenians conquered the island, put to death all men, made slaves of the women and children, and "then colonized the island, sending thither five hundred settlers of their own."[6]

Various attempts have been made, throughout history, to inject ethics into the unceasing struggle of each group to prevail over the others (see Chapter 7). At the end of the seventeenth century, for example, Fénelon wrote:

> One must count on what is real and happens every day, which is that each nation seeks to prevail over all the others that surround it. Each nation is therefore obliged to be unceasingly watchful in order to prevent the excessive enlargement of each neighbor, for his own safety. To prevent the neighbor from being too powerful is not at all to do evil; it is to protect oneself from slavery and likewise to protect one's other neighbors. In a word, it is to work for liberty, for tranquility, for the public well-being....This attention to maintaining a kind of equality and equilibrium among neighboring nations is what assures their common peace.[7]

In the early part of the twentieth century, on the other hand, Douhet, the theoretician of air power, took a more pessimistic position:

> It is useless to delude ourselves; all the restrictions, all the international agreements made during peacetime are fated to

be swept away like dried leaves on the winds of war. A man who is fighting a life-and-death fight—as all wars are nowadays—has the right to use any means to keep his life. War means cannot be classified as human and inhuman. War will always be inhuman, and the means which are used in it cannot be classified as acceptable or not acceptable except according to their efficacy, potentiality, or harmfulness to the enemy. The purpose of war is to harm the enemy as much as possible; and all means that contribute to this end will be employed, no matter what they are. He is a fool if not a patricide who would acquiesce in his country's defeat rather than go against those formal agreements which do not limit the right to kill and destroy, but simply the ways of killing and destroying.[8]

In this discussion, the term "amoral" has been used in the common meaning of "neither moral nor immoral." Although this has been, so far, satisfactory for our purposes, some clarification is now in order.

It is commonly stated that geometry, for example, is amoral. If the canons of ethics are not applied to foreign politics, the question arises whether foreign politics should be defined as amoral in the same sense as geometry. It is evident that if we were to say that a triangle, or the study of a triangle, is immoral, we would be stating an absurdity. But if we declare that country A has not honored a treaty with country B and therefore has committed an immoral act, we are not dealing with the same degree of absurdity even if it is agreed that ethical principles do not apply in the relations between nations. In fact, the statement that, in the above case, country A acted unethically may appear a valid statement to many. Obviously then, even if conventional moral principles are not applied to the breaking of treaties (or any other act of international politics), they could be, and the statement "war is immoral" is not as inane as "geometry is immoral." It would appear then that although in no circumstances could the study of geometry be considered immoral, the breaking of a treaty could be if the usual ethical standards were applied. In other words, two types (or degrees) of amorality may be identified: in one, what is amoral is so under all circumstances (e.g., geometry); in the other, what is amoral is so only because usual moral standards are not applied (e.g., the breaking of a treaty). These two types of amorality may be defined as amorality of the first order and amorality of the second order. The objection might be raised that amorality of the second order includes any conceivable act no matter how reprehensible because, obviously, a theft or a murder (obviously immoral acts) could be declared amoral by simply deciding not to judge them by the usual ethical standards. The objection is not valid simply because, historically, ethical standards, usually, *have been* applied to theft or murder and *have not been* applied to war and acts of foreign politics in general (attempts to do so will be discussed later).

Moreover, even in the case of theft and murder, conventional moral standards have not been applied with absolute consistency. If an individual steals military secrets from a hostile country to the benefit of his own, or in war kills enemy soldiers, he is not considered a thief or a murderer. Those acts are amoral of the second order. It is, in fact, to be underlined that, although a spy caught in the act is punishable by death according to the laws of war (Article 68 of the 1949 Geneva Convention), spying is not considered a criminal activity (Article 31 of the 1907 Hague Convention). Thus the death penalty is imposed not for punishment but for deterrence.[9]

At this point two questions arise: (i) is it really true that ethical principles are not applied in war and foreign politics as asserted above, and (ii) if not, why?

As for the first question, even a superficial study of history shows that this is the case indeed. Concerning all the wars and all the treaties of the past, from the Punic to the Napoleonic wars, from the conquest of Gaul to the subjugation of India, from the Peace of Westphalia to the Treaty of Versailles, from the various and common non-aggression pacts to commitments to settle disputes by pacific means, one notes a vast display of oratorical flourish about noble principles and very little else besides naked self-interest from all countries involved. Examples are extremely easy to find; here is one that is both recent and dramatic.

150 MAN AND WAR

The following is a document that should be remembered, together with the events that followed it, not because it is unusual or because it shows the perfidy of one or both parties; just the contrary, it should be remembered because it is so typical of the way foreign policy has been conducted since the beginning. This is not to say that all acts of foreign policy are followed by such dramatic reverses, nor that in all cases there is such obviously naked self-interest and disregard of ethical principles. In other cases the self-interest may be less blatant or the disregard of ethical principles less obvious (especially when the act is of less overall importance for the countries involved), but morality has always been conspicuously absent except in words.

On the 28th of September, 1939, the following joint statement was issued by the German and Soviet Governments:

> Moscow, September 28, 1939.
>
> The Government of the German Reich and the Government of the USSR having, by means of the treaty signed today, definitely settled the problems of the disintegration of the Polish State and having thereby created a firm foundation for a lasting peace in Eastern Europe, they mutually express their conviction that it would serve the true interest of all peoples to put an end to the state of war existing at present between Germany on the one side and England and France on the other. [England and France had declared war on Germany because the latter had invaded Poland; Russia had then invaded on the other side, and the country was partitioned between Germany and Russia. Italy, Japan, and the U.S. had not entered the war yet.] Both Governments will therefore direct their common efforts, jointly with other friendly powers if occasion arises, toward attaining this goal as soon as possible.
>
> Should, however, the efforts of the two Governments remain fruitless, this would demonstrate the fact that England and France were responsible for the continuation of the war; in which event the Governments of Germany and the USSR shall engage in mutual consultations with regard to necessary measures.[10]

As to the question of why morality is not applied to foreign policy, the answer is that no country could afford to do so unless all others would do the same, and man has not yet reached the level of evolution that would make this possible. In other words, unilateral application of ethics in war is self-destructive and asinine, as pointed out by Mao Tse-tung:

> In the year 638 B.C..... the two feudal states of Sung and Ch'u fought a battle at the Hung River in central China. The army of Sung, led by its ruler Duke Hsiang, was drawn up in battle formation on the river's northern bank; the Ch'u army had to ford the stream. When its soldiers were halfway across, one of Hsiang's ministers came to him and said, "They are many, and we are few. Pray let us attack them before they are all crossed over." The Duke refused. When the enemy army had reached the northern bank but had not yet re-formed its lines, the minister again asked leave to begin the fight; again the Duke refused. Only after the Ch'u soldiers were properly marshalled did he signal the attack. And then, in the ensuing battle, the Duke himself was wounded and his army put to flight. According to the chronicles, the people of Sung blamed their ruler for the defeat, but he said, "The superior man does not inflict a second wound, and does not take prisoner anyone of gray hairs. When the ancients had their armies in the field, they would not attack an enemy when he was in a defile; and though I am but the poor representative of a fallen dynasty, I will not sound my drums to attack an unformed host."
> ...Mao Tse-tung drew his story out of the chronicles in order to make a modern point. "We are not the Duke of Sung," he declared in one of his lectures "On Protracted War" (1938), "and we have no use for his asinine ethics."[11]

No government could, in the name of ethical principles (e.g., that killing is immoral), let another country occupy a part of its territory without armed resistance. However, especially if the disproportion between its military power and the enemy's is sufficiently great, or if armed resistance is of no avail, it is usually expedient for the government of the invaded country to invoke ethical principles.

It is implicit in the concept of amorality of the second order that the quantity of human actions that it encompasses varies with time. In a hypothetical primitive society in which ethical concepts had not yet evolved, every act would have been amoral of the second order by definition. As primitive societies evolved, the creation of the first taboos marked the beginning of ethics, which decreased the number of acts that we call amoral of the second order. For example, it might be conceived that parricide or cannibalism, at a certain point, ceased to be amoral and became immoral. On the other hand, we can speculate that, in the ideal society of the future, amorality of the second order will be reduced to a minimum because most acts will be considered from an ethical point of view. It is evident that between the two extremes there will be a continuous process of change during which different actions previously considered amoral would become immoral. Although this process advances at an exceedingly slow pace, the change can be easily detected during historical times. The physical elimination of large groups of civilians, for example, was not considered particularly repugnant during the classical wars, but during the Second World War caused horror and revulsion. Similarly, the mutilation, the killing of children as a game, the boiling of human beings, and some of the other atrocities mentioned in Chapter 3 would not be tolerated today. In other words, what were before, at least for some, acts amoral in the second degree have become immoral for all.

This means that, although war and foreign politics in general are regulated by amorality of the second order, the most extreme acts related to these activities tend more and more to become immoral as humanity slowly progresses on its evolutionary path.

For centuries, moralists and theologians have tried to apply ethical principles to the practices of foreign politics. The concept of just war (see Chapter 7) was, in part, the result of such efforts. The Crusades were examples of just wars, from the Christian side; the other side had a different opinion. Colonial wars were also considered just because the conqueror, among other things, brought a true religion to the conquered barbarians; the barbarians sometimes thought otherwise. Although the doctrine of the just war has religious roots, attempts to apply ethical principles to the conduct of war and foreign affairs have often been made without reference to religion. In our time, the Vietnam War was the most deeply influenced by such attempts, which usually have deleterious results. During that war, for example, by injecting into the conflict the question whether it was moral or immoral, just or injust, good or bad, details of secondary importance were allowed to become central and important issues faded into the background. Great discussions and debates, for instance, were held to decide if some of the guerillas were in reality North Vietnamese soldiers, or if North Vietnam had invaded the South from the beginning or simply helped the South Vietnamese to carry on a war of liberation, or if the American advisors were really advisors, or if the South Vietnamese Government, being oppressive and corrupt, was really a legitimate government. On the other hand, the question of how the various possible outcomes of the war would affect the equilibrium of forces in the world did not receive much attention. The result was defeat for the United States and, consequently, a serious blow for the Western World.

Nuclear deterrence will be discussed later (Chapter 9); however, it is of interest to note here the deleterious effects of attempts to apply ethics to the subject. Here are two examples:

> [Concerning nuclear deterrence] the threat produces a "balance of terror".... But is the threat itself morally permissible?... The reason for our acceptance of deterrent strategy, most people would say, is that preparing to kill is not at all the same thing as killing. Indeed it is not, but it is frighteningly close—else deterrence wouldn't work—and it is in the nature of that closeness that the moral problem lies....The secret of nuclear deterrence is that it is a kind of bluff....The immorality lies in the threat itself, not in its present or even its likely consequences....[12]

> Whatever is wrong to do is wrong to threaten, if the latter means "mean to do".... If counter-population warfare is murder, then counter-population deterrent threats are murderous.[13]

154 MAN AND WAR

The above authors, by rejecting deterrence on moral grounds, seem to disregard the point, in this case crucial, of its effectiveness: suppose deterrence is capable of preventing war, shall we nevertheless continue to slaughter each other (as we have done for millennia) because we do not want to soil our noble spirits with the immorality of deterrence? The notion seems, at best, bizarre.

Others have tried to apply ethical principles to the ghastly arithmetic of war:

> Several years ago, in deploring the assurance of scientists that "not many deaths" would result from nuclear testing, George Kennan wrote: "I recall no quantitative stipulation in the Sixth Commandment. Whoever gave us the right, as Christians, to take even one innocent life? I fail to see how any of this can be reconciled with Christian conscience." It is a small step from Kennan's view to the view expressed by Kenneth W. Thompson that "there is some sophism in the claim that taking many lives is morally more offensive than killing one man. War in terms of any ultimate moral judgment is evil; by any absolute standard it is as wrong to bomb a city with cannons as it is with atomic bombs."[14]

Surely the notion that there may be no difference, even if only in ethical terms, between dropping atomic or conventional bombs can only have academic interest.

At this point one could ask: why are ethical principles not applied to international politics if the final goal, we all agree, is an international system based on such principles? Because only confusion and deception can arise from their application to something that is inherently immoral (if we were to apply usual standards), as war is, or as foreign politics is (the latter being, to paraphrase Clausewitz, war conducted by other means). Trying to understand and analyze, in the light of ethical principles, activities that involve killing of innocents, destruction, and deception is like attempting to measure subzero temperatures with a thermometer registering only those above the boiling point of water; we would simply get an "out-of-scale" reading. If, on the other hand, such an attempt were in reality an effort to *solve* the problems of international politics by morality, then it would be like trying to solve the problem of overpopulation by preaching the virtues of chastity.

In addition, it is evident that the application of ethical principles to international relations is unacceptable even to those who advocate it. For example, how would the most enthusiastic Canadian supporter of ethics in international affairs react if his Prime Minister were to advance the proposal of giving, in the name of international cooperation and brotherhood, the largely uninhabited Northwestern Territories to an overpopulated and underdeveloped country, such as India or China? How many generous people could be found, among the most righteous, who would be ready to reduce their standard of living to the level of the average, let us say, Albanian so that the dismally poor people of the most underdeveloped countries could also reach the Albanian level?

To the observer, it appears that relations between countries are regulated, not by ethical principles, but by a few, and at first sight, simple rules:

1) Each country pursues only and exclusively its own interest.
2) The desirable is nothing, the possible is all.
3) Conventional ethics do not apply.

It is clear that not only are these rules governing international relations in our time, but, since they have done so since the beginning of history, it is logical to assume that they will continue to do so for quite some time to come. Countries that violate these rules do so at their own risk. Let us consider a few examples.

Take the recent Falkland War. Rule number three indicates that the question "who was right and who was wrong" has no answer because in the international arena there is no right and wrong in the usual sense. It is obvious, however, that Argentina made a mistake as shown by the fact that it lost the war. What was the mistake? Considering again the three rules, it is easy to see that, although Argentina followed rule number one, it neglected rule number two. Annexation of the islands was desirable (from the Argentine point of view) but was not feasible. England, on the other hand, respected all the rules.

What about the invasion of Afghanistan by the Russians?

It is in the interest of the Soviet Union to secure the allegiance of the governments of all neighboring countries; therefore rule number one seems to have been respected. As for rule number two, time will tell. Russia of course, has no problem with rule number three except as far as international public opinion is concerned.

Although these three rules may appear simple, in fact simplistic, they are more complex than they appear at first sight:

If the United States were to invade Canada, would this be in contradiction of any of the rules? Canada is a large country, rich in natural resources and with the same language and culture as the United States. No doubt, therefore, rule number one would seem to be respected. What about rule number two? Surely Canadian armed forces are no match for the United States Army; invasion and annexation would undoubtedly be feasible. Rule number three tells us to ignore ethical scruples. Everything seems to be all right according to our rules. Should then the United States invade and annex Canada? No. Rule number one would be violated.

Rule number one indicates that every country always acts in self-interest. What is to be decided, of course, is what in a given situation constitutes self-interest. In the example just mentioned, it is obvious that the invasion of Canada would not be in the interest of the United States because of political considerations (world opinion, reaction of the Canadians, internal reactions, etc.). The acquisition of Canada, not its invasion, would be in the interest of the U.S., and in this case the two are not equivalent. The modalities of application of the various rules vary with the historical period; there was a time, in fact, when invasion and acquisition were equivalent.

Even the third rule is not as simple as it seems. It is true that individual morality does not apply to international relations, but for the man in the street, the voter, to a certain extent it does, and it is the voter who, in a democracy, decides who will be in power. Those who conduct foreign policy, on the other hand, usually follow the third rule and play the game accordingly, but are in the very difficult position of acting as if they were not. In other words, they must show that their actions in the international arena are governed by principles of conventional morality even though they are not. For example, they must act as if their country were faithful, honest, and even altruistic in dealing with other countries and as if it were always pursuing the desirable, possible or not. This is what causes confusion and obfuscation, and this is the reason for the difficulty that the governments of the Western democracies (especially of the United States) experience in conducting foreign politics. Totalitarian regimes, of course, do not have such problems.

For centuries there was no such thing as public opinion in the modern sense. Sometimes in this century a sufficiently powerful public opinion was born and, since then, for better or for worse, politicians have a new element to consider in the international game. Because public opinion affects international politics, and conventional morality has some influence on public opinion, the effect of individual ethics on international relations is not altogether negligible. Is this a positive or a negative effect? It depends. It is positive, for example, when it prevents the most extreme acts of cruelty in war; it is negative (for one side and positive for the other) when it interferes with the conduct of the foreign policy of the Western world toward the Soviet Union (in which public opinion is more easily manipulated)—as when, for example, it forced the United States to abandon Vietnam.

Will rule number three govern international politics forever? Nothing in this world is immutable and the three rules are no exception. It would appear that what we call ethical principles will become more and more important as civilization progresses, not only in the life of the individual, but in the international arena as well. What this means is that, in the far future, as the "biological need" for war decreases with the increased distance from our animal ancestors, the number of actions that we call amoral of the second order will diminish, and countries will operate more and more according to the principles of conventional, individual morality. It is to be underlined immediately, however, that this may happen only in the distant future and that, therefore, it has little or no importance as far as the present and the foreseeable future is concerned.

Another problem related to the application of moral principles to war concerns responsibility for acts committed by members of the armed forces while executing orders.

The main function of the army is, of course, to fight wars. As discussed above, war is an amoral act of the second order and an immoral act by conventional standards. For this reason, if, in time of war, the individual member of the armed forces were to execute orders only if morally acceptable by conventional standards, he would have to disobey most of them and the armed forces' reason to exist would disappear. It is evident, therefore, that as long as there are wars, obedience to orders is essential for the survival of the group. Only in certain extreme cases may refusal to obey be justified. If under usual circumstances a soldier were ordered to kill a toddler, for example, he would have not only the right but also the duty to disobey. This is so because, as stated before, although war in general is regulated by amorality of the second order, its most extreme acts are not. In practice there may be borderline cases in which a decision may be difficult, but it would appear that obedience to orders must be considered a very strong defense argument for anybody accused of war crimes. It is unfortunate that in the climate of self-righteousness that prevailed among the victors of the Second World War the reverse was upheld. The Western democracies, in so doing, undermined, without realizing it, the effectiveness of their own armies. During the Vietnam War, it was reported that a few American pilots refused to carry on bombing missions because, in their opinion, the raids were immoral. The pilots apparently invoked the principles established at the Nuremberg trials. It is evident that if, in any air force, enough pilots were to follow those principles, their usefulness would be limited to the spraying of crops.

The Nuremberg "law" stating that obedience to orders, even in time of war, is no justification for acts that can be questioned later for their legality applies, of course, to all ranks. According to this principle, a general must not obey the orders of his government if such orders are in conflict with the dictates of his conscience. The framers of this principle felt, undoubtedly, a sense of self-righteous relief in having contributed so brilliantly to the betterment of human behavior. They did not think, however, that every coin has an opposite side, as became evident a few years later in the Truman-MacArthur controversy.

General MacArthur's conscience dictated to him a much more bellicose action toward the North Koreans than the orders of his Commander-in-Chief; as a result, the General was fired. In his speech before the Massachusetts Legislature on July 25, 1951 the general said among other things:

> ...I find in existence a new and heretofore unknown and dangerous concept that the members of our armed forces owe primary allegiance and loyalty to those who temporarily exercise the authority of the executive branch of government, rather than to the country and its constitution which they are to defend. No proposition could be more dangerous.... Yet so inordinate has been the application of the executive power that members of the armed services have been subjected to the most arbitrary and ruthless treatment for daring to speak the truth in accordance with conviction and conscience.[15]

It is evident that the general's statements are the stuff of which military coups are made. For this reason, many felt that the business of the military commanders is to obey their civilian superiors no matter what their own opinions, feelings, or dictates of conscience may be. In fact, most people were relieved that Truman held firm and that MacArthur faded away as all good soldiers do. Few realized at the time that what they were asking MacArthur to do, they reproached the German generals for having done. Bosch says:

The complexity of the problem of military obedience was indicated clearly by the fact that many who had demanded that the German generals follow their conscience, even to death, now demanded just as vehemently that American military leaders should leave all decisions to the civilian branch of the government and concern themselves exclusively with fighting war as they were paid to do.[16]

It is interesting that the staunchest supporters of the judgment of conscience in the matter of orders would undoubtedly be the first to agree that the generals should just do what they are told by their civilian superiors.

It may also be remembered that, during the Vietnam war, the Government of North Vietnam mentioned the possibility of trying captured American pilots as war criminals according to the Nuremberg principles. President Johnson stressed that the pilots were military men carrying out military assignments and therefore not war criminals,[17] and it was hinted that if the trials and executions took place he might have to ask for a declaration of war and then pursue the conflict to total victory. The incident passed but, although the execution of American pilots would have been a crime, the *Minneapolis Tribune* of July 19, 1966 wondered if the Administration's "proposal to obliterate tens of thousands of non-combatant North Vietnamese [in case of declaration of war and pursuit of the conflict to total victory] in retaliation for the execution of thirty-seven Americans—unjust though it would be—dangerously [resembled] the Nazis' retaliatory slaughter of non-combatants in Lidice and other towns and villages."[18]

And so Nuremberg came back to haunt the victors.

In spite of their amorality, foreign relations are nevertheless governed by certain rules that influence each country's status in the international community.

In 1940, Italy entered the Second World War as an ally of Germany. In 1943 the Italian Government and Victor Emmanuel III, the King, escaped to the part of Italy occupied by the enemy and declared war on Germany. Italy became a "co-belligerent" of her former enemies. At that time, Italy had fought beside Germany for three years and had lost all its African territories, and the Allies had seized a large section of Italy's metropolitan area. The Italian armed forces had shown a singular lack of preparation, both psychological and material, from the beginning of the war, with consequent and increasingly serious military reverses. The war, on the side of the Axis Powers, was more and more fought by the Germans alone, with their Italian allies a hindrance rather than a help. Naturally, under the circumstances, suing for peace, even if not consonant with the heroic mystique of Mussolini, was a valid option for Italy. It was decided, however, not only to sue for peace, but to turn completely around and declare war on Germany (and Japan) in an attempt to reduce to the minimum, at the peace table, the effects of military defeat.

During the Vietnam war, the peace movement in the United States forced the U.S. Government to stop most support for South Vietnam. This, of course, meant defeat of the Asian ally who had fought the war with the support and encouragement of the United States.

There is no doubt that, if conventional ethical principles were applied to these episodes, condemnation would be inevitable.

We have seen, however, that, except in extreme cases, conventional ethical principles do not apply in foreign politics. The Government of Italy was trying to work out a solution in the interest of the country, and the peace movement in the U.S. was following what it considered overriding ethical principles, perhaps believing that, in so doing, the interests of humanity, or of the country, or of both, were best served. No matter what the reasons and the intentions were, however, the actions taken by the two governments entailed deleterious consequences for the two countries. Among the complex and numerous elements that determine the status of a country in the international community, credibility is one of the most important. It is evident, for example, that the political equilibrium in Europe is now dependent on the credibility of American determination to defend the Western countries; similarly,

Japan's non re-armament policy relies on American protection, and the outcome of the Arab-Israeli conflict hinges on the validity of the United States' guarantee of Israel's existence. Credibility is so important that diplomacy, as we know it, would be impossible if the countries involved, especially the superpowers, lost it completely. The United States, by abandoning the South Vietnamese, lost some of it. In addition, because the foreign policy of Western Europe after the Second World War was based on the assumption that the American defense umbrella was both valid and adequate, when its credibility became questionable, that policy had to be reassessed. While before Vietnam American friendship meant security, after Vietnam it became a possible liability. In fact, if the Americans were not able to follow words with deeds, as in Vietnam, then pacifism and disarmament became more and more attractive, given the obvious impossibility of Europe's defending herself against a Russian attack. What good would it do to start a resistance against such an hypothetical attack, sustain horrible losses, and then end up under Russian domination anyway because the American Congress came to the conclusion that the war was unethical, unpopular, or dirty? The same applies to Japan, which may now feel much more uncomfortable under the American umbrella than before the Vietnam war.

The consequences of the 1943 Italian exercises in Machiavellism were, of course, of less importance. Italy, already known as a feeble enemy, lost her credibility as an ally, even if a weak one, and had to renounce playing a significant role in international politics at least for some time.

The above discussion should not be taken as meaning that denunciation of an alliance or a treaty on the part of a given country always produces a loss of credibility. This is obviously not the case. The breaking of a treaty or an alliance is an amoral act of the second degree and as such is commonly practiced by all countries in the international arena. The continuous shifts and changes in international relations are accompanied by the abolition of old alliances and treaties and the creation of new ones. The loss of credibility is not associated with reversal of alliances or denunciation of treaties but with the circumstances in which this is done. Italy exchanged enemies for allies *during* the war when it became more and more evident that its outcome would be favorable to the enemy. The peace movement in the U.S. forced the Government to abandon, *during* the war, a previously supported and encouraged ally because of weariness produced by a long conflict. That conflict had not been won long before because of American indecision, and had caused no serious hardship in the United States in comparison with the hardship that South Vietnam had to endure.

It is to be underlined that, although the abandonment of an ally in time of war would be censurable by conventional ethical principles, the loss of credibility suffered by Italy and the United States was not caused by ethical but by purely utilitarian considerations. Their friendship and support, which collapsed in time of stress, became, like weaker currency, just less valuable.

Later (Chapter 7) we shall discuss how "mass" may modify our ethical judgement. Here we will try to show, with a few hypoethetical examples, how war necessity may force us to consider acts to be amoral that, at first, would be judged immoral.

Imagine the following:

Case 1:
A pilot steals a military airplane and proceeds to bomb a population center in another country. The bombs fall on an orphanage and one hundred children are killed.

Case 2:
Country A is at war with country B. A pilot from the air force of country A is ordered to bomb a population center in country B. The bombs fall on an orphanage and one hundred children are killed.

We all agree that the first is a criminal act and, as such,

obviously immoral. The second case is more complicated but, before passing judgment on it, we need more information. Here are two alternatives, at opposite ends of the scale of possibilities:

Case 2a:
Because of faulty intelligence, the population center was thought to be in reality a disguised military-industrial center very important for the war effort of the enemy.

Case 2b:
It was well known that it was a civilian center with no military objectives and that many children would die, because it was also known that they had been evacuated there to protect them from raids on more industrialized areas.

With this information we could conclude that case 2a is an accident and that, in war, such episodes, regrettable as they are, are bound to happen. What about case 2b? Our first reaction is anger and we are ready to declare, without any further ado, that those who ordered the raid are indeed criminals. We may want, however, to ask for more information. Again we could distinguish two cases at the two ends of the scale of possibilities.

Case 2b i:
It was firmly and sincerely believed that if Country B were to win the war, enslavement and mass deportation for the population of Country A would follow, with reduction of its remnants to a state of abject primitivism. It was calculated that a military defeat of Country A would result in the murder of millions of its citizens and slavery for tens of millions. The leaders of Country A felt that the chances of military defeat were high. It was believed that the will to fight of the population of Country B could be undermined by terror-bombing. It was felt that the bombing of the civilian population was one of the main ways of avoiding military defeat. The killing of children was, by its very nature, particularly apt to terrorize

the population of Country B. In fact this case was only one episode of a campaign of terror-bombing of civilians.

Case 2b ii:
The order to bomb the civilian population of Country B was given with the express intent of killing as many of its people as possible so that the job of finishing them off at the end of the war would be easier.

Now that we know more, we may be willing to concede that Case 2bi may include a set of extreme circumstances that, in spite of the monstrosity of the act, may require a less harsh judgment than we were ready to give before. The reader may in fact recognize a similarity between this hypothetical case and the terror-bombing of Germany by the Allies in World War II. One would think that there is no need to spend time on Case 2bii, which does not even seem to belong in a human world. It seems impossible to find any set of circumstances that would justify it.

It is, in fact, difficult but not altogether impossible.

Case 2b ii—1
The population of Country B has been infected by an extra-terrestrial virus contained in a meteorite that fell on Country B one year ago. It has been proven that the virus goes through reproductive cycles and that the infection becomes contagious at the end of each one. Larger and larger numbers of humans are infected with each cycle. Practically the entire population of Country B was infected by the previous cycle. The next one, due in one year, will infect the rest of the world. The infection causes a terrible death. There is no cure. The only alternatives left are the killing of the entire population of B or the extinction of human life on the planet. The virus, acting on the central nervous system, makes the citizens of B violent maniacs whose purpose is to infect the rest of humanity.

Case 2b ii—2
The leaders of Country A wanted to eliminate all the popu-

lation of Country B because of hate based on feelings of racial superiority.

Obviously, with Case 2bii-2 we have reached the end of the line. But what about case 2bii-1? Forgetting for a moment the unlikelihood of the science-fiction situation, one surely should hesitate to condemn offhand any measure, no matter how horrendous, to save humanity from extinction.

Persual of these hypothetical cases shows that only in Case 1 and Case 2bii-2 is there no doubt about the immorality of the act. What makes the other cases different? The other cases consist of acts that would be condemned under ordinary circumstances, but that in those particular cases may be justified—if not by all, at least by a sufficient number of people so that they could be considered amoral of the second order.

It may be easily perceived that the cases that may be justified by necessity have in common a sufficiently large difference between the importance of the end and the heinousness of the means. This indicates another element that governs international relations: the end justifies the means. Without disturbing the great shade of Machiavelli, clear examples can be found of the application of that tenet throughout history:

Here is the speech of Chancellor von Bethmann Hollweg to the Reichstag on August 4, 1914:

> Gentlemen, we are now in a state of necessity, and necessity knows no law. Our troops have already entered Belgian territory.
>
> Gentlemen, that is a breach of international law.... A French attack on our flank on the lower Rhine might have been disastrous. Thus we were forced to ignore the rightful protests of the Government of Belgium. The wrong—I speak openly—the wrong we thereby commit we will try to make good as soon as our military aims have been attained.[19]

Another case:

During the Second World War, before the German invasion of Norway, iron ore was shipped from Norway (a neutral

Ethics and War Crimes 167

country) to Germany to the great distress of the British Government. Churchill urged the mining of Norwegian territorial waters (an act against international law), so as to force German merchant ships out into the Atlantic where the British navy could sink them. He explained his reasons for such a breach of international law in a Cabinet memorandum in terms that echo the German Chancellor's speech at the time of the invasion of Belgium in 1914:

> We are fighting to re-establish the reign of law and to protect the liberties of small countries. Our defeat would mean an age of barbaric violence, and would be fatal, not only to ourselves, but to the independent life of every small country in Europe. Acting in the name of the Covenant, and as virtual mandatories of the League and all it stands for, we have a right, indeed we are bound in duty, to abrogate for a space some of the conventions of the very laws we seek to consolidate and reaffirm. Small nations must not tie our hands when we are fighting for their rights and freedom. The letter of the law must not in supreme emergency obstruct those who are charged with its protection and enforcement. It would not be right or rational that the aggressive power should gain one set of advantages by tearing up all laws, and another by sheltering behind the innate respect for law of its opponents. Humanity, rather than legality, must be our guide.[20]

In accordance with the above memorandum, the British decided to proceed and the Norwegian waters were mined. The next day, Germany invaded Norway. The Germans were indicted at Nuremberg for the invasion of Norway.

Yet another example is the British air raids on Germany during the Second World War, when the *primary* objective of the bombing was the destruction of civilian targets.[21]

> As a direct result of the adoption of a policy of terror bombing by the leaders of Britain, some 300,000 Germans, most of them civilians, were killed and another 780,000 seriously injured.... And the British policy had further consequences: it was the crucial precedent for the fire-bombing of Tokyo and other Jap-

anese cities and then for Harry Truman's decision to drop atomic bombs on Hiroshima and Nagasaki. The civilian death toll from allied terrorism in World War II must have exceeded half a million men, women, and children.... by early 1942, aiming at military or industrial targets was barred: "the aiming points are to be built-up areas, *not*, for instance, the dockyards or aircraft factories."[22] The purpose of the raids was explicitly declared to be the destruction of civilian morale. Following the famous minute of Lord Cherwell in 1942, the means of this demoralization were specified: working-class residential areas were the prime targets. Cherwell thought it possible to render a third of the German population homeless by 1943....from the beginning, the attacks were defended as a reprisal for the German blitz. This is a very problematic defense....First of all, it appears possible, as one scholar has recently argued, that Churchill deliberately provoked the German attacks on London—by bombing Berlin—in order to relieve pressure on R.A.F. installations, until then the major Luftwaffe targets...So the raids continued, culminating in the spring of 1945—when the war was virtually won—in a savage attack on the city of Dresden in which something like 100,000 people were killed.[23]

The bombings of civilians are, in fact, often justified with the argument that "the end justifies the means":

...had victory been clearly impossible without these practices [Allied terror bombing]...the purposes for which the war was fought would have sanctioned them.[24]

The same principle is also applied on the battlefield:

In July 1944, Omar Bradley, in command of American forces in Normandy, was engaged in planning a breakout from the invasion beaches established the months before. The plan that he worked out, code-named COBRA and approved by Generals Montgomery and Eisenhower, called for the carpet bombing of an area three and one half miles wide, and one and one half deep, along the Périers road outside the town of St. Lô. Air bombing, we calculated, would either destroy or stun the enemy in the carpet and so permit a quick advance. But it also posed a moral problem, which Bradley discusses in his autobiography. On July 20, he described the coming attack to some American newsmen:

"The correspondents listened quietly to the outline of our plan, craned their necks as I pointed to the carpet and...tallied the air strength that had been assigned to us. At the close of the briefing, one of the newsmen asked if we would forewarn the French living within bounds of the carpet. I shook my head as if to escape the necessity of saying no. If we were to tip our hand to the French, we would also show it to the Germans...the success of COBRA hung upon surprise even if it meant the slaughter of innocents as well."[25]

There are, in history, enough examples to show that the principle that the end justifies the means has been applied in war as a matter of routine. Usually the end was military victory and the means killing and destroying. For the same end, surely other means (e.g., torture) have also been used; in fact, one can easily think of hypothetical situations in which such a means would be justifiable:

A politician who has won office with an honest pledge to end a prolonged colonial war goes off to the colonial capital to open negotiation with the rebels. The capital is in the grip of a terrorist campaign and the new leader's first decision is this: he is asked to authorize the torture of a captured rebel leader who knows or probably knows the location of a number of bombs hidden in the city and timed to go off in the next twenty-four hours. He orders the man to be tortured "convinced that he must do so for the sake of the people who might otherwise die in the explosions—even though he believes that torture is 'always wrong.' "[26]

Of course, if there were a single bomb that was planted, in a way that the life of a single man was endangered, we would not feel that the decision of torturing the prisoner could be justified. It is evident that the larger the number of lives endangered, the more the action seems necessary.

(b) War Criminals

Man needs to find causes. Science is a consequence of this need, but so is superstition. Primitive man invented various deities to explain natural phenomena, and the more important the phenomenon was, the more necessary it was to find a cause. Such catastrophes as the barbarian invasions of the fifth century and the Black Death of the Middle Ages were explained as the result of the punishment of God for our sins and corruption. Both of those calamities were of gigantic proportions and imposed on humanity a burden that seemed intolerable. The active intervention of the deity was needed to explain them because a natural cause was felt to be inadequate for such tremendous events. Naive as such explanations are, they were not limited to those remote ages. In the seventeenth century, when a great plague afflicted the north of Italy and central Europe, it was believed to be caused by evil persons, working for the devil, who were going around smearing walls and clothes and public places with a substance that propagated the disease. In Milan, those evil doers were called *untori* (smearers), and innocent people lost their lives because their acts looked suspicious to the righteous.[27] The belief that the *untori* were responsible for the plague was almost universal and not limited to the superstitious; in addition, the killing and torture of the *untori* did not occur only in Milan:

> ...in Palermo in 1526; in Geneva in 1530, then in 1545 and again in 1574; in Casal Monferrato in 1536; in Padua in 1555; in Turin in 1599 and again in 1630, here a few, there many unhappy innocents were tried and condemned to torments, often the most atrocious, as guilty of spreading the plague either with powders, or with ointments, or with incantations, or with all of those.[28]

It is evident that pinning the responsibility on the *untori* is much better than accusing the deity—this for various reasons. First, if God did it, we are faced with the necessity of placating Him by abandoning our vices and becoming virtuous, a task known by long experience to be very arduous; second, even if we were to succeed in placating Him, we could again get into the same trouble for the same reasons, knowing the penchant of man; third, if the *untori* are responsible, all we have to do is kill them and live happily ever after. No wonder then that, as soon as he could, man switched the responsibility for disaster from God to the *untori*.

While the other major disasters that afflicted humanity needed a scapegoat, war did not seem to need one. In antiquity, after deciding in a perfunctory sort of way that there was a specialized god in charge of it, man did not seem to give the matter a second thought inasmuch as war was a common activity. It is true that the enemies were always the culprits and in the heat of battle, or immediately after, one could decide to exterminate all or parts of them, but once the war was over, any question of ethical responsibility would have been considered absurd. Caesar, for example, would have thought it ridiculous if somebody had suggested that Vercingetorix deserved to be executed because he had done something ethically wrong. He was executed because he was the ringleader of a revolt, because he could have caused more trouble, because that was the common fate of the loser, as a warning to others, or perhaps because there was no reason not to do so, but surely not because it was felt that he had committed an unethical act. Later, when the primitive custom of executing the enemy chief was abandoned, even when a "just war" was distinguished from its opposite, nobody would have dreamed of hanging the defeated enemy leaders even if they were fighting a war that was not just. During the First Crusade, surely Urban II would not have tried the caliph, had he been taken prisoner, nor the caliph Urban II in the reversed situation, and Charles V did not dream of executing Francis I after the Battle of Pavia.

Why were no scapegoats sought for war? Probably because, for millennia, it was considered a "normal" activity, something like a natural phenomenon, such as disease or drought, and like them unavoidable, frequent, and usually unwelcome. Because of its frequency, therefore, man had acquired a resigned endurance and did not expect to avoid it by finding scapegoats. The rarity and more intense destructiveness of the plague over a shorter period of time (it was not unusual for 20 to 30 percent of the population in a given area to die in one or two years in comparison with the 30 to 35 percent of the population lost in Germany during the entire Thirty Years War, for example) did not result in this state of resigned "habituation."

As civilization continued its ceaseless if slow progress, man became more and more sensitive to the horrors of war, which began to be perceived not as an inevitable recurrence similar to a natural phenomenon, but as a horror to be made less cruel and eventually to be eliminated. For this reason, international agreements on warfare started to be developed.

The First World War, with its horrible massacres, was perhaps the most atrocious of recent times. Man recoiled, refused to believe that "good men" could be responsible for such a thing, and started to look for *untori*. So, after the defeat of Germany in 1918, the Allies demanded that about 900 Germans, including military and political leaders, be handed over for trial on war-crimes charges. The Germans resisted, a compromise was reached, and the trials were allowed to take place in Germany. They were conducted in Leipzig (not by military courts but by the German Supreme Court) in 1921 and 1922. Only a few were tried, nearly all were acquitted, and the others were allowed to avoid their very short prison sentences.[29] That meant that no *untori* were really found. Many felt that such an episode should not happen again. Therefore after the Second World War the *untori* were found, many were hanged, and others were given very long prison terms. Many people were confident that this would forever eliminate war crimes and even war.

The war-crimes trials were absurd and unjust for many reasons, the main ones being:

a) they were a step backward toward the primitive practice of finding scapegoats;

b) they were conducted by the victors and therefore the judges could not be unbiased;
c) they were based on retroactive laws;
d) the victors had often committed the same kind of crimes as the accused; and
e) they were an attempt to apply moral principles to an activity (war) that is amoral.

Critics of the trials were at the time, and are now, not lacking:

> A serious objection to planning war-guilt trials is, one authority believed (Hoover, *"War-Guilt" Trials*, p. 47), "that such planning fosters the belief that world peace can be assured by the elimination of a few bad men. The assumption that the woes of this world are caused by devils, whether spiritual or terrestrial, is a popular error that continually thwarts realistic analysis and intellectual action. It would be tragic if we ever believed that the creation of a special tribunal to judge the Axis leaders *ex post facto* would materially contribute to the preservation of peace.[30]

> For many the [Nuremberg] trial was faulted from the beginning. State and federal judges, including the Chief Justice of the United States Supreme Court, were dubious of its morality and its dicta, as were jurists and politicians in the United States, England, France, and Germany....Chief Justice Stone, speaking of the power of the victors over the vanquished, wrote: "It would not disturb me greatly if that power were openly and frankly used to punish the German leaders for being a bad lot, but it disturbs me some to have it dressed up in the habiliments of the common law and the constitutional safeguards to those charged with crime".... Senator Taft said much the same thing: "My objection to the Nuremberg Trials is that while clothed with the forms of justice they were in fact an instrument of government policy determined months before at Yalta and Teheran"....Judge Radhabinode Pal, a member of the Calcutta High Court and of the International Military Tribunal of the Far East, wrote, "The so-called trial held according to the defi-

nition of crime now given by the victors obliterates the centuries of civilization which stretch between us and the summary slaying of the defeated in a war. A trial with law thus prescribed will only be a sham employment of legal process for the satisfaction of a thirst for revenge." Protests against the trials were also made by, among others, the secretary of the American Association of International Law, Pitman B. Potter, and Federal Judge Charles E. Wyzanski.[31]

That trial [Nuremberg] was a sort of legalistic prayer that the Kingdom of Heaven should be with us.[32]

It hardly needs stressing that the Nuremberg Tribunal was established by the victors to try the vanquished. If Allied nationals committed crimes under international law during the Second World War, they were not brought to trial before any international tribunal....a number of jurists considered that the Nuremberg procedure was partially defective. It is no doubt for this reason that the General Assembly [of the United Nations] was careful not to endorse the entire Nuremberg procedure, but only to affirm those "principles of international law" which are to be found in the Charter and the judgment of the Tribunal.[33]

International hypocrisy probably reached its highest point in the trials of thousands of Germans and Japanese for alleged war crimes....[Nuremberg was an] all-time low point in the prostitution of the forms of law to the purposes of political revenge....[34]

[the trials were] pseudo-legalized vindictive retribution...[35]

[punishing the defeated enemy] gratifying [as] it may have been to wartime passions of hatred, revenge, and self-righteousness, seems in retrospect a colossal blunder, morally, legally, and politically.[36]

In spite of all that, the vast majority at the time supported the trials:

... Walter Lippmann compared Nuremberg with the Magna

Charta, habeas corpus, and the Bill of Rights: "A development in human justice which our descendants may well consider the event of modern time."[37]

Some even thought that more trials should be held:

> Telford Taylor [chief U.S. counsel for the prosecution at Nuremberg who, later, was to be so bewildered by the horrors of Vietnam] prepared a plan to bring two hundred to four hundred more Nazi leaders before a half-dozen tribunals distributed throughout the four zones of occupation. But the United States Army objected because of the expense involved. The Russians, strapped for foreign exchange, did not want to participate in any further trials unless they were held in Berlin....[38]

Telford Taylor also reproached Judge Wennerstrum:

> ...Charles F. Wennerstrum, an Iowa judge who presided over the trial of army leaders involved in mass executions and the rounding up of slave laborers, returned to America early in 1948 to denounce the trials and the American prosecution. Taylor, who by then was frustrated, fed up, and to some extent heartsick at the lack of interest in the execution of justice prevalent in the United States, replied to Wennerstrum: "Your behavior arises out of a warped, psychopathic mental attitude."[39]

The indictment at the Nuremberg Trials consisted of four counts: Count 1—conspiracy; Count 2—crimes against peace (starting "wars of aggression"); Count 3—war crimes; Count 4—crimes against humanity.

Not all the accused found guilty on Count 4 were condemned to death (e.g., Funk, Speer, Von Neurath, Von Schirach). The accused condemned to die by hanging were: Goering, Von Ribbentrop, Keitel, Kaltenbrunner, Rosenberg, Frank, Frick, Streicher, Sauckel, Jodl, Seyss-Inquart, and Bormann. All were hanged except Goering, who committed suicide shortly before his execution, and Bormann, who was tried *in absentia*.[40]

In Japan there were many trials, the Tokyo one being the most important. Some 5,700 Japanese were tried on war crimes charges, and 920 were executed.[41]

The most significant legal innovation of the Nuremberg Trials was the legal definition of aggression as the "supreme crime." Until then, international law considered that war was legally justified if a state considered it in its national interest. The court not only declared that aggressive war violated international law (a law that was created for the occasion), but also set itself as a judge of ethics and declared that war was immoral.[42] Aggression, being the supreme crime, deserved the death penalty. Another legal innovation was that government leaders were personally responsible for their policies. Previously, a head of state, for example, was immune from criminal liability related to political decisions because such decisions were "considered referrable to an abstract entity which was independent, sovereign, and supreme in its own affairs [the state]."[43]

Aggression as the supreme crime could have perhaps deserved serious consideration if it were not for the fact that the accusers were guilty of the same crime. Following the Molotov-Ribbentrop Treaty, Russia had attacked Poland from the East while Hitler invaded from the West. Yet at Nuremberg the "rape of Poland" was held to be a crime committed only by the Germans and not, of course, by the *particeps criminis* on the seat of judgment—who was also guilty of aggression against Latvia, Estonia, Lithuania, Finland, Rumania, and Hungary.[44] If Russia was guilty of those same crimes for which the Germans were tried, she was not alone. The Americans had bombed Rumania while technically at peace with that nation, and the invasion of Norway by Hitler possibly "frustrated Great Britain's invasion of Norway by anticipating their move by only a few weeks."[45] Admiral Doenitz was found guilty because he gave the military orders (issued by political leaders) for the same invasion.[46] The conviction was also based on

...the fact that Doenitz "waged" aggressive war because his submarines "were fully prepared to wage war." On that basis every commander of combat troops or ships would have been equally guilty, but the Tribunal's opinion showed no awareness of these far-reaching implications.[47]

Admiral Raeder was accused of urging Hitler to convince the Japanese to seize Singapore. These judges simply overlooked the fact that the Americans and the British had tried very hard to convince the Russians to breach their non-aggression pact with Japan at the very end, when Japan was trying to get the Soviet Union to act as a mediator in the war.[48] At the beginning of August 1945, Japan was on the brink of total military defeat. From July 13 on, its leaders, seeing the inevitable, had asked the Soviet Union to mediate an end to the war.[49] They had sought the help of the U.S.S.R. because a neutrality pact between the two countries, signed on April 13, 1941, was still in effect. In spite of this step to end the war taken by the Japanese, on August 6 the first atomic bomb was dropped on Hiroshima. On August 8 the Soviet Union declared war on Japan. The declaration of war read in part:

> ...Taking into account the refusal of Japan to capitulate, the Allies approached the Soviet Government with a proposal to join the war against Japanese aggression....the Soviet Government has accepted the proposal of the Allies....[50]

Incredibly, the Tokyo tribunal found Japan guilty of aggression against the Soviet Union. The verdict read: "...they [the Japanese] had long been planning and preparing a war of aggression which they prepared to launch against the U.S.S.R...."[51]

The idea that aggression was the supreme evil was almost an obsession for the Allies. The Nuremberg Judgment contains the characteristic observation: "to initiate a war of aggression...is not only an international crime; it is the supreme international crime differing only from other war crimes in that it contains within itself the accumulated evil of the whole."[52] It is to be noted, however, that the definition of what constitutes aggression (and its mirror image, self-defense) is practically non-existent in international law. The Kellogg-Briand Pact of 1928 (see Chapter 5), for example, was designed to stop once and for all aggressive wars; yet the U.S. Senate Committee on Foreign Relations, commenting on the Pact and self-defense, expressed itself in the following terms:

> The Committee reports the above treaty with the understanding that the right of self-defense is in no way curtailed or impaired by the terms or conditions of the treaty. Each nation is free at all times and regardless of the treaty provisions to defend itself, and is the sole judge of what constitutes the right and the necessity and extent of the same.[53]

A commentator on this statement writes: "This is worthy of Humpty-Dumpty. Self-defense is what I say it is, and so is the right and necessity and extent of the same."[54]

Practically of the same worth is the definition of aggression adopted, after much discussion, dissent, and soul-searching, by the General Assembly of the United Nations on December 14, 1974. Article 2 reads:

> The first use of armed forces by a State in contravention of the Charter shall constitute *prima facie* evidence of an act of aggression although the Security Council may, in conformity with the Charter, conclude that a determination that an act of aggression has been committed would not be justified in the light of other relevant circumstances....[55]

So, it is up to the Security Council to judge; in practice, it means that each member's decision depends on its political allegiance and not on an objective evaluation of the facts and circumstances. The partisan reactions to the events in Algeria, Suez (1956), Afghanistan, Czechoslovakia, Cambodia, Grenada, Vietnam, etc., are well known.

Count 4 of the Nuremberg indictment dealt with crimes

against humanity. The fact that the Germans were not condemned for the bombing of civilian populations was probably due to the fact that all over Germany the signs were still evident of the savage Allied attacks. German bombs killed 60,000 British civilians during the war; on the other hand, Allied bombs killed 300,000 Germans and 500,000 Japanese, of whom over 100,000 died in the two atomic bomb attacks on Hiroshima and Nagasaki in August 1945.[56]

Concerning bombing of civilians, it is of interest to remember that Secretary of State Cordell Hull declared on June 11, 1938, after the bombardment of Canton by Japan, that the Administration disapproved of the sale of aircraft to countries that had engaged in the bombing of civilian populations. In his speech of December 2, 1939, President Roosevelt declared a similar moral embargo against the Soviet Union, because of Russian bombing of Finnish civilians.[57] It is also of interest that

> The Tokyo tribunal held that evidence concerning the dropping of the atomic bombs was inadmissible, and the majority judgment did not mention the issue; but three justices did. In his "Concurring Opinion," Justice Jaranilla of the Philippines endorsed the dropping of the bombs in these terms: "If a means is justified by an end, the use of the atomic bomb was justified."[58]

It is not clear if Justice Jaranilla realized that he was uttering the unutterable: the end justifies the means.

Another serious charge at Nuremberg concerned the infamous Commando Order. This was an order issued by Hitler (after the Dieppe raid of August 19, 1942) which instructed the German armed forces to kill all captured enemy commandos even if they were in uniform. The record shows that the orders issued by the British authorities to the commandos (and found on the captured ones) was as brutal and barbarous as anything that Hitler could have thought up. It read:

Your value to the war effort as a live and effective killer is great... The only way to achieve this is never to give the enemy a chance; the days when we could practice the rules of sportsmanship are over. For the time being every soldier must be a potential gangster and must be prepared to adopt their methods whenever necessary.

In the past we as a nation have not looked upon gangsters and their methods with favor; the time has now come when we are compelled to adopt some of their methods....

Remember you are not a wrestler trying to render your enemy helpless, you have to kill.

And remember you are out to kill, not to hold him down until the referee has finished counting...

In finishing off an opponent use him as a weapon as it were, beating his head on the curb or any convenient stone. Do not forget that good weapons are often lying about ready at hand. A bottle with the bottom smashed off is more effective than a naked hand in gouging an opponent's face....The vulnerable parts of the enemy are the heart, spine, and privates. Kick him or knee him as hard as you can in the fork. While he is doubled up with pain get him on the ground and stamp his head in.[59]

And one must also consider that

At least some of the [British] Commandos were provided with an ingenious device: two guns strapped under the armpits of a trooper fired when his arms were raised in seeming surrender. The chain used on the prisoners who were trussed in the Dieppe raid were called "death slings" in the Commando handbook. A noose was passed over the head and around the neck of the man shackled, then the end of an attached chain was tied to his bent legs. Thus with every movement the victim helped to strangle himself. The time of death could be determined, for no human being could long lie in this position without being forced to stretch out his legs; the muscle tension became unbearable. This handbook, however, could only be produced in a later trial. The President of the Court at Nuremberg reminded the defense that they were not trying the victorious powers and the British Commando orders, and the events at Dieppe were brought into the trial record only by witnesses' reference to them.[60]

Concerning massacres, the Germans were surely not innocent but, while the British and Americans killed thousands of innocent civilians by bombing, the Russians were responsible for the massacre of Katyn for which they accused the Germans:

> Unwisely, they pinned the Katyn Massacre onto the person of Herman Goering, and thus it appeared in the indictment. Meanwhile Dr. Markov, the Bulgarian member of the International Medical Commission, had been tried in Sofia for his life for anti-Soviet activities and had revoked his statement that the murders must have been committed not later than 1940 (i.e., that it was committed by the Soviets), Dr. Markov repeated his revocation at Nuremberg, and there were other apparent witnesses produced. But after a few hearings the Soviet prosecution itself dropped the indictment.[61]

As for mistreatment of prisoners, especially Russians, the Germans were indeed guilty. However, even in this case the Court showed lack of impartiality. When Goering's lawyer wanted to introduce evidence concerning the treatment of German prisoners by the Russians, the President of the Court said:

> Well, we are here to try major war criminals; we are not here to try any of the signatory powers....The question is, how can you justify in a trial of the major war criminals of Germany evidence against Great Britain, or against the United States of America, or against the USSR, or against France? If you are going to try the actions of all those four signatory powers, apart from other considerations, there would be no end to the trial at all.[62]

Other examples of the partisan behavior of the Court are not difficult to find:

> The Russian treatment of German prisoners of war and the use of German forced labor could not be described nor could Paulus be questioned on the subject, although he could have

testified on what had happened to the survivors of the Sixth Army, only some 5,000 of whom eventually returned to Germany out of the 123,000 who had surrendered at Stalingrad. The bombing of German cities...could play no role in the issue under debate, although the German air attacks on Warsaw, Belgrade, Rotterdam, and other population centers were brought up many times and the bombing of Rotterdam was part of the indictment. The millions of German men, women, and children who had been driven from their homes in Poland, Hungary, Czechoslovakia, Rumania, and Bulgaria, where their families had been settled for centuries, could not be mentioned, nor could the alleged atrocities committed against German troops by any of the Allied nations.

The British handbook of irregular warfare, instructing the Commandos to act like gangsters, not soldiers, could not be brought into the trial, although Jodl's lawyer, Franz Exner, pleaded that the British orders affected the German reprisals against the Commandos and that the British Government had officially defended this kind of warfare as acceptable (copies of the handbook had been found on captured British Commandos)....*Tu quoque* was permitted as a defense only in one instance, with regard to the German Navy and the defense of Admirals Doenitz and Raeder, whose lawyers argued that they had conducted submarine warfare under the same rules as the Allies, and in its verdict the court accepted the defense as justified. The court quoted the testimony of British and American officers, most importantly of Admiral Chester Nimitz, who in an affidavit declared that American submarines from the first day of the war against Japan had orders to sink any Japanese ship in the Pacific without warning. The British Admiralty also conceded that British submarines had orders to sink any ship on sight in the Skagerrak.[63]

An English patrol, operating in Burma, killed between twenty and thirty unarmed Japanese prisoners because to leave them unharmed where they were would have betrayed the whereabouts of the British troops. The German lawyer pointed out the inconsistency between these men going unpunished and the case of the German submarine commander Eck, who tried to kill the survivors of the ship he had sunk for the same reason—that they would betray the presence of his U-

Ethics and War Crimes 183

boat in the shallow Mediterranean waters—and who was subsequently sentenced to death by an Allied court.[64]

The Germans were guilty of executing hostages in practically all countries that they occupied during the war. The Allies did the same on a much smaller scale (see Chapter 4), but one must consider the possibility that the scale would have been much bigger if they had been confronted with the guerrilla warfare that the Germans faced. In fact, a 1940 American field manual stated:

> "Hostages taken and held for the declared purposes of insuring against unlawful acts by the enemy forces or people may be punished or put to death if the unlawful acts are nevertheless committed...."[65]

Nobody contests that the Germans indeed committed atrocities but

> After the fall of Poland, the Soviet occupiers matched the Germans in beheading their newly annexed territory of its native elite. More than a million Poles were forcibly deported to Siberia and Central Asia, from which many of them never returned.[66]

In addition French, British, and American military men had stated clearly that war and atrocities are practically synonymous:

> The use of atrocity...had been advocated and taught before 1914 by a French lieutenant-colonel: "Terrify, in order to terrify and destroy. The immediate object of fighting is to kill and to go on killing, until there is nothing left to kill." To this....a British major general made his contribution: "War is a relapse into barbarism. There is no disloyalty in war save that which forbears to spare; no morality, save that which ends quickly. Love and sentiment are out of place in the struggle for existence....It is the exercise of the sterner barbaric qualities which governs the day. Atrocities are the last recourse of strategy in its efforts

to force an enemy to his knees." And an American lieutenant-general [Lt.-Col. S.B.M. Young in 1902] added his opinion: "To carry on war, disguise it as we may, it is to be cruel; it is to kill and burn, burn and kill, and again kill and burn."[67]

The absurd consequences of the Nuremberg Trials' rejection of the principle according to which a soldier's first duty is to obey orders, with the implication that he cannot be held responsible for their legality, are well illustrated by the question of the new West German Army's oath:

> One suggestion for the reform of the military oath would have permitted an officer to refuse to carry out a lawful order twice, if he felt that it would lead to an inhumane act. The third time he received the order he must then carry out, under protest, the command given. The two refusals to obey would be entered in his personal file. "No doubt," remarked a critic, "to be of use at a future Nuremberg Trial." The solution finally hit upon simply left the problem of obedience unanswered by not mentioning it in the oath. Instead there is a relevant passage in the law which states: "An order may be ignored when, through carrying it out, a crime or misdeed would be committed. If the subordinate carries out the order, his guilt is only excusable if it can be shown that he obeyed the order unaware of the crime or misdeed which might result..." How the framers of this proposal planned to operate it with a real army is not entirely clear.[68]

All that because, as Telford Taylor says:

> The notion of individual accountability before the bar of international law lies at the heart of the Nuremberg judgments, and the reluctance of the Germans to resist oppressive acts of state is widely held to have greatly aided the Nazi seizure of power.[69]

With admirable composure, the same Telford Taylor recognizes that the notion may involve some problems:

> The imposition of responsibility on those giving illegal

orders, but not the secondary responsibility of subordinates who carry out the orders known to be illegal, was provided for in the British and American manuals published in 1914. Both explicitly exempted from liability those whose violations of the laws of war were committed under orders of their "government" or "commanders," while declaring that the commanders who ordered or authorized the offenses might be punished. These provisions raised questions whether anyone at all could be held liable if the "commanders" were themselves acting under orders from still farther up the military chain of command. At the outbreak of the Second World War, accordingly, military law on the question of superior orders was in a state of considerable confusion.[70]

Although the Nuremberg Trials were tragic examples of miscarriage of justice, the limits of the absurd were reached in the trials of the Japanese. One of the best known is the case of General Yamashita.

Early in the Pacific war, Singapore, defended by a force of 100,000 men, surrendered to 30,000 Japanese commanded by General Tomayuki Yamashita. It was a great humiliation for the British Empire. It was not forgotten. During the closing months of the war, while General Yamashita was the commander of the Japanese forces in the Philippine Islands, horrible atrocities were committed against the civilian population. After the surrender of Japan, the General was accused of war crimes and tried by a United States military commission in Manila.

At his trial:

> Small children described how they had seen their parents bayoneted, mothers wept as they recalled the deaths of their babies, men who had hidden themselves told of watching others being decapitated. Day after day, tales of bestiality and horror were recounted by the Filipinos, Chinese, and occasionally Americans, until the listener wondered whether he was living on this green earth or in a bloody gash on the corpse of hell. There *had* to be revenge. Not vengeance by flame-thrower, blockbuster, or atomic bomb—such devices were impersonal, that retribution was past, those victims were not to be seen here

in the Manila courtroom. There had to be a personal vengeance, somehow—on *someone*. And here he was in this chamber for all to see, an individual, a creature, a man, not only a Japanese soldier but THE Japanese soldier, the TOP Japanese soldier [General Yamashita].[71]

Yamashita had taken command a few months before the end of the war and the evidence showed that he had not approved, much less ordered, these barbarities.[72] In fact, as he took command, his communication and control of his troops rapidly disintegrated as a result of victorious American military operations. The Japanese troops behaved as soldiers without a commander in a situation of defeat, chaos, and disruption often do. Yamashita had no possibility of preventing or stopping what was happening in those terrible days. Yet the tribunal found him guilty on the ground that he had "failed to provide effective control of his troops as required by the circumstances" and sentenced him to death by hanging.[73] The sentence was confirmed at lower levels before it reached General MacArthur, who, in his statement of confirmation, in addition to his piece on the soldier quoted in Chapter 2, wrote:

> ...I have reviewed the proceedings in vain search for some mitigating circumstance on his behalf. I can find none....This officer, of proven field merit, entrusted with high command involving authority adequate to responsibility, has failed this irrevocable standard; has failed his duty to his troops, to his country, to his enemy, to mankind; has failed utterly his soldier faith. The transgressions resulting therefrom as revealed by the trial are a blot upon the military profession, a stain upon civilization, and constitute a memory of shame and dishonor that can never be forgotten....[74]

Yamashita's appeal was carried to the U.S. Supreme Court, which declined to review the case despite the dissents of Justices Murphy and Rutledge.[75] He was executed on February 22, 1946.

The following serves to put the case in perspective:

In 1901, Americans in the Philippine war were harried by guerrilla activity that was similar in nature, if not equal in power and scope, to that faced by General Yamashita. How did our generals meet the problem? We know of what happened in Samar, one of the Visayan group of the Philippine archipelago. Extensive guerrilla activity there was countered by a "punitive expedition" of American forces commanded by one Brigadier General Jacob H. Smith. In autumn, 1901, General Smith ordered a Major L.W.T. Waller of the Marine Corps to conduct the raid of Samar, saying in so many words: "I want no prisoners. I wish you to kill and burn; the more you kill and burn, the better you will please me....The interior of Samar must be made a howling wilderness." As reported by Mr. John Bassett Moore (in his Digest of International Law), General Smith "wanted all persons killed who were capable of bearing arms." Major Waller was a precise soldier who, understandably, wanted precise directions. He asked the general what he was to consider the age limit in carrying out his order of extermination—in other words, how young a child would have to be to escape the massacre. "Ten years of age," was the reply. Because he gave this order, Brigadier General Smith was court-martialed in the spring of 1902. He was charged with "conduct to the prejudice of good order and military discipline." He was found guilty, and he was sentenced to be admonished by his superior. General Yamashita gave no such order.[76]

If one were to think that this was an isolated case of *vae victis*, other sentences of the Japanese war crimes tribunals would show otherwise. The case of Koki Hirota is one in point.

Koki Hirota was Foreign Minister of Japan between 1933 and May 1938, after which he held no office. The so-called "rape of Nanking" by Japanese forces took place in the winter of 1937-38, while Hirota was Foreign Minister. Atrocities were committed and he demanded and received assurances from the War Ministry that they would be stopped. They continued. Hirota resigned in May 1938. The Tokyo tribunal found him guilty because

...[he] was derelict in his duty in not insisting before the

Cabinet that immediate action be taken to put an end to the atrocities, [and] was content to rely on assurances which he knew were not being implemented.[77]

Because of this, and because he was convicted of being guilty of the aggressive war charge, Hirota was sentenced to hang.[78]

Finally, as is common in human affairs, the tragic may have been accompanied by the grotesque:

> ...consider the issue of Chief Prosecutor [at the Tokyo trial] Keenan's sobriety. One spectator at the trial, Courtney Browne, writes: "Evident too were the unfortunate occasions when Keenan's naturally florid complexion was flushed more than usual and when he might charitably have been described as being unfit to be in court."[79]

In spite of the evidence to the contrary, many still believe that the war-crimes trials were a step in the right direction, even if not terribly effective in achieving the objectives that their supporters were attempting to reach (abolition of aggression, of unacceptable behavior in war, of immorality in international relations, and even of war itself). Here, for example, is a supporter of the justice meted out at Nuremberg who meditates on the good that has resulted from the trials:

> ...power politics in the name of self-interest has continued as before, and none of the Nuremberg prosecuting nations has been without sin. The United States has, on and off, practiced ideological imperialism. The French, in attempting to perpetuate colonialism, engaged [in Algeria] in some of the same kinds of terror for which the Nuremberg defendants were condemned. The British, French, and Israelis attacked Egypt in 1956. The Soviets have crushed nationalist movements in East Germany, Hungary, Czechoslovakia, Poland, and Afghanistan. Brushfire wars have proliferated....The genocide in Cambodia exceeded, proportionately, Hitler's exterminations in Eastern Europe. In Argentina, Chile, Iran, and a host of other nations, political opposition has been crushed with Gestapo tactics. The

Ethics and War Crimes 189

Christian Falangist action in the Beirut refugee camps had all the elements of a German ghetto clearance; and the Nuremberg tribunal would doubtlessly have considered the Begin [Prime Minister of Israel until 1983] Government culpable for its involvement....The impact of Nuremberg has faded. Nuremberg has become an abstract concept rather than a dire precept....

The world, however, can ignore the lessons of Nuremberg only at its peril....what would happen if Hitler were regenerated in the guise of another dictator—if there were to be another all-powerful leader who grows more and more lunatic in office, and cannot be removed? Had Hitler possessed atomic weapons and believed it to be his advantage to use them, he would have had no scruples about doing so. What if a paranoid tyrant, surrounded by toadies and nonentities, labors under the delusion he is about to be subjected to attack and orders a "retaliatory" strike?[80]

It is difficult to believe that anyone could really think that the hangings and the "principles" of Nuremberg and Tokyo could prevent dictators who grow "more and more lunatic in office" from giving insane orders.

One wonders if the Allies knew what they were doing at the war-crimes trials. The Russians most probably did, while measuring, for future use, the incredible naiveté of their colleagues in judgment.

At Teheran, Marshal Stalin raised his glass in a macabre toast. "I propose a salute to the swiftest possible justice for all Germany's war criminals—justice before a firing squad. I drink to our unity in dispatching them as fast as we capture them, all of them, and there must be at least fifty thousand of them."

Elliott Roosevelt, a primary source for this story, reported that Churchill was instantly to his feet, enraged by the adoption of a policy in morbid humor which he considered unjust and illegal. "Any such attitude," he cried, "is wholly contrary to our British sense of justice! The British people will never stand for such mass murder. I take this opportunity to say that I feel most strongly that no one, Nazi or no, shall be summarily delt with, before a firing squad, without proper legal trial, no matter what the known facts and proven evidence against him."

Roosevelt, attempting to dissipate the tenseness of the situation, interposed the comment that the Russian Marshal's number was perhaps too high. The President said he would be satisfied with 49,500....

...Elliott Roosevelt related that his father told him in private that all was said in jest and that it was Churchill's misunderstanding to take it seriously.[81]

Churchill, in his history of the Second World War, reports the same episode with little variation in the details.[82] Stalin himself may or may not have been jesting; nevertheless, before the Nuremberg Trials started, the Russian Judge Nikitchenko said:

"We are dealing here with the chief war criminals who have already been convicted and whose conviction has already been confirmed by both the Moscow and Crimea declarations and by the heads of the governments." He thought that the tribunal, therefore, should carry out the just punishment immediately. Nor was there any necessity, he said, "to create a sort of fiction that the judge is a disinterested person who has no legal knowledge of what has happened before.... [that] would lead only to unnecessary delays."[83]

The Western concept of justice may have required creating that fiction but, tragically, the Allies did not realize that it was a fiction.

There are...certain similarities to be found in all these war-crimes trials. They are, for example, all subject to the objection that they are not really trials in the sense that there is an honest possibility of acquittal. Although it seemed likely from the beginning that a few of the Nuremberg defendants would be acquitted, it was even more obvious that such important German prisoners as Herman Goering had no more chance of being found not guilty than there was of our military commission letting Yamashita go. The fallacy is that we have been

Ethics and War Crimes   191

trying to cover what is essentially a political act with a cloak of legalism.

...The significant defendants at Nuremberg were those charged with conspiring and undertaking to initiate a war of aggression, a far cry from the allegations against Yamashita. Yet here too there is an important similarity. Both convictions are subject to the accusation that they were for *ex post facto* offenses. Never before had it been a crime to plan an invasion, any more than it had been a crime to be in command of troops who committed crimes. Ever since the days of the Magna Charta, our judicial canons have had no place for the idea of punishing a man for having done something that was not illegal at the time that he did it.[84]

Retroactive laws, in fact, are so repugnant that the United Nations took a clear position against them:

Not only had the United Nations not endorsed all the principles of Nuremberg, it had enacted a law which many considered a censure of the Tribunal. The General Assembly on December 9, 1948 had adopted the Declaration of Human Rights of which Article 11 (4) provides that: "No one shall be held guilty of any penal offense on account of any act or omission which did not constitute a penal offense, under national or international law, at the time when it was committed."[85]

In the same way as the doctrine of the just war did not deter armed conflict, the "principles" of Nuremberg and Tokyo have not deterred and will not deter the waging of wars that, if judged with the conventional standards of individual morality, would be considered immoral.

The chief counsel for the prosecution at the Nuremberg war-crimes trials, Telford Taylor, when confronted with reports of American atrocities in Vietnam (especially My Lai), advocated a full inquiry into the higher ranks stating:

Little as the leaders of the Army seem to realize it, this is the only road to the Army's salvation, for its moral health will not be recovered until its leaders are willing to scrutinize their behavior by the same standards that their revered predecessors applied to Tomayuki Yamashita twenty-five years ago.[86]

The investigation that Mr. Taylor advocated was never carried out; the Army's salvation must have been reached by some other road. The standards of the revered predecessors were not applied and the conduct of all the wars that followed Vietnam proceeded in the manner common to all wars.

The fact, however, remains that in the war-crimes trials the Allies forgot what Thomas Paine said:

> He that would make his own liberty secure must guard even his enemy from oppression; for if he violates this duty he establishes a precedent that will reach to himself.[87]

Goya — *What a Tailor Can Do!* (From Los Caprichos)

Chapter 7

> La notte che morí Pier Soderini,
> l'anima andó de l'inferno a la bocca;
> gridó Pluton: Ch'inferno? anima sciocca,
> va su nel limbo fra gli altri bambini.
>
> Machiavelli,
> *Epigrammi*[1]

JUST WAR AND PACIFISM

(a) The Just War Doctrine

Quite early in history man felt the necessity of justifying war. Although, as we have seen, he did not search for scapegoats and, in early times, probably considered war unavoidable like a natural phenomenon, soon he must have felt that, unless the war was "just," there was also something shameful and reprehensible in it. This was possibly due to man's capacity for identification: even the cruelest must have felt on occasion that a child slaughtered or sold as a slave resembled his son, that the old man whose white hair was sullied with blood could have been his father, or that the young man with the slit throat and the stare frozen in death could have been himself. Probably because of this, war, in spite of its overwhelming attraction, could also have caused a certain secret horror in the heart of even the bravest. The horror was quickly overcome, of course, but reassurance from the priests that the war was "just," that the gods were pleased and that the victims deserved their fate, must have been welcome.

In royal and early republican Rome a war became "just" (*bellum iustum*) and therefore rightly (*iure*) waged if a strict ceremonial was observed. A Roman herald (*fetialis*) would ask satisfaction from the "offending" people. If within thirty-three days there was no acceptable response, the herald was dispatched to declare war by hurling a javelin dipped in blood into the territory of the foe.[2] In addition to being "just" (*iustum*) the war had also to be *pium*, that is, in accordance with the rules dictated by religion and, therefore, with the express or implied commands of the gods.[3] Historians who, like Livy, wanted to preserve for posterity the glory of their country tended to underline the justice of its wars, sometimes with arguments that may not be the most objective. Roman preoccupation with the "justice" of their wars is illustrated by the following passage reporting the speech to the Roman senate of a Rhodian envoy:

> ...vos estis Romani, qui ideo felicia bella vestra esse, quia iusta sint, prae vobis fertis; nec tam exitu eorum, quod vincatis quam principiis, quod non sine causa suscipiatis, gloriamini.[4]

In fact, "to the Romans with their incessant exaltation of 'justice' and formality, the conception of conducting a war *more latronum*, in the manner of brigands, was repugnant."[5] Even the ancient Greeks, a people with a much less legalistic mind than the Romans, never started a war unless there was a justification judged, by them, valid, and without an attempt to avoid it by demanding reparations or satisfaction from the foe.[6]

As the civilized world came more and more to be identified with the Roman Empire, the justification for war became less important because it was considered that the populations outside the Roman pale were barbarians and therefore that war against them was justified as a matter of patent necessity—either to protect the integrity of the Empire (in times of defensive warfare) or to increase its security and power when the legions were on the offensive.

The Empire was very tolerant in matters of religion. The governing elite, composed of men well versed in the elegant sophistication of Greek philosophy, had discarded, long before, the crude beliefs of their ancestors and treated the endless proliferation of cults and religions with a tolerance born of indifference. At the beginning, Christianity was one of those insignificant sects and, as such, ignored. Later, when it became the most important religion of the Empire, it was found to have a most unsettling belief: pacifism.

Justin Martyr, Lactantius, Eusebius Pamphili, and practically all other Christian writers before the fourth century, took it for granted that military service was incompatible with Christian faith.[7] Origen (c.185-c.254) wrote:

> To those who ask from where we come and who is our leader, we answer: we come, following the precepts of Jesus, to break the rational swords of our confrontations and violences, to make with them ploughshares and to forge into sickles the spears which were used for war. Because we will not brandish the sword anymore against anybody, nor will we train for war: we have become the children of peace through Jesus who is our leader....[8]

Tertullian (c.155-after 220) wrote:

> But, once we have embraced the faith and have been

baptized, we either must immediately leave military service (as many have done); or we must resort to all kinds of excuses in order to avoid any action which is...forbidden.[9]

Many cases of martyrdom suffered by soldiers are recorded in this period.

This pacifist and anti-militarist attitude was due not only to the message of Jesus, but also to the belief that the Second Coming was near and that the Empire was wicked and doomed. This attitude was, of course, dangerous for the integrity of the Roman world. Perhaps as the result of pressure from the government, perhaps because the Church Fathers recognized that uncompromising opposition to war, with the barbarians pressing at the borders, would be suicidal, such strict pacifism was soon diluted:

> Here is what we could say to the strangers to our faith who ask us to kill and fight as soldiers, for the common good....We, who with our prayers overcome the devils that cause wars, break oaths, and disturb peace, we help the emperor more than those who fight....We fight for the emperor more than anybody. We do not serve with his soldiers, even if he orders us to do so, but we fight for him by raising a special army, an army of pity, with our supplications to God.[10]

Although the effectiveness of prayers and supplications was not doubted, the problem remained. Soldiers had to be found to defend the borders of the Empire, and the task was increasingly difficult because, by then, Christians constituted a very large portion of the population. The situation was in the process of becoming critical.

Then, in a dramatic move, the Emperor and the Empire became Christian. All of a sudden, with the conversion of Constantine, the Christians were called to defend not a wicked institution but their own kingdom. The change took many by surprise:

> ...All this was to throw the Church into confusion. Some retreated into monasticism. Some joined utopian sects which

were regarded as heretical, and in due course died or were coerced out of existence. The majority took the view that they should seize the opportunity to extend the frontiers of Christianity into the political realm, even if this meant some modification in putting into practice the high ethical standards of the Christian gospel.[11]

As Christians became "the establishment" and therefore started to wield the power of the Empire, they realized that the spiritual message of the gospels had to be embedded in a temporal organization and that power had necessities. Compromise became necessary, and corruption, injustice, prevarication, and the other evils of temporal institutions started to afflict the body of the Church. Soon the pacifists started to become soldiers, and a few years after the Empire became Christian, the circle was complete when the persecuted became persecutors and non-Christians were prohibited from serving in the army:

> In 380 the Emperor Theodosius I declared...[that] non-Christians were but "foolish madmen" and should be "branded with the ignominious name of heretics." They would be punished with "the chastisement of the divine condemnation" as well as with "the punishment which our authority...shall decide to inflict." Christians were learning to live with the ambiguities of politics. The emblem of the cross was inscribed in the shields of the Roman soldiers, and early in the fifth century non-Christians were excluded from serving in the army.[12]

If this solved the problem from a military and political point of view, serious difficulties remained. Now Christians were being asked to fight and to kill, and this was still, for too many, in serious contradiction with the principles of the faith; on the other hand, the menace of the barbarians pressing at the borders was real. A new solution was needed.

St. Augustine (354-430) solved the problem by resuscitating the concept of just war and adapting it to Christian needs. He declared that Christians could fight provided that the war was just, and outlined the criteria to be applied so that it could be so classified. First of all, like Cicero, he insisted that war should only be a means to obtain peace. In addition, no war should be fought purely for power.[13] His definition of just war also included the notion that it was legitimate to start a war to avenge an injury suffered, such as when a city or a nation is unwilling to punish a misdeed of its citizens or refuses to restore what has been unjustly taken.[14] Isidore of Seville (c.560-636) followed as an authority on just war, but St. Thomas Aquinas (1225-1274) contributed the most to the systematic formulation of the concept. These are his criteria for a just war:

> ...quod aliquod bellum sit iustum, tria requiruntur. *Primo* quidem auctoritas Principis, cuius mandato bellum est gerendum: non enim pertinet ad personam privatam bellum movere....*Secundo* requiritur causa iusta; ut scilicet illi, qui impugnantur, propter aliquam culpam impugnationem mereantur; unde August. dicit..."iusta bella solent definiri, quae ulciscuntur iniurias, si gens, vel civitas plectenda est, quae vel vindicare neglexerit quod a suis improbe factum est, vel reddere quod per iniuriam ablatum est." *Tertio* requiruntur ut sit intentio bellantium recta; qua scilicet intenditur, vel ut bonum promoveatur, vel ut malum vitetur....Potest autem contingere, ut sit legitima auctoritas indicentis bellum, et causa iusta, nihilominus propter pravam intentionem bellum reddatur illicitum: dicit enim August...."Nocendi cupiditas, ulciscendi crudelitas, impacatus, et implacabilis animus, feritas rebellandi, libido dominandi, et si qua sunt similia, haec sunt, quae in bellis iure culpantur."[15]

With St. Augustine and later St. Thomas, the problem was solved in such an effective manner that the solution, with minor modifications, is still considered valid by some.[16]

In spite of being a brilliant and necessary solution to a great problem (the defense of the Empire), the doctrine of just war as an ethical norm could not be applied in practice because, as we have seen, international relations, and therefore wars, were not (and are not) conducted according to moral principles. Consequently, nothing changed:

>...moral insensibility and ruthlessness were conspicuous in the public life of the...[Christian] Empire....when the Christian Armenians rebelled against Persian rule after the conclusion of the peace, the Emperor Justin [in 572] claimed the right to assist them regardless of the peace. Under such conditions a discerning doctrine of "just war" obviously could not exist....The unbridled cruelty of the [Christian] Greeks was notorious; it included the blinding of prisoners of war....[17]

Cruelty, lack of compassion, lust for power, etc.—all those faults that were sufficient to transform the most just war into an injust one—continued to be the rule. In fact, with a perverse reasoning that is so common in human affairs, those same acts that were condemned became objects of admiration and joy if the war was "just" enough. For example, Raymond d'Agile, canon of the cathedral of Puy, describes the horrible carnage during the conquest of Jerusalem in 1099—pieces of human bodies in the streets, blood up to the knees near the Temple, etc.—and comments: "Spectacles célestes...dans l'Église et dans toute la ville, le peuple rendait grâce à l'Éternel."[18]

Later, cruelty and barbarism were not limited, of course, to Catholic soldiers, and Protestant theologians were as ready as their Catholic counterparts to justify similar behavior. Calvin warns against imprudent leniency, and Luther writes that it is "both Christian and an act of love to kill the enemy without hesitation, to plunder and burn and injure him by every method of warfare until he is conquered." Almost as an afterthought, he adds "except that one must beware of sin, and not violate wives and virgins."[19]

It turned out that it was also impossible to reach a consensus on the matter of just war. "Historians frequently tell us how difficult they find it to mention even a single case of war about which opinion as to whether the war was just or unjust has been unanimous."[20] Curiously enough, it would appear that, among political thinkers, those who find that there is no difficulty in distinguishing a just from an unjust war are the Communists. Mao Tse-tung, for example, declared, "All wars in history may be divided into two kinds according to their nature: just and unjust wars."[21] He then proceeded, with magnificent simplicity, to define as just all the Communist and revolutionary wars and unjust those fought by their adversaries, that is to say, the imperialists.[22] At a session of the Geneva Conference of 1974-77, the Chinese delegate reaffirmed that wars are indeed of two kinds, just and unjust, and that this distinction should be made in the protocols: just are the wars of national liberation and unjust those generated by the imperialist policy of aggression of the capitalist countries. It is of considerable interest that, on the same occasion, the delegate of the Holy See, Monsignor Luoni, affirmed that the distinction of the just and unjust war was a thing of the past, and that it would be extremely dangerous to introduce such a distinction into the protocols.[23]

As already discussed, another flaw of the doctrine of just war was that it represented an obstacle to the formulation and application of international agreements concerning armed conflict. As mentioned in Chapter 5, the views of Hugo Grotius (and of others), who concluded that "by the consent of nations, a rule has been introduced that all wars, conducted on both sides by authority of the sovereign power are to be held just,"[24] are considered essential for meaningful and effective international laws.

The difficulty in finding an example of a just war, the fact that the doctrine has consistently failed to moderate the horrors of armed conflict, and the advantages of considering all wars "just" from a legal point of view would seem to be enough to conclude that the just war doctrine has a very limited value from a practical point of view. Its faults, however, are not limited to those.

Implicit in the concept of just war is the corollary that it can be just only on one side. In the absence of a supernational structure capable of enforcing its decrees on the members of the international community, in the final analysis only the victor can impose his decision concerning which side was in the right; and even if agreement on the identification of any given war as just or unjust were possible, the incapacity of enforcing any meaningful punitive action against the winner (if his war were unjust) would make it useless. Most often the losing side, after being declared as the one that was fighting the unjust war, would become liable to punishment. In addition, as mentioned before (Chapter 5), the limits of warfare (e.g., prohibition against the killing of war prisoners) could conceivably be applied only to fighters for the just cause.

The enemy who is wrong is readily considered wicked and is easily dehumanized: this is one of the reasons for war atrocities.

> The tendency to stigmatize the enemy, at least in certain circumstances, as a criminal makes the humanization of warfare more difficult. Already the prohibition of the use of force in international relations, necessary as it was, has unfortunately revived the doctrine of *bellum iustum* and led to the inclination to refuse to the enemy rights provided for by international law.[25]

The fact that up to the eighteenth century the Church decided, in Catholic countries, whether a war was or was not just inevitably injected religious partisanship into international relations:

> Despite the treaty of Francis I with Suleiman the Magnificent, they [Spanish authors of the sixteenth century] still considered the [heretic] Saracens *per se* as born enemies of Christianity, necessarily on the "unjust" side. And the Dominican Domingo de Soto—often mentioned as one of the initiators of international law—declared as late as 1556, with characteristic casualness, that heretics were to be burned.[26]

For these reasons, the just war doctrine was abandoned, for all practical purposes, in the eighteenth and nineteenth centuries:

> From about Vattel's time until the early twentieth century, there was not much meaningful talk about the just war except by Christians; especially Roman Catholic scholars in whose

academic tradition (which had, however, become rather remote from the world of affairs) the concept had retained all its ancient centrality to the discussion of international relations, and others religiously and historically inclined who found that it offered a convenient entry into the discussion of the subject of the rights and wrongs of war itself. From the professional language of international law, however, the just war virtually disappeared, and with it the itch to discover which side in any particular war was "right" or "wrong." Vattel and the other publicists who mixed traditional natural law philosophy with proto-positivism firmly concluded that no good practical purpose was served by seeking to apply just war distinctions. From a pragmatically humanitarian standpoint, the just war seemed better forgotten about. It was simpler and in practice better (better, that is, in terms of limitations and restraints and of the likelihood of their being observed) to take war as it came and to set up the *jus in bello* as a law which required to be observed, irrespective of the *jus ad bellum*, about which, in the heyday of the positive school, the would-be legislators of international affairs hardly bothered to think. That did not stop almost everyone else thinking about it, especially when a war was in view or in progress. It would be difficult, I imagine, to find any war...which was not pronounced a just one by the religious pontificators of each belligerent country as well as by its political leadership, and which was not felt to be so by the men enthusiastically fighting it. But the law schools and the foreign offices remained aloof, preserving their principles from the contagions of popular politics and propaganda.[27]

Concern about the *ius ad bellum* (laws concerning the starting of war, *ius in bello* being the laws concerning the conduct of war)[28] was reintroduced on the international scene in the twentieth century. In fact, after the First World War, the entire concept of just and unjust wars was reintroduced, the winning side having fought, of course, a just war. The loser's war was unjust, and, this being the case, he had committed a punishable act. For this reason, Article 231 of the Versailles Treaty declared that Germany and its allies had been responsible for the war, and attempts were made to bring the Kaiser and other "war criminals" to trial (as discussed in Chapter 6).

The moral fervor of President Wilson after the First World War was paramount in the establishment of The League of Nations, the body that was going to bring justice and enduring peace. The climax of those efforts to ban war as an instrument of national policy was reached in 1928 with the General Treaty for the Renunciation of War, also known as the Kellogg Treaty from the name of President Coolidge's Secretary of State, whose exertions succeeded in securing the signatures of all major powers (see Chapter 5). Germany's signature was later made part of the grounds for indictment of the Nazi leaders for "crimes against peace: namely, planning, preparation, initiation, or waging of war of aggression...."[29]

During the Second World War, the idea that there are just and unjust wars was kept alive for obvious propaganda reasons, but afterward the winners, declaring that they were on the just side, proceeded to prosecute the losers.

With the Vietnam war, the question again came to the fore in a more acute way because there had not been episodes like Pearl Harbor or the concentration camp exterminations to show clearly the causes of American involvement. It was forgotten that Pearl Harbor was no more the real cause of the Second World War (for the United States) than the assassination at Sarajevo was the real cause of the First. As for the attempted extermination of the Jews, it was surely not the cause of the war (nor was it an act of war—the Jews not being at war with anybody), but an act committed during the war by deranged criminal minds.

During the Vietnam war, therefore, there was much soul-searching to decide whether the United States was fighting a just or unjust war. In the meantime the doctrine had been modified to disown the principle that "aggressive" war (aggressive in the sense of initiation of hostilities) could be justified in certain cases (e.g., to redress an injury or to forestall injurious action);[30] war could not be used for vindictive justice, nor was it considered a legitimate means for changing the status quo. Only the defense of territorial integrity and political independence against "aggression" could justify war. In the case of Vietnam, as the territorial integrity and political independence of the United States was not in jeopardy, the war was unjust. By the same token, the United States would have fought an unjust war against Japan and Germany in 1940-45, because American territorial integrity and political independence were not menaced.

The absurdity of trying to limit the interests of a country to the defense of territorial integrity and political independence is obvious: this would mean preserving the status quo in a kind of frozen eternity that is incompatible with the realities of international politics. The problem related to the definition of "aggression" has been discussed in Chapter 6. In addition:

> In the absence of a society possessed of effective collective procedures for protecting the rights of its members as well as for changing conditions that have become oppressive and inequitable, it is argued that the attempt to deny states this ultimate means of self-redress [armed force]—save as a measure of self-defense against attack—is bound to fail....
>
> Thus Paul Ramsay writes: "No sweeping proscription of 'aggressive' war can hope to stand....Aggression has to be defined so as to include within its meaning, not only the first resort to arms, but also any basic challenge to the security of a rival nation, to its *pax-ordo-iustitia* and the laws of its peace, against which the only effective defense may be, and is known to be, a resort to armed force."[31]

Even the concept of self-defense is not immune from criticism:

> ...the objection...is simply that a state may be unable to preserve its vital interests—above all its political independence—if self-defense is only legitimate where the measures taken to endanger the state's interests take the form of an armed attack. [Example: the U.S. took forcible measures to prevent further shipments of missiles to Cuba after they were discovered there in October 1962. Strictly speaking, the Soviet Union had done nothing illegal and there was no armed aggression.]
>
> ...Within a state a right of self-defense is denied the individual short of an armed attack or the imminent threat of armed

Just War and Pacifism   207

attack precisely because the individual may seek and receive protection against other acts endangering his vital, and legally protected, interests. The same assurance evidently does not obtain for states in international society....

These uncertainties marking the scope of self-defense in international law are equally apparent in current versions of *bellum iustum*.[32]

Modern modifications of the concept of the *bellum iustum* include also a principle of proportionality according to which the force used in self-defense must be proportional to the good expected by taking up arms. In other words, the values preserved by the use of force must be proportional to the values sacrificed. This also is not immune from justified criticism:

> Even if all the relevant facts were known, and all the consequences of action (or abstention from action) foreseen, the application of the principle of proportionality would give rise to uncertainty and, in consequence to disagreement. This is so for the apparent reason that the principle of proportionality is devoid of substantive content. Nor is there any real consensus among theorists of the just war with respect to the values that should form the content of the principle of proportionality.[33]

In addition:

> Even a defensive war may not be an "apt and proportionate means"; even a defensive war, then, may be an unjust war if the good secured by such a war is outweighed by the evil attendant upon—or expected to attend the conduct of war. This is precisely the issue raised by the prospect of thermonuclear war; even if defensive in character, a thermonuclear war may nevertheless be an unjust war. On the other hand, if a defensive war may nevertheless be an unjust war, it does not necessarily follow from the principle of proportionality that under present conditions an "aggressive" war must be an unjust war. The presumption is not self-evident that war—any and all war— can no longer serve as an apt and proportionate means for resolving international conflicts. (Nor, for that matter, is it self-evident that war—any and all war—can no longer be

waged with "right intent" and the proper means.) To say this is not at all to dismiss our experience with war in this century; it is simply to say that despite this experience, and despite the possible consequences of thermonuclear war, there may still be wars and wars.[34]

It is of interest that the proponents of the principle of proportionality find a very closely related principle unacceptable. In the proportionality principle, values sacrificed by the use of force should be "proportional," that is, not more important than those preserved by the use of force. In other words, the "bad" means (use of force) is justified or permitted if the "good" end (preservation of certain values) is worthwhile. The principle which this very much resembles is, of course, "the end justifies the means." In fact, supporters of the principle of proportionality (as applied to the just war doctrine) could be accused of accepting the tenet that the end justifies the means.

The usual way of trying to avoid this accusation is to invoke the so-called principle of double effect. According to this, there are no "bad" means that can be used to achieve "good" ends because the "bad" means are eliminated by a distinction made between what a man does with intention and what he merely foresees as a result of his action. In other words, an act with evil "side effects" may be morally acceptable if those side effects are not intended, even if foreseen, and what is intended is only the "good" end result. In the case of just war, some evil resulting from the use of force (e.g., the unavoidable killing of innocents) is the foreseen but not intended "side effect" (and, therefore, not a "bad" means), while what is intended is the "good" result (e.g., the preservation of certain values).

Serious flaws have been found in this argument:

> If it is known that an act will have certain evil consequences, and that act is nevertheless taken, it is plausible to contend that some of these consequences were not intended only if intent is made synonymous with wish or desire. This equation, however, accords neither with ordinary usage nor with com-

mon sense. We may not wish or desire something to happen, yet we may intend it to happen. The reason for this distinction is simply that to intend means to have in mind something as to be done or brought about. Thus we may not wish or desire a certain consequence of an action and consider this consequence as tragic or as an evil. Even so, we intend this consequence if we know that it will result from a certain action and we nevertheless take this action....There is a further point to be made in this connection. To say, as do the theorists of *bellum iustum*, that an act must "positively intend only the good effect and merely tolerate the evil effect" is to give a moral significance to the notion of intent without resolving the real difficulty. Objectively, we still intend the one effect just as much as we intend the other effect. It does not alter the matter to characterize the one effect as positively intended and the other as merely tolerated.[35]

Indeed, the criticism seems valid and it is difficult to accept an argument that attempts the *ethical* justification of, for example, the killing of civilians on the ground that such killings were not "intended," even if clearly foreseen, as in massive aerial bombing. An even more serious flaw of the double-effect argument, however, is that it would lead to absurd choices in certain situations.

Consider, for example, these two:

Situation A:
A terrorist has hidden a nuclear device in a large metropolitan area and has decided to detonate it at a certain time by remote control. He is many miles away from the area to be destroyed, hidden in a small city of ten thousand inhabitants. The police know that he is hiding in that small city but do not know exactly where. If the nuclear bomb is detonated one million will die. There is no time to do anything except to destroy the small city where the terrorist is hiding. If this were to be done, ten thousand would die.

Situation B:
As above, except that the terrorist—and we believe him—

has declared that he will give himself up without detonating the nuclear device if a certain innocent person is killed.

The doctrine of double effect would allow the killing of ten thousand innocents (as an unintended evil effect—the good intended effect being the destruction of the detonating device—Situation A) but, to achieve the same result, would not allow the killing of the one innocent because, in this last case (Situation B), the act would be an intended means and not an unintended effect. It is absurd that in one situation ten thousand could be killed to save a million, but in the other a single one could not.

In defence of the doctrine of double effect, Philippa Foot says:

> Suppose for example that some tyrant should threaten to torture five men if we ourselves would not torture one. Would it be our duty to do so, suppose we believed him, because this would be no different from choosing to rescue five men from him rather than one? If so, anyone who wants us to do something we think wrong has only to threaten that otherwise he himself will do something we think worse. A mad murderer, known to keep his promises, could thus make it our duty to kill some innocent citizen to prevent him from killing two. From this conclusion we are again rescued by the doctrine of the double effect. If we refuse, we foresee that the greater number will be killed but we do not intend it: it is he who intends (that is strictly or directly intends) the death of innocent persons, we do not.[36]

The first part of the above may sound, at first, quite convincing until one realizes that its apparent strength rests on two points: (a) the use of small numbers, and (b) the natural repulsion to using the group to commit injustice.

In the Introduction it has been discussed how the utilitarian solution of a similar problem becomes the only one acceptable if we consider numbers much larger than those used by the author. Suppose the above tyrant would threaten not to torture five men but to destroy millions, in fact to wipe out humanity, with his stockpile of nuclear weapons. Suppose also that we are sure that he will do so unless we kill, or torture, an innocent. It is evident that, in this case, when the ratio between the rescued and the sacrificed is in the billions instead of in the single digits, the above argument, at least from a practical point of view, loses its force. Of course, it can be argued that, in theory, there is no difference between killing one person and killing millions or destroying humanity, but it is obvious that, in practice, there is. If society were confronted with the necessity of choosing between the two alternatives outlined by Ms. Foot, it would undoubtedly choose not to intervene, but if the alternatives were the sacrifice of one innocent person or the end of humanity, there is no doubt that it would become necessary to sacrifice the innocent.[37]

This suggests that, although under usual circumstances moral attitudes are not affected by the quantities involved, when some of the elements have a mass that reaches extreme values, the ethical situation becomes "deformed" and the usual ethical principles become inapplicable. A similar phenomenon occurs in the physical world: bodies of relatively small mass do not affect their environment (or their effect is negligible from a practical point of view), but bodies of very large mass produce a "deformation" of the space around them so that observable effects result. We may have to modify our ethical tenets by taking into account the concept of "mass." This is made necessary by the advent of the nuclear age, which has given us the capacity of producing cataclysmic events of planetary size that were beyond the capability of our technology until very recently.

The fact that mass "deforms" the ethical situation so that moral principles are not applied means that "mass," in certain situations, makes some acts (otherwise considered immoral) amoral of the second order (or degree). We have seen, however, that "mass" is not the only agent capable of doing so: self-defense, war (the defense of the group), protection of the innocent, etc., can also produce the same effect in the appropriate circumstances. This suggests that we can state the principle in more general terms: *necessity can transform immoral acts into acts amoral in the second degree.* In the case of war, for example, necessity is created chiefly by the drive to survive, as discussed in Chapter 1.

Man's repugnance for injustice committed by the group is due to the strong identification between the individual and the group to which he belongs. This identification makes the individual feel that he is personally responsible for the "official" activities of the group. Consider, for example, the current controversy about abortion. The anti-abortionists are particularly repelled by the fact that society officially sanctions abortion because this makes them feel directly involved in what, to them, is a crime. If, however, abortion were illegal but the law rarely enforced, the movement against abortion would likely be much less vocal and active even if the number of abortions were the same.

It would appear that our repugnance to having the police or the army—in other words, society—kill an innocent, even if to save many, is based on the same feelings. This is not to imply that such a feeling is irrational or that it is devoid of importance or value, but that it has to be taken into consideration when trying to analyze reactions to a given situation.

As for the second part of Ms. Foot's argument ("If so anyone who wants us to do something we think wrong has only to threaten that otherwise he himself will do something we think worse"), surely she has not missed all reports about the activities of blackmailers and kidnappers. They try to force somebody to do something wrong (e.g., to pay ransom) by threatening to do something worse (e.g., kill the child). Very often they succeed.

From the above discussion we must conclude that the doctrine of double effect is unacceptable and that, far from avoiding it, it allows the application of the principle that the end justifies the means, even if without the pangs of guilt that this causes in many people. However, although this principle is acceptable and accepted in practice (see Introduction), the doctrine of double effect must be rejected for the reasons stated above, including the fact that it seems to lead to absurd

Just War and Pacifism   213

moral guidelines in certain situations (e.g., to save millions it would allow us to kill ten thousand but would forbid us to kill one—situations A and B considered above).

The just war doctrine as an attempt to apply moral principles to an amoral act was, and is, bound to fail, but as a practical device to allow Christians to fight, it has been useful for sixteen centuries. Considering that wars are inevitable and that the side that does not fight is soon eliminated from the scene of history, we may speculate that the doctrine may have saved Western Civilization from its external enemies (e.g., from the Moslem onslaught). At the same time, however, it would appear that the same doctrine did not have much effect in preventing war among Christian countries.

We must recognize that the old myth of just and unjust wars should be abandoned, not only for the reasons discussed above but also because of the existence of nuclear weapons. (Who would dare to start an all-out nuclear war even if "just"?) As repeatedly stated, man still behaves as if war were an act amoral of the second degree, but if, on the other hand, we want to consider it in the light of conventional ethics, it is impossible to justify its horrors no matter how desperately we may try to patch up our moral principles with the doctrine of double effect or with other sophisms. In fact, perhaps, the most disturbing feature of the just war doctrine is its attempt to transform an act that, from a strictly ethical point of view, cannot be just or moral (for instance the killing of an enemy soldier who is a human being doing his duty in the service of his country) into a "meritorious deed":

> ...the moral "object" of the same physical acts changes when the situation to which they pertain becomes...different. In our civilized societies it is not a murder, it is a meritorious deed for a fighting man to kill an enemy soldier in a just war. In utterly barbarized societies like a concentration camp, or even in quite particular conditions like those of clandestine resistance in an occupied country, many things which were, as to their moral nature, objectively fraud or murder or perfidy in ordinary civ-

ilized life cease, now, to come under the same definition and become, as to their moral nature, objectively permissible or ethical things. There are still, there are always good and evil actions; not every means whatever is permissible; it is still and it is always true that the end does not justify the means; moral principles keep on still and will always keep on dividing bad and good means from each other: but the line of demarcation has shifted.[38]

Not at all. "Many things which were, as to their moral nature, objectively fraud or murder or perfidy in ordinary civilized life" remain fraud or murder or perfidy. What changes is not the morality of the acts, but the degrees of necessity that force us to "suspend" the application of ethical principles. There is nothing ethically meritorious in killing the enemy soldier, it is a necessary and grim act that all good soldiers may have to do for an end that transcends in importance the negative aspects of the act. What is meritorious, therefore, is not the act in itself (killing an innocent cannot *ever* be meritorious) but the consequences of the act—in this case the protection of the group achieved through the killing of the enemy soldier. In the same way, there is nothing meritorious in amputating a cancerous leg. The surgeon maims the patient, in itself a grim act, because it is judged that the life of the patient is more important than his physical integrity. Again, what is meritorious is not the amputation itself but the protection of the life of the patient achieved through it. Therefore, those who insist on applying ethical principles to war should not speak of just and unjust war but of *unavoidable or necessary* war, acknowledge the immorality of it, and, with the recognition of its necessity under certain circumstances modify the doctrine so that it avoids inconsistencies and the confusion between acts that are ethical and acts that are unethical but necessary.

To conclude, it would appear that the concept of just war even in the modern form,[39] does not seem to be able to solve the problem of our revulsion for war and our incapacity to abolish it.

Just War and Pacifism 215

(b) Pacifism: Another Dream

War is as old as man, but so is man's desire for peace. Even the most bellicose have, on occasion, proclaimed their inclination toward peace. After the conquest of Aleppo in 1400, Timour (Tamerlane) saw the doctors of the law among the captives and he invited them to a personal conference. After asking various questions he said:

> You see me here a poor, lame, decrepit mortal. Yet by my arm has the Almighty been pleased to subdue the kingdoms of Iran, Touran, and the Indies. I am not a man of blood; and God is my witness that in all my wars I have never been the aggressor, and that my enemies have always been the authors of their own calamity.[40]

During this peaceful conversation the city was being sacked:

> ...the streets of Aleppo streamed with blood, and echoed with the cries of mothers and children, with the shrieks of violated virgins. The rich plunder that was abandoned to his soldiers might stimulate their avarice; but their cruelty was enforced by the peremptory command of producing an adequate number of heads, which, according to his custom, were curiously piled in columns and pyramids.[41]

A few months later, the conqueror moved toward Damascus. The inhabitants resisted. Timour agreed to raise the siege if "they would adorn his retreat with a gift or ransom." The inhabitants agreed, he entered the city "under color of a truce" and massacred the entire population. It was the year of our Lord 1401. Gibbon adds that Tamerlane also "erected on the ruins of Bagdad a pyramid of ninety thousand heads."[42]

In classical antiquity war and conquest were exalted and sung by poets, but men were dreaming of a past "Golden Age" of peace (created by their yearning), forever hoping for its return when

> Ipsae lacte domum referent distenta capellae
> ubera, nec magnos metuent armenta leones.[43]

The *Pax Augusta* was considered the beginning of that new Golden Age and Rome dreamed, for a time, of being able to impose by force a *"Pax"* that the world did not seem to be able to achieve without the might of the legions. The dream was short, however, and peace continued to be an object of desire that occasionally blessed humanity but that could not be expected to continue indefinitely.

Christianity brought a renewed message of peace and, although the message remained only a hope, man continued to dream of peace: Charlemagne added *"pacificus"* to his titles and the German Kings called themselves *"Friedennsfürsten"* ("peace princes").[44] Dante, at the beginning of his divine poem, sang the coming of the *"Veltro,"* a mysterious being who

> ...non ciberá terra né peltro
> ma sapienza e amore e virtute...[45]

In our days, man continues to dream of perpetual peace.

The term "pacifism" encompasses the many forms that the efforts to eliminate war have taken through the ages. Max Scheler, in an essay published between the two wars (1931), distinguished eight kinds of pacifism: heroic and individual, Christian, economic, juridical or legal, semi-pacifism (Marxist), the imperialist pacifism of universal empire (*pax Romana*), the international class pacifism of the great capitalist bourgeoisie, and the cultural pacifism of cosmopolitanism.[46] In this book, only the two forms that seem the most important are considered: the "juridical or legal" pacifism and the kind that Scheler calls "heroic and individual"—the doctrine of non-resistance to violence in principle—which will be called simply "pacifism." Only the latter will be discussed here, as the former was examined in Chapter 5.

Two types of pacifism are usually distinguished: absolute and relative. The absolute pacifist holds that violence is the supreme evil and agrees to submit to it, rather than commit it, in all circumstances, even in case of self-defense or when the life of members of his own family are at stake; he preaches non-resistance in all cases and, therefore, the elimination of violence by surrender. In other words, the absolute pacifist assumes that if violence were to encounter no resistance, it would eventually disappear. This is, of course, wrong.

> Although it is true that if in every conflict one side were to surrender, war itself would be eliminated, it is also true that ...violence would not. If it were, the best way to eradicate rape would be to instruct the victims to simply agree and submit to the act. It is evident that if all rape victims were to do so, rape (defined as sexual intercourse without the consent of the victim) would disappear.[47]

The relative pacifist holds that violence can be resisted and can be used, but only in extreme cases. Most pacifists belong to this second category:

> Ghandi...would certainly not do as an example of the absolute pacifist....In a much-quoted paragraph, he said: "I do believe that, where there is only choice between cowardice and violence, I would advise violence. Thus, when my eldest son asked me what he should have done had he been present when I was almost fatally assaulted in 1908, whether he should have run away and seen me killed or whether he should have used physical force which he could and wanted to use,'and defend me, I told him that it was his duty to defend me even by using violence."[48]

Another example of a relative pacifist is Bertrand Russell, who advocated pacifism, disarmament, and conscientious objection in the Thirties, armed resistance against Hitler in the Forties ("forgetting that if they [his compatriots] had listened to him, they would have nothing to resist Hilter with"[49]), then again, pacifism, disarmament, and conscientious objection thereafter.

To this category also belong the majority of the pacifists

who demonstrate, as they did during the Vietnam war, in the so-called "peace campaigns," and against rearmament, atomic weapons, and the military establishment. These peace groups are composed of various subgroups, but if we disregard the so-called "alienated" who want to protest no matter what, the faddists who participate because it is the "thing to do," and those who, for various reasons, desire the victory of the other side, we are left with a nucleus of sincere believers whose purpose is to eliminate war by eliminating nuclear weapons and promoting good will toward the foe and anti-militarism.

The futility of such endeavors has been discussed in previous chapters. The question, however, arises whether the actions of these groups, who always stigmatize the immorality of war, may have some value in accelerating the slow process of moralization of foreign politics. There is no doubt that these activities tend to remind the public of the horrors of war and the desirability of peace. Also, by advocating the application of the canons of morality to international activities, and therefore by depicting as immoral anything related to war, they tend to produce a certain amount of public pressure against armaments, the military establishment, and any form of foreign policy other than tolerance and compromise. In view of the fact that public pressure often tends to be effective in producing changes, one may conclude that such groups accelerate the process of the abolition of war and moralization of foreign policy. Unfortunately it is not so.

The activities of those groups may have a certain weight in the Western democracies, where there is freedom of the press, speech, and assembly, but are almost completely ineffective where such freedoms do not exist. For this reason, they tend to have an impact only on one side of the world political arena, and therefore to cause dangerous alterations in the equilibrium of the forces on which peace is based. By weakening the capacity of one side to apply power—in other words, by weakening the military capabilities of the West—they may induce the other side to take advantage of the situation, with catastrophic consequences, because one of the most important among the causes of war is the real or imagined power deficiency of the other side. For these reasons the endeavors of those groups, far from being valuable to the cause of peace, are dangerous to it.

Often, relative pacifism, more than a form of true pacifism, is simply a reaffirmation of belief in the doctrine of just war. Russell was in favor of armed conflict when the war was just according to his judgment, and Ghandi used non-violence as the only form of effective power that he could bring to bear, under the circumstances, to achieve the goals of the struggle that he considered just. He was ready to advocate the use of violence in particular cases—such as, for example, in the protection of his own life. One wonders if he would not have advocated violence if this was the only way to achieve Indian independence.

Absolute pacifists are those who condemn the use of violence in all circumstances, as stated before. Often their conviction is derived from religious beliefs, in which case they see themselves as advocates of a return to purer and more innocent times (e.g., to an idealized primitive church). Their position, considered by themselves as consonant with the highest standards of ethics, is considered immoral and contemptible by others. Many, in fact, agree that it is despicable and immoral to let a human being be tortured, raped, or killed without trying to defend him or her with all possible means including violence.

The absolute pacifist belief is more consistent and straightforward than the relative one, because it avoids the distinction between the just and unjust use of violence—that is, war—and all the pitfalls related to that distinction. Nevertheless, it has its own difficulties; not only is the assumption that violence can be eliminated by non-resistance wrong, as we have seen, but more importantly, absolute pacifism is bound to entail the death of the group—except in the most improbable case that all groups embrace it at the same time. Therefore, as war is motivated by the desire for survival and as such, paradoxically, represents man's rejection of death (see Chapter 1), absolute pacifism, the total renunciation of struggle, may be interpreted as the expression of a death wish, akin to suicide, the supreme renunciation of all conflict. This, of course, has to be understood from a collective and not from an individual point of view: pacifism is the suicide of the group, not of the individual. The individual pacifist, in fact, may think that his position, by rejecting war's slaughter, is an affirmation of his belief in life and not the manifestation of a suicidal wish. His conviction, however, could cause the death of the group because of his concern for the physical safety of himself and others and his unwillingness to take risks for the protection of the group.

A subgroup of "absolute pacifism" is "unilateral nuclear pacifism." Because it allows the use of conventional weapons in extreme circumstances, this type is not, strictly speaking, absolute pacifism. However it must be considered a subgroup—at least for the superpowers—because for them unilateral renunciation of nuclear weapons is the equivalent of surrender and would have the same practical result as absolute pacifism. It is evident that a small power can unilaterally renounce nuclear weapons because its subjugation may not be worth the risk of upsetting the general equilibrium of forces, or because of the protection of a nuclear ally.

Even if the adoption of either type of pacifism (absolute and nuclear unilateral) would have the same result for the group, namely destruction or subjugation, the unilateral renunciation of nuclear weapons does not represent the expression of a death wish but rather the falling back on the next line of defense in the rear. As mentioned in Chapter 1, oneself, family, country, civilization, humanity, earth, solar system, universe, and God could be considered lines of retreat in man's struggle against death. Unilateral nuclear disarmament means the abandonment of the more forward positions, country and civilization, and the falling back on the next line, humanity. The unilateral nuclear pacifist "sacrifices" country and civilization to be sure that humanity will not be destroyed in a nuclear holocaust. As for the nuclear pacifists who preach bilateral (as opposed to unilateral) nuclear disarmament, they simply indulge in a form of wishful thinking. Their protestations and demonstrations, although well inten-

Just War and Pacifism 221

tioned in many cases, have the same value that protests and demonstrations against cancer or old age would have.

It is to be expected that, in a society in decline, pacifism and appeasement (perceived as moderation and good sense) should be particularly widespread as the death wish of a structure that has reached the end of its life. The following is of interest in this connection and concerns the dying society of pre-revolutionary France:

> What but a death wish could bring about so complete a reversal of all normal worldly considerations of good sense, self-interest, and desire to survive? I remember reading in Taines's *Origines de la France Contemporaine* of how, shortly before the Revolution, a party of affluent liberal intellectuals were discussing over their after-dinner cognac all the wonderful things that were going to happen when the Bourbon regime was abolished, and freedom à la Voltaire and Jean-Jacques Rousseau reigned supreme. One of the guests, hitherto silent, suddenly spoke up. Yes, he said, the Bourbon regime would indeed be overthrown, and in the process—pointing around—you and you and you will be carried screaming to the guillotine; you and you and you go into penurious exile; and—now pointing in the direction of some of the elegant ladies present—you and you and you will hawk your bodies round from sans-culotte to sans-culotte. There was a moment of silence while this, as it turned out, all-too-exact prophecy sank in, and then the previous conversation was resumed. I know several fashionable and affluent households in London and Washington and Paris where similar conversations take place, and where similar exact prophecies may be made, without, as on the occasion Taine so appositely described, having the slightest impact.[50]

The challenge to the establishment came, in the case described above, from an internal revolutionary group and not from an external fore. For that reason France underwent profound transformations but did not die as a protagonist of history; if the challenger had been a foreign power, France would have been reduced to a geographical expression.

Pareto noted this phenomenon (the renunciation of struggle) and described it as characteristic of elites:

> Elites often become effete....It is amazing to see how in imperial Rome the members of the elite committed suicide or allowed themselves to be assassinated without the slightest defense, as long as it pleased Caesar. We are equally amazed when we see the nobles of France die on the guillotine, instead of going down fighting, weapon in hand....If Louis XVI had had the spirit of Silano, he would have saved himself and his family, and perhaps saved the country much blood and pain.[51]

For much of history the elites were the movers of history and the masses played only a secondary role. For this reason, renunciation of struggle occurred mostly among the elites, and this was enough to produce the fall of the group. Only in the twentieth century, especially in the Western democracies, has the phenomenon become evident among the public, in the form of pacifism, although those affected are still a small minority.

Pacifism, as we have seen, is the expression of a death wish for the group. But, of course, if it were to become universal and, therefore, war were eliminated, a world situation would come into being in which the survival of one group would not be menaced by the bellicosity of others. In that hypothetical case, naturally, pacifism would cease to be the expression of a death wish and become a great boon for humanity. But, and this is one of its great weaknesses, the pacifist among non-pacifists is like a lamb among lions, a lamb that by his very presence encourages the lions to keep their carnivorous habits instead of encouraging them to become vegetarians:

> The pacifist argument that it pays everyone not to have wars runs up against the fact that it would pay some people, in a world where others are pacifist, to make war on the pacifists.[52]

In spite of being ineffective and even dangerous, one could think that pacifists might at least claim a certain moral superiority because of their opposition to violence, which is indeed a sign of barbarism and bestiality. Unfortunately, in this respect, they display a curious attitude: their opposition seems

Just War and Pacifism

to be directed not toward violence per se but only toward violence associated with war. This is shown by the common attitude of pacifists toward violence associated with crime. Not that they are indifferent to crime, of course, but it is evident that its violence is not among the targets of their crusades. Let us take two examples to illustrate the point— Kim and the murders of Interstate 57.

> In 1972, during the war in Vietnam, there was a famous picture of a little Vietnamese girl named Kim running from a napalm attack with her clothes and flesh afire. This became one of the classic horror photographs of that war. For many people it took napalm and Vietnam out of the abstract, and it touched the consciousness of many Americans who had been viewing the war through rose-colored glasses of patriotic cliché. The response was one of moral shock. What was happening to that girl was wrong....It was wrong to dump napalm on Kim...[53]

Indeed it was wrong to drop napalm on Kim, even if it was an accident. Nobody wanted to dump napalm on Kim but such (and even worse) cases take place during the nightmares that we call wars. As stated in the previous quotation, the picture that everybody could see on television and in all the newspapers caused a furor, and the pacifists showed it as proof of the immorality of war. "The response was one of moral shock" indeed. The degree of moral shock and indignation, however, does not seem to be the same when wilful horrible acts (not accident's as in the case of Kim) are committed, not in war, but in peacetime. Here is the case of the murders of Interstate 57, which received only scant attention:

> On the night of June 3, 1973, a Chevrolet Caprice, driven by a woman, was forced off Interstate 57 in southern Cook County, Ill., by a car carrying four men. One of them pointed a 12-gauge pump shotgun at her, ordered her to strip and then to climb through a barbed-wire fence at the side of the road. As she begged for her life, her assailant thrust the shotgun barrel into her vagina and fired. After watching her agonies for several

minutes, he finished her off with a blast to the throat. Less than an hour later, the marauding motorists stopped another car and told the man and woman inside it to get out and lie down on the shoulder of the road. The couple pleaded for mercy, saying that they were engaged to be married in six months. The man with the shotgun said, "Kiss your last kiss," then shot both of them in the back, killing them....The man ultimately convicted of the "I-57 murders" now sits confined in the Menard Condemned Unit, the official name for death row in the Illinois prison system. Yet...[he] does not face execution for those three killings nearly ten years ago. Illinois' death penalty was invalidated in 1972 and was not restored until 1977....It took....[him] less than one year to kill again, this time stabbing a fellow inmate at Stateville Correctional Center with the sharpened handle of a soup ladle....[54]

The different reaction to the two episodes was in part due to the fact that the burning of Kim, even if accidental, was the result of action taken by the army—that is, by the group (see earlier in this chapter)—and in part by the fact that man, being still a primitive being, is much more impressed by pictures than by words. If there had been a television camera to record the scene so that the blast of that shotgun could have been shown in living color together with all the various expressions of agony on the face of the victim, then more righteous indignation would have been aroused. The written word, requiring a little more abstraction, is not capable of producing the same moral shock as the picture. Consequently, in terms of the reaction of pacifists, it would appear that it is not as wrong to fire shotguns into innocent victims as it is to dump napalm on Kim (even if by accident). The selectivity of pacifist indignation is further underlined by the fact that the brutality of criminal violence can reach such levels of unspeakable horror that not only the episode of Kim but even the murders of Interstate 57 pale in comparison: in a news broadcast, for example, a national wire service reported that a group of persons was accused of murder committed while making films showing children being sexually abused and killed on camera.[55] There is no need to dwell on the abomination of the deed and on the implications of any commerce involving these movies.

One could object that the violence of crime does not compare with the magnitude of war's violence, but this would be inaccurate. In 1965, for example, during the Vietnam war, 2,800,000 major felonies were reported to the police in the U.S., where about 5,000,000 arrests occur annually.[56] In addition there are about 20,000 murders per year in the United States alone, 10 to 20 per cent of which are "recreational" homicides, that is, murders committed

> for reasons outside the traditional motives of jealousy, greed and revenge....What's terrifying is...what it takes in terms of a world view to think that shooting you is a way to fill a Tuesday afternoon....[57]

In 1983, for example, there were in the United States 21,000 murders, 500,000 robberies, and 100,000 arson cases.[58] These are annual figures that must be compared with the 46,000 American deaths in the entire Vietnam War. Of course those were not the only deaths caused by that war; nor is the violence of war measured only by the number of dead. But if one considers that many crimes of violence are not reported and that crime is a continuous, ongoing phenomenon in all countries, whereas war is intermittent and involves only a few countries at a time, one is forced to conclude that the tragedy caused by violent crimes is of the same order of magnitude as the one caused by war. It would appear, therefore, that the violence of crime should be as much the target of the pacifists as the violence caused by war. Yet it is not so.

Because, usually, non-resistance results in elimination (or subjection) of the group at least as an historical entity (by eliminating or reducing its influence on subsequent historical events), it would appear that the aim of the pacifist is not the elimination of violence but (unconsciously perhaps) the elimination of his group, at least as a protagonist in history. In this sense is pacifism the expression of a death wish.

Albrecht Dürer — *The Fall of Icarus*

Chapter 8

> Quivi si vede Memfi e Tebe doma,
> Babilon, Troia e Cartagin con quelle,
> Ierusalem, Atene, Sparta e Roma.
> Quiva si mostran quanto furon belle,
> alte, ricche, potenti; e come, al fine,
> fortuna a' lor nimici in preda dielle.[1]
>
> Machiavelli,
> *I Capitoli, Di Fortuna*.

POWER AND DECLINE

(a) Power

In general, power means the capacity to modify the environment. In the more restricted political sense, it means the capacity "of a political unit to impose its will upon other units."[2]

228 MAN AND WAR

Many languages distinguish between power and force (*puissance et force, Macht und Kraft, potenza e forza*), and often the word meaning power (e.g., *potenza, puissance*) indicates the concept of "potentiality" implicit in the concept of power. Power, in fact, is not force but the capacity to apply force—in other words, potential force. In addition, power is the energy source for the pressure that every group exerts on others, as discussed in Chapter 6.

The components of the power exerted by groups have been variously identified by many authors. Spykman enumerates: surface of territory, nature of frontiers, size of population, absence or presence of raw materials, economic and technologic development, financial power, ethnic homogeneity, degree of social integration, political stability, national morale.[3] Morgenthau lists: geography, natural resources, industrial capacity, state of military preparedness, population, national character, national morale, quality of diplomacy.[4] Aron distinguishes three fundamental elements: milieu (the space occupied by the group), resources (raw materials plus technology), collective capacity for action (organization, discipline, etc.).[5]

All the above definitions recognize that the power of a group or country finally rests on three main elements: psychological, economic, and military. Other elements contribute, in varying degrees, to the capacity to use or to resist power. For example, Switzerland is geographically favored by nature for defensive warfare; Venice was, at a certain time in the evolution of nautical technology, at a disadvantage being in a marine cul-de-sac; distance, until recently, decreased Russia's offensive capability and increased its defensive capability. Size of population and territory, availability of raw materials, industrial capacity, etc., are also important, of course, and are part of the economic component. Until the Renaissance a city with tens of thousands of inhabitants and a few hundred square miles of territory could become great. Then the modern countries emerged and millions of inhabitants and hundreds of thousands of square miles of territory became necessary. Today, the so-called superpowers have hundreds of millions of

Power and Decline 229

inhabitants and millions of square miles of territory. The military and economic necessities in the modern world are such that we can be certain that, in the future, India may conceivably become a superpower but Albania will not. It is evident, however, that countries with about the same population and territory may have a different importance in the international arena.

The psychological component of power includes unity. Not only political unity but also that particular unity of purpose and uniformity of positive feelings toward the country that is called patriotism. The intensity of patriotism is proportional to the degree of conformity (in its meaning of congruity, harmony, and accordance), while diversity, especially political and cultural, tends to be inimical to it.

Patriotism and conformity are the expression of a force that encourages the identification of the individual with the group so that he sees the group's interest as his own and sometimes even puts it ahead of his own. We call this force centripetal and it will be discussed in the second part of this chapter. Conformity, as already mentioned, is closely related to patriotism and one tends to encourage the development of the other. We may note that, in the United States, the intensity of patriotism has decreased *pari passu* with the increase in tolerance for the so-called "unconventional lifestyles"—in other words, with a decrease of conformity which, in fact, has become, for many, a word that elicits derision and contempt. Nevertheless, conformity and patriotism are essential for the survival of the group. For this reason, governments encourage them and dictatorial regimes try to impose them.

As all human convictions, however, conformity and patriotism, when extreme, become oppressive and even grotesque. Here is an example reported by Gibbon:

> His learning and virtue introduced him to my father; and at Putney he [Mr. John Kirby, a learned and indigent curate] might have found at least a temporary shelter, had not an act of indiscretion driven him into the world. One day reading prayers in the parish church, he most unluckily forgot the name of

King George: his patron, a loyal subject, dismissed him with some reluctance, and a decent reward; and how the poor man ended his days I have never been able to learn.[6]

On the same page it is also noted that Swift mentions the following:

...Dr. Sheridan, the grandfather of R. B. Sheridan, lost preferment by selecting through inadvertence, as the text for a sermon on the anniversary of the accession of the House of Hanover, "Sufficient for the day is the evil thereof."[7]

One of the main pillars on which patriotism rests is the conviction that one's country is superior to all others, which implies that to injustice elsewhere corresponds justice in the homeland, to oppression freedom, to incompetence competence, to stupidity intelligence, and so on. In other words, in a way that has little relation with objective reality, the superiority of one's country implies that the fatherland has all the desirable characteristics that a country may have and the others lack. In the past, the ignorant masses, helped by the propaganda of governments, were easily convinced. Members of the affluent classes, who were also the educated, traveled and came in contact with other societies, and it must have been evident to them that, even if differences existed between countries, they were hardly sufficient to inspire and support wild patriotism and nationalism. Yet there is no doubt that patriotic ferver was as widespread among the educated as among the uneducated.[8] The persistence of the belief that one's side is so much sluperior, in spite of direct experience to the contrary, can be explained, not only by the great capacity of man for self-deception, but also by remembering that patriotism means identification with the group and that it is therefore related to the capacity of the group to guarantee survival (as discussed in Chapter 1).

It is to be underlined that patriotism, as one of the essential elements of the psychological component of power, is of the utmost importance for the survival of the group, in spite of the fact that it rests upon an assumption that is usually false (the belief in the superiority of one's own group over all the others). In fact, patriotism is so important that its being considered, in the Western world today, a quaint survivor of the past is either a temporary phenomenon or, if not, a serious symptom of decline. Patriotism, like war, is an expression of the survival instinct, and lack of patriotism, like pacifism, is an expression of a death wish (Chapter 7).

Because a powerful group, by definition, must have a strong economic basis, to be powerful means to be prosperous. On occasion, a given country may suffer economic hardship because of the effort needed to industrialize and build its military machine (e.g., Russia since the Communist Revolution) but, once the desired level of military capability is achieved, an increase in the standard of living will follow. Economic prosperity, on the other hand, may be achieved without great military power, as, for example in the case of Switzerland, Sweden, Belgium, Canada, and Australia. It becomes immediately apparent, however, that these are small countries (either in size or in population or both) that exist and prosper because, for geographical and political reasons, their more powerful neighbors do not consider it to be in their interest to eliminate them as independent entities. Concerning the United States and Canada, for example, we see that when it would have been politically possible for the former to annex its northern neighbor (e.g., at the beginning of the nineteenth century), it was judged that the necessary economic and military effort would be too great for the conquest of some millions of acres of semi-frozen and frozen land. When the value of Canadian resources became fully appreciated, in the twentieth century, and the conquest became worthwhile from an economic point of view, it was politically impossible.

Even if for geographic and political accidents it is possible today to achieve economic prosperity without great military power, weak countries do not exert significant cultural influence, at least of the ethno-marked type (as defined below), and they must, by necessity, belong to the cultural and political "sphere of influence" of one of the superpowers.

If we measure cultural influence by its most obvious index, namely the geographical diffusion of a country's language—that is, by counting how many people speak its tongue outside its borders—it is easy to see that such diffusion is proportional to the present or past power of the country of origin. Beauty, literature, and other attributes are obviously of secondary importance. Latin, spoken in most of the Western world at the height of Roman power, has left a lasting imprint in many languages, and English is spoken by a large segment of mankind. But, in spite of the Renaissance and Dante, Italian is a secondary language in terms of geographical diffusion. Past military power spread French, Spanish, and Portuguese, but Polish, Hungarian, and Rumanian are spoken in only a very limited area. Russian is more important than Hindi although it is spoken by roughly the same number of people (136,000,000 and 133,500,000 respectively). It may safely be predicted that Albanian will not be one of the most studied languages in the world in the foreseeable future.

The language of Malta exemplifies the relationship between power and diffusion of a language. Malta was occupied by the Romans in 218 B.C. and was part of the Empire until 870 A.D. (having been assigned to the Eastern half in 395 A.D.). The Romans found the local population speaking a Phoenician tongue. After a thousand years, when the Romans were replaced by the Saracens, the people of Malta spoke a Latin tongue. The Saracens imported Arabic and one of its dialects became the Maltese, a language spoken mostly by the common people. After the Norman conquest in 1091 the Western influence returned, and later Italian became the official language of the island. At the beginning of the nineteenth century Malta became a British possession and English became an additional official language. In 1934, Maltese replaced Italian as one of the two official languages. Since then, and especially since World War II, the number of Italian-speaking Maltese, although still significant, has been declining. This is particularly significant if we remember that Malta is 58 miles from Italy, 180 miles from Africa, and 1700 miles from England. It is evident that the decline of Italian is related to the weakness of Italy and that the roles of English and Italian in Malta would be reversed had Italy won the Second World War.

Languages, of course, continuously change, and today we have no more reason to believe that the French will always speak French, the Italians Italian, the Germans German than somebody in the fifth century B.C. had to believe that the Romans would always speak Latin, the Greeks Greek, and the Egyptians Egyptian. In the never-ending process of language change, however, the idioms of powerful countries will have a stronger influence on the others and not vice versa. This influence accumulates over the centuries and, although no language is eternal, very likely the works of Shakespeare will be understood in the original by a larger number of readers, for a longer time, than the *Divina Commedia*.

One may object that cultural influence is not always related to power because ancient Greece and Renaissance Italy, for example, had a cultural impact on the rest of the world well out of proportion to their negligible power.

Two points must be considered with regard to ancient Greece. First, its power was shortlived and small in comparison with Rome's but it was far from negligible. The victories of Marathon and Salamis could not have been won by a weak country, and the empire of Alexander, though not lasting long, spread Greek culture over a very large part of the ancient world. Second, the great disproportion between Greek and Roman power would have, in fact, produced an earlier demise of Greek as an important language and caused Greek culture to have a smaller impact if it were not for an historical accident. The Greeks were conquered when the Romans were civilized enough to appreciate Greek culture but not enough to have a well-developed one of their own. They therefore proceeded to assimilate Greek culture and spread it throughout the world with the swords of the legions—"Graecia capta ferum victorem coepit."[9] Greece then, with the arms of Rome, exerted its cultural influence like a great power.

Concerning Renaissance Italy, it is true that her military power was negligible, but her economic power was not. The Florentine bankers financed wars, governments, and kings, and the Genoese and Venetian sailors and merchants were the commercial masters of the Mediterranean. If not a military power, Italy was an economic power of first magnitude until the seventeenth century.

The fact that the power of ancient Greece and Renaissance Italy (military in one case, economic in the other) was not negligible, and that Greece was helped by the power of Rome, may perhaps be sufficient to answer the objection. However, another consideration may be even more important: the cultural influence exerted by the achievements of Renaissance Italy belongs to a special category that is defined below as ethno-neutral.

Cultural influences that diffuse across borders may be divided into two categories: ethno-marked and ethno-neutral. The ethno-marked are those on which the imprint of the group that originates them is permanent or long lasting; ethno-neutral those on which the imprint of the originating group is non-existent or transitory. Ethno-marked influences are those exerted by language and philosophy of life. For example, the imprint left by Latin on the Romance languages has already lasted a thousand years and the end is not in sight; the diffusion of the English language, behind British conquests first and American power later, will possibly last a long time. By philosophy of life is meant the general approach or attitudes of a group confronted with the problems of existence—in other words, those ethico-philosophical principles that, for example, made Western civilization oriented toward action, efficiency, and concrete achievements in the concrete world, as opposed to Oriental mysticism, introspection, and concern with problems less related to the material world. This philosophy of life of Western civilization is of Greco-Roman heritage and in its essential points has not changed since classical times.

Ethno-neutral cultural influences are those that, even if very important, either do not have the "seal" of a particular country or group, or have it only for a short time. For example, we may agree that modern science started with Galileo, his experimental method being the cornerstone on which our science is based. It is evident, however, that although Galileo was Italian, the experimental method is no more Italian than the laws of gravity are English. The language spoken by Americans, on the other hand, *is* English and the one spoken by the French *does* bear the profound imprint of Latin. Other more superficial influences are of short duration. It is to be assumed, for example, that either blue jeans and fast-food restaurants will fade away in a comparatively short period or that the American imprint that they now carry will soon disappear. Other examples of ethno-neutral influences are easy to find. The "French way" or the "English style" of the past were ethno-neutral cultural influences well known in Europe in the nineteenth century. Now the American style among youth (dress, rock music, etc.) is the rage in most of the world, often to the dismay of governments hostile to the U.S. Velasquez was a Spanish artist but the beauty of his works is not Spanish. Conversely the Spanish legal code *does* bear the seal of the Roman one and the American of the English, the latter being examples of ethno-marked influences.

Power is always related to the diffusion of the ethno-marked influences but not always or necessarily to those of the ethno-neutral, which have a spontaneous tendency to diffuse among civilized people. Interestingly enough, however, power seems to be related to the cultural achievements that are the source of both types of influence: in any given group, the association of group power with intellectual achievement is so common in history that it would appear to be the rule rather than the exception. The "golden age" of intellectual achievements coincides or closely follows a period of military power and economic expansion in almost all countries: in the Rome of Caesar and Augustus, in the England of Elizabeth, in the France of Louis XIV, in the Florence of Lorenzo il Magnifico, in the Spain of the Conquistadores, in the Portugal of Henry the Navigator. The explosion of Greek genius and civilization occurred after Salamis and Marathon.[10]

Because of the psychological component mentioned previously, power depends not only on a country's capabilities but also on its will to apply such power. The analogy between military power and money is of interest:

> Many political theorists have dealt with the analogy of military power to money or credit....For, like money, military power is an indispensable means for meeting future, unspecified, and largely unpredictable contingencies. It is common currency in international intercourse. A nation's reputation for using force to support its vital interests is much more important to it than is an individual's reputation for solvency or wealth to him.[11]

A country which lacks the will to apply power is weak no matter what its capability (e.g., the United States in Vietnam). In a well-organized dictatorship (e.g., Nazi Germany, Communist Russia) the government can impose its will on the country and all the available power can be more easily applied. In Fascist Italy the will to fight was successfully mobilized at the beginning of the Second World War, although it disappeared after the first military defeats started to shake the foundations of the regime. In a Western democracy, on the other hand, the government must take into account the willingness of the public to bear the hardships that inevitably accompany the application of power.

To stimulate and sustain the public will, governments usually use propaganda which tends to depict the enemy (or the potential enemy) as wicked and despicable so that it may become the object of public hate. Propaganda becomes an instrument that facilitates the application of power. If the enemy commits some action that can easily be recognized as wicked and despicable, the achievement of the goal is, of course, enormously facilitated (e.g., the attempted extermination of the Jews and the bombing of Pearl Harbor in the Second World War). If the enemy does not commit such acts, events are distorted and modified to achieve the goal. With the debasement of the enemy, the propaganda campaign also uses, as the other face of the same coin, the stimulation of patriotic fervor. In view of the fact that, most often, the enemy is not particularly wicked and that the motivations for patriotic fervor, in some cases, are not particularly noble, one could conclude that propaganda, by trying to convince the public of the contrary, is deceiving and should therefore be declared immoral and discarded. This would be a simplistic solution.

During the Vietnam war, for the first time in the U.S., the propaganda campaign against the enemy was almost a complete failure. Large segments of the American people were unable to see the soldiers of their side as knights in shining armor and those of the other as bloodthirsty fiends. They were also unable to see how noble principles could be defended by supporting a Vietnamese government that seemed to be as oppressive as the enemy's and how lofty humanitarian ideals could be furthered by the killing, bombing, and destruction shown every night in "living color." Many declared themselves against the war and produced, by their demonstrations and counterpropaganda, such a paralysis of the American will to fight that the war ended in Western defeat in spite of the enormous difference in military capability between the two contenders.

Most of those who opposed the war, however, failed to realize that what was true for the Vietnam war was true for all wars; therefore, the distinction between just and unjust wars was again invoked so that many could justify their opposition to the "unjust" Vietnam war while declaring themselves ready to support a theoretical, future, "just" war. Because the Vietnam war was no more "unjust" than wars fought before were and future wars will be, and because the factors that produced widespread revulsion toward that particular war will be operating in future wars as well, we must expect that classical propaganda campaigns may fail again, at least in the Western world. However, even if classical war propaganda may be obsolete, it must be underlined that it is so not because of its immorality and deceitfulness but because it may have lost its usefulness. In fact, ethical scruples concerning war propaganda are ridiculously exaggerated considering that war is much more "immoral" (if usual ethical standards were to be applied) than any deceit that a propaganda campaign may attempt. It would be as if a thief, while robbing a bank, were to feel pangs of guilt for having parked his car illegally.

This does not mean that propaganda should be abandoned. If wars are to be fought, the capacity to apply military power is essential, and a propaganda campaign to support such capacity is necessary. To assume that the public will sustain the war effort without propaganda is unrealistic; in addition, the propaganda of the adversary must be counteracted. Propaganda will simply have to become more attuned to the modern world (see Chapter 9).

As mentioned before, lack of power condemns a group to the "sphere of influence" of a more powerful one. Because of this, many so-called non-aligned or neutral countries are so either temporarily or in name only. Geopolitics, and its concept of spheres of influence, is somewhat in disrepute today but, as often happens, fashion has little effect on political reality. The "spheres of influence" continue to be a reality as they were in the past. In 1956 the U.S. did not dare to help the insurgents in Hungary because the revolt was taking place inside the Russian sphere of influence. For this same reason, among others, the Soviet Union did not make any substantial move to counteract the U.S. invasion of Grenada in 1983.

There is a tendency on the part of the well-intentioned to consider the concept of "spheres of influence" as immoral because it implies a sort of enslavement of the weak by the powerful. This is a false perception caused, again, by attempting to apply conventional ethical standards to international relations. It is evident that equality between states (as between individuals) exists only when each side does not depend on the other or when the interdependence is symmetrical. If A depends on B more than B depends on A, then A is in the "sphere of influence" of B. The precise relationship between B (the predominant) and A (the dependent) varies with historical circumstances from that of master and slave to that of leader and follower. In theory, all countries are "equal," if not in size or importance, at least in their capacity of "deciding their own destiny." Reality is different, of course. For example, if a very militant Communist Party were on the point of taking over, by perfectly legal means, the government of Canada, the United States would have no choice but to intervene, as the Soviet Union did when an insufficiently friendly regime was taking control of Czechoslovakia. Naturally we must not expect an automatic response by a great power every time a small country slips out of its sphere of influence. The reaction of the predominant power is one of the numerous graded options that exist between no response and military occupation. The choice is dictated by considerations of distance, prestige, importance of the dependent country, degree of hostility, etc., and eventually it is the algebraic sum of all these elements that determines the final decision. We must, however, expect that if the apostate country is important enough and close enough, the superpower will intervene. Unless the U.S. were to decide not only to renounce playing any significant role in world politics but also to become a "satellite" of the Soviet Union, no degree of risk would deter its government from intervening to stop a Communist takeover of Canada. On the other hand, we would not see the Marines in Rome if the Italian Communist Party were to obtain a majority in the next elections. In the same way, Yugoslavia left the Russian sphere of influence with impunity but Czechoslovakia could not.

The degree of hostility that the dependent country may display before provoking a reaction from the predominant country (we could call this its "degree of freedom") is directly proportional to the distance between the two countries and to the power of the dependent country in comparison with that of the predominant. It is also inversely proportional to the importance of the dependent country (strategically and otherwise) and to the capacity of the predominant country to re-establish the status quo. Such a capacity depends, of course, on political as well as military considerations, so that, in the Western world, military actions to re-establish the status quo are more difficult to carry out. The foreign policy of the Western countries is more influenced, for example, by public opinion than that of the Soviet Union. Therefore, the latter can more easily re-establish the status quo in apostate countries.

Thus the "degree of freedom" of countries in the American sphere is higher than that enjoyed by countries in the Russian sphere. In addition, because of the vagaries of public opinion and of Congress, the capacity of the United States to apply power in general is much less than that of the Soviet Union. This is underlined by the difference between the degrees of internal opposition in the U.S. to American support for the guerrillas in Nicaragua and in the U.S.S.R. to the invasion of Afghanistan. In the latter case, internal opposition has been negligible; in the former, Congress and the media have exerted such a negative effect on U.S. action that American capacity to conduct an effective foreign policy has been significantly reduced.

Power is the source of energy in intergroup relations. Many well-intentioned people wonder whether it would not be better if all groups were to abandon all dreams of supremacy so that man could live in peace. It should be obvious that the question has the same value as asking if it would not be better if all disease were to disappear so that man could live in health. The quest for power, like disease, is here to stay and the logical thing to do is not to dream the impossible, which is often dangerous, but to study the consequences and implications of this quest in an attempt to deal with it in the best possible way.

(b) Decline

In the first paragraph of the *De Bello Gallico*, Caesar makes an astonishing statement:

> Horum omnium fortissimi sunt Belgae, propterea quod a cultu atque humanitate provinciae longissime absunt, minimeque ad eos mercatores saepe commeant atque ea quae ad effeminandos animos pertinent important.[12]

The *propterea quod* clearly establishes a relation of cause and effect between the strength and fortitude of the Belgians and their distance from the civilizing influence of the Roman province. In other words, Caesar seems to have perceived that culture and civilization cause weakness by, among other things, exposing man to "the goods that make for effeminacy" (*ea quae ad effeminandos animos pertinent*). He did not elaborate on the causal relation between weakness and civilization because he may have considered it one of the those natural phenomena that by their very ineluctability make any discussion vain; civilization has in itself the seeds of ruin as maturity carries the germ of death.

Groups (countries and civilizations) rise and decline. Some never rise to prominence but sooner or later all decline, or so they have done in the past. The rise to prominence starts with the acquisition of power and with the exerting of pressure on other countries as discussed in Chapter 6. The pressure is often followed by "cultural infiltration" when the way of life, the style, of a certain country is imitated. This particular cultural infiltration is ethno-neutral, not because it does not bear the "seal" of the country of origin, but because its life span is usually ephemeral. Occasionally the cultural infiltration is much more profound and the language and/or "philosophy of life" of a given culture or civilization is transplanted in another. We are then dealing with ethno-marked influences as discussed before. Finally, during its decline, the group gradually loses its capacity for exerting pressure on others and progressively yields to their pressure.

Two opposing forces seem to operate in any organized group: one centripetal and one centrifugal. The centripetal tends to increase the cohesion of the group, the centrifugal to increase particularism. In other words, one induces the individual to seek his private interest, the other to seek the interest of the group. Extreme examples of the effects of the centrifugal and centripetal force on the individual are the deserter and the kamikaze respectively. There is no doubt that among competing groups, all other things being equal, the one in which the members are ready to sacrifice themselves for the common good (in other words, the one with the stronger centripetal force) will be more successful. In contrast, when the members prefer their own advantage (when the centrifugal force is predominant), the group will be unable to compete as successfully. Although in history we have examples of countries in which either the centrifugal or the centripetal force seems to be prevalent (e.g., Athens and Sparta, Italy and Japan in the Second World War), usually in each group or country there is a mixture of the two tendencies and a struggle to achieve a compromise between anarchy (the result of extreme particularism) and fanatical discipline (the result of extreme cohesion).

Many factors influence the relative proportions of the two forces in different countries. It has been suggested, for example, that war not only increases national cohesion, but also creates it. The example of Bismarck's use of the Austro-Prussian War of 1866 and the Franco-Prussian War of 1870 to forge a German nation, is often cited.[13] Others, who disagree, assert that the effect of war on national cohesion is just the opposite. They mention the examples of the Vietnam war on the United States and of the Russo-Japanese War of 1905 plus the First World War on Russia. One could ask if the type of war (e.g., "just," aggressive, defensive, etc.) has some bearing on the argument. It would appear that this is not the case. The distinction between aggressive and defensive war does not seem to make a difference on the cohesion of the group. The history of Rome is not exactly a sequence of defensive wars and there is no doubt concerning Roman cohesion. One could then say that it is perhaps a question of defending the "sacred soil of the fatherland." No, the French and the Italians in the Second World War did not react with a great surge of national unity when the invader broke through the borders. War seems to unmask the lack of group cohesion (e.g., Italy in the Second World War), or to underline its intensity as, for example, in the case of Japan:

> As the Marines pushed northward on Saipan, they did not realize the macabre scene that awaited them...hundreds of civilians had chosen, for one reason or another, to stay with their

troops. Along with the Japanese soldiers they had been cornered near the cliff of Marpi Point. As these Japanese began their self-destruction, many Marines watched in horror.

Japanese men would stab what appeared to be their wives and children and then jump into the sea. Women were seen adjusting their hair and then, clad in their finest kimonos, leaping to their deaths. Elderly Japanese literally had to be carried to the edge of the cliffs and then hurled into the sea.[14]

It is easy to dismiss the above as fanaticism or, at best, as behavior generated by a culture that we Westerners cannot understand. In fact, it is not fanaticism (if we mean by this word the frenzied behavior of maniacs possessed by irrational beliefs) and we can understand it quite well. What we cannot do is duplicate those feats because the centrifugal force operating in our groups is too strong. It is easy to understand what those brave people were doing: they were defending their country with the last weapons at their disposal, namely their lives. Saipan, it was obvious to everybody, was a stepping-stone for the invasion of Japan itself. Those men and women were simply convincing the enemy that the conquest of Japan would have been terribly difficult. The thought of invading an island whose millions of inhabitants were willing to die would undoubtedly have convinced the Americans that a negotiated peace was unavoidable. Those men and women would have succeeded if it were not for the atomic bomb. But they did not know about it.

Stein describes a method to measure the effects of war on domestic disunity; for any given country, the author can provide an index of "domestic disunity" by combining three indicators: crime, strikes, and domestic conflicts (defined as "all collective non-governmental or governmental attacks on persons or property, resulting in damage to them, that occur within the boundaries of an autonomous political system"— that is, violent demonstrations, riots, etc.). The variations of the index, plotted against time, show that disunity in the United States increased during the period analyzed, namely from 1935 to 1972, with peaks during World War II, the Korean war, and the Vietnam war. The author concludes that

> ...the empirical work presented...provides strong evidence in support of the hypothesis...that domestic cohesion decreases during wartime as a function of the process of mobilization, despite any positive effects that war may have in bringing a society together.[15]

One wonders if such a conclusion can be reached by analyzing such a short period of time (from 1935 to 1972) and, even assuming that it can, if the findings are valid only for the United States or if they have a more universal value. Would they apply to more warlike societies? Suppose it were possible to measure the same parameters in Rome from the beginning of the first Punic War to the end of the Third (a span of one hundred and eighteen years), would the same variations be found and would Stein be able to reach the same conclusions? It is possible that the answer to these questions is no, and that the observed reactions to war are only characteristic of contemporary American society. In fact, it may be very significant that the index of domestic disunity, as obtained by Stein, increases steadily in the intervals between wars as if it were a phenomenon not caused but affected by them, in the same way as, for example, fire is not caused by wind but is affected by it. It would appear, therefore, that war is a test of the centrifugal and centripetal forces but does not affect their long-term intensity.

Although an effective centripetal force is beneficial for the survival of the group, the proper quantity cannot be imposed by legislation. In authoritarian societies this is attempted, but it creates an oppressive system that sooner or later is destroyed by violent revolution or is forced to modify itself in a structure that, by allowing more freedom, would eventually have to face the same problems as democratic societies. When a group possesses the proper equilibrium between centrifugal and centripetal forces, it has the proper psychological component for the acquisition of power. Failure to achieve such equilibrium (usually because of a preponderance of the centrifugal force) prevents a group from becoming prominent. Example: Spanish-speaking South America is fragmented into many countries while English-speaking North America is divided into two large ones. The difference in intensity of the centrifugal forces at work in the two continents is obvious. The most celebrated example of failure due to prominence of the centrifugal force is ancient Greece. After the defeat of Xerxes, a centripetal flickering induced the formation of the Delian League in 478 B.C. This was, however, short-lived. Less than fifty years later, in 431 B.C., the suicidal Peloponnesian War started, and with it the beginning of the end.

History is full of dead civilizations and empires. In fact, they are so numerous that it can be affirmed with a high degree of certitude that all the presently existing ones will eventually decay and disappear. This means that, except in the few cases of inevitable decline due to external circumstances,[16] no matter how well adjusted is the equilibrium between the two forces, eventually the centrifugal one will prevail and the country, the civilization, the empire will decline. This appears to be the most common *causa mortis*; in fact, history shows that decline due to unavoidable external circumstances is rare and that most of the time it starts inside the group itself.

Why is this so? Why do countries, civilizations, and empires grow, reach maturity, and then, inevitably, decline? Many have tried to answer these questions, from Saint-Simon to Spengler, from Gibbon to Toynbee to anybody who has pondered on the fall of the Roman Empire. Why does the centrifugal force always triumph at the end? In view of the uniformity of the process and the lack of exceptions, it is obvious that the main causes must be related to some basic, fundamental process in the structure of the social group. As the process of senescence in the individual is probably related to the basic mechanisms of growth and life itself, the decline of the group, the final increase of the centrifugal force, must be closely connected with the forces that make the group rise and reach maturity.

Although man's intelligence probably has not changed appreciably since the emergence of *Homo Sapiens*, we know that his assessment of the external environment and his reaction to situations has changed (and changes) according to cultural and social influences. For example, the reaction of modern man to the idea of eating human flesh is different from the one that may have been characteristic of our early ancestors. Similarly, the attitude toward sex may be different today from what it was in the Victorian Era. Obviously what has changed is not the drive toward food or sex but the intellectual reaction to such drives. Similarly, during the growth, maturation, and decay of a society, man's intellectual reaction to the opposite forces that we have called centrifugal and centripetal varies.

One of the by-products of civilization is an increasingly sophisticated cultural life. As a society rises and reaches its zenith, more and more people, relieved from the need to labor continuously for the necessities of life, have the possibility of devoting part of their energies to intellectual endeavors. Philosophers, artists, scientists, and intellectuals in general become increasingly numerous, and a larger number of the members of the group tend to use more sophisticated intellectual powers in their analysis of the external environment. As culture spreads and becomes more and more refined, the evaluation of the various elements of the environment tends to produce a continuous reassessment of the traditional values of society. This is sometimes called "progress." Religion, ethics, and politics are scrutinized, discussed, and evaluated. Among the structural elements to be re-examined are particularism and cohesion, which, as we have seen, are the sociopolitical expressions of the centrifugal and centripetal forces. When this happens, the principles of cohesion invariably lose, the principles of particularism invariably win, the centripetal force is enfeebled, the centrifugal strengthened, and the civilization declines, to be replaced by a new, young one, composed of relatively uncouth, ignorant, coarse members who are ready to start the cycle all over again.

The conflict between centripetal and centrifugal forces always ends with the victory of the latter because, from a logical point of view, the particularist position is more easily justifiable. As stated before, particularism represents the tendency to seek private advantage, and cohesion to disregard the interest of the individual in favor of the interest of the group. If we examine the tenets of cohesion in one of its expressions, namely patriotism, we see that they are not easily defensible against the attacks of the other side.

The table below shows the opposing points of view, as might be expressed by the average member of the group.

	COHESION		PARTICULARISM
1.	God is with us.	1.	So the other side says.
2.	The enemy is wicked.	2.	The enemy is not more wicked than we are.
3.	My country is always right.	3.	Well...
4.	I am ready to die for my country.	4.	My country is the place where I happen to have been born and where I happen to live. I do not see why I should die for it.
5.	The honor of the flag is sacred.	5.	The flag is only a piece of cloth. To speak of the honor of a piece of cloth is ridiculous.
6.	The flag represents the principles in which I believe.	6.	The enemy flag represents principles too, and our principles may or may not be more noble.
7.	I am ready to fight so that my children may live in peace.	7.	My children will live in peace if we give up fighting or if I move to Switzerland.

248 MAN AND WAR

8. It is noble and glorious to die in battle.

8. No more than in a car accident.

9. If you die as a hero your name will be remembered forever.

9. How many names do you remember of the heroes who died in the Spanish-American War?

10. Better to die than to live in servitude.

10. Always better to live than to die.

11. When I hear the National Anthem my heart is full of pride.

11. I prefer the Ninth Symphony.

12. The honor of our Armed Forces...

12. I have never met the Armed Forces, but I have met Colonel X, who was a drunkard, Captain Y, who was not very bright, General Z, who was a heroin addict....

13. Our leader...

13. The one who cheated on his income taxes?

14. Our civilization is at stake.

14. Look around. If you do not like what you see it means that their civilization may be better.

15. Our Armed Forces exist to defend peace.

15. If they were not there we would surely have peace because we could not fight.

16. Better dead than Red.

16. Better Red than have humanity wiped out by atomic war.

17. I like men, not cowards who are afraid to fight.

17. I like reasonable men who live in peace, not bulls who

			get enraged by a piece of cloth.
18.	If necessary, we will destroy them.	18.	We shall live in peace.
19.	The law should be obeyed.	19.	Only good laws should be obeyed. The conscience of each man should be the judge.

Even a cursory review of this table shows that the banalities used by the particularist side are easier to defend and somehow seem more sophisticated than the platitudes used by the other. Cohesion, being based on the assumption, which is obviously false, that one's group is superior to all others, is bound to be less easily defensible than particularism, which is based on the immediate advantage of the individual. In addition, considering that, in a civilization that has reached its zenith, the principles of cohesion have been held for the long period of growth, it is understandable how the increasing number of people who become converted to the particularistic point of view feel that their position is new and therefore modern and enlightened. When this conclusion is reached by a sufficiently large number of people, the group (the country, the civilization) declines.

It is obvious that there would be no comparative decline if all competing groups were to reach the same point at the same time. Clearly this is not the case. The group with the predominant centripetal force will take its turn as *prima donna* (or as one of the *prime donne*) on the stage of history, while the group in which the centrifugal force is predominant will step down. If this continuous change of actors could be accomplished in a peaceful way, we could accept it with the same equanimity as the eternal change of the seasons. We might even try to consider it, like the death of the individual, a beneficial, if sad, necessity. The change, unfortunately, is usually accomplished by war, destruction, and suffering, and the search for an alternative should go on no matter how difficult. The centrifugal force contributes to the decline of the group with consequent turmoil: the strong Empire of Augustus maintained peace for one and one half centuries, but the weak Empire of the fifth century was continuously involved in wars and convulsions. Cohesion, on the other hand, may also cause turmoil when the aggressive, cohesive group is in the process of overcoming the weaker.

One of the elements that influences both the use of power and the process of decline is freedom, especially the so-called negative freedom—that is, freedom from society's interference.[17] It is clear that society must impose limits to individual freedom when its exercise endangers the existence of society itself. It is also generally agreed that limitations are justified when the exercise of a particular freedom impinges on the freedom of others or tends to produce damage to the individuals who exercise it. When concrete cases are examined, however, difficulties often arise. Let us consider two phenomena related to individual freedom that are actual and present some features that can be generalized: the use of drugs and pornography.

By drugs, in this context, we mean compounds that alter the state of consciousness and the perception of reality, and that are taken for voluptuary purposes. Usually, discussions concerning these drugs hinge on their toxicity. Advocates of free use endeavor to show that such and such a compound does not produce physical or mental damage and that therefore its use should be allowed. The other side strives to show that the drug produces ill effects and that therefore its use should be forbidden. In other words, it is stated by one side and tacitly accepted by the other that, if any one of these drugs were found to be really devoid of damaging side effects, it should be freely available. The assumption, therefore, is that an altered state of consciousness *per se* is acceptable. Suppose now that in fact a harmless drug capable of immersing the user in a temporary artificial paradise is found. Should its use be allowed? Having assumed that it is physically harmless to the individual, we must consider if it would be also harmless to society. It is evident that, if a sufficiently large number of the members of a group are often enough under the influence of a drug that distorts the perception of reality, harm to the group would follow. The question therefore becomes: would such a drug be likely to be used by a dangerously large number of people?

The social history of alcohol may help us here. Alcohol is a drug that alters the state of consciousness and the perception of reality, but, far from being innocuous, produces a vast number of deleterious effects ranging from hangover to cirrhosis of the liver and death. In spite of that, it is drunk in excessive quantities by a large segment of the population in many parts of the world. This being the case, it is logical to assume that our hypothetical drug, being innocuous, would be used by a much larger number of individuals: a number that could easily reach a level that would cause damage to the group. Contrary to commonly held opinion, therefore, the more a drug that alters the state of consciousness and distorts reality is innocuous to the individual, the more it is necessary for society to forbid it.[18] It is the interaction between the individuals and a properly perceived reality that makes the continuation of civilized social life possible. The principle of prohibiting such drugs is therefore justified because it constitutes self-defense for society and this takes precedence over the unlimited exercise of individual freedom. As for the enforceability of a prohibition, the American experience with alcohol may suggest pessimistic conclusions, but this, a problem of law enforcement, is not relevant to the present discussion.

Pornography flourishes because of man's voyeuristic tendencies, which make the observation or description of the sexual act stimulating. Society, from the beginning of history, has imposed rules that tend to regulate and limit the sexual behavior of the individual. At present the conflict between the limiting rules imposed by society and the voyeuristic tendencies of the individual shows the limiting side losing many battles. The main difficulty in enforcing limitations is in defining pornography and in deciding if there is or is not a "redeeming" element (namely artistic value) in the pornographic material. However, even if we had an infallible method for the clarification of these points, should society allow pornography? Let us suppose that even the few restrictions left are eliminated and that a very large percentage of the population is given to the "consumption" of pornographic material. Would that present a danger for society?

The indulgence in pornography by a section, no matter how large, of the population would not in itself constitute the same danger as if the same number were to become alcoholics or drug addicts. In addition, it is true that pornography promotes sexual promiscuity, but this in itself has no effect on the capacity of society to evolve or defend itself. The conclusion therefore could be that pornography is quite innocuous and that the problem is rather trivial. Such a conclusion, however, would be simplistic.

The structure of society rests on rules and traditions that change slowly with time so that the more restrictive tend to be eventually eliminated. If the change is too fast, and therefore goes beyond the limits acceptable to the majority in a particular historical period, it becomes permissiveness and causes conflict because of the opposition of some sectors of the group. The observance of rules and traditions requires discipline. Discipline in a socio-political sense inevitably involves not only the principle of control of one's own tendencies in favor of the common interest but, among other things, a degree of conformism, obedience to the laws, and the following of certain patriotic rituals (saluting the flag, singing the national anthem, etc.).

Relaxation of discipline (the development of permissiveness) in a Western society seems to follow a stereotyped pattern: as discussed earlier in this chapter, among the more educated members of society certain individuals (few at the beginning and then more and more) start to feel ill at ease with rituals because they are often based on beliefs that are easily ridiculed. For example, because the flag *is* a piece of colored cloth, eventually it is felt that it is silly to fine the girl who makes a "bikini" out of it; often the patriotic anthem *is* a mixture of atrocious music and ludicrous words and the feeling develops that, to be a good citizen, one does not need to stand when the national anthem is played. Similarly, restrictions on sexuality come to be considered repressive, and sexual promiscuity and indulgence in pornography become, by the law of opposites, activities of the "liberated" and of those who aspire to be sophisticated.

When the feeling that these rituals and restricting rules are ridiculous or oppressive becomes sufficiently widespread, their observance slowly starts to be seen as characteristic of the simple-minded and the unrefined. Soon a feeling of contempt is felt for those who follow them and a new conformism spreads: non-observance of rituals and rules.

The human mind is so made that, once a given premise is accepted, the logical consequences, even the most extreme, are sooner or later followed by at least a certain number of members of the group. The worst abuses of the Inquisition, for example, were an expression of this phenomenon. Once it was accepted that the teachings of the Church were the only true ones and therefore the only ones that led to eternal salvation, it followed that *any means* was justified to save the soul of the heretic, since eternal damnation was the worst possible fate for a human being. A few hours (or days or weeks) of torture were obviously nothing if it meant that it would save souls from *eternal* torture. In fact it would have been cruel and inhumane to spare the heretic and commit his soul to eternal damnation. Torquemada possibly felt that he was being compassionate.

Although the chain of reasoning involved does not produce the tragic results of this example, lack of discipline and disregard of rules and rituals does nevertheless start a series of consequences that are deleterious for society. When the rejection of traditional customs and rituals is accepted, the next step is to feel that some of the underlying principles, formerly accepted without discussion, are false and even despicable. The "establishment" becomes contemptible and attitudes and behavior that are interpreted as revolt against the establishment become acceptable, and are even interpreted as a sign of intellectual sophistication (for example, long hair, outlandish clothes, nudity, sexual promiscuity, etc.).

In addition, lack of discipline and lack of observance of traditional restrictions often tend to degenerate into bizarre activities that are mistaken for original approaches to old problems:

> Civilizations, like individuals, in their decrepitude develop a death wish, which makes them seek to encompass their own destruction by damning their friends and lauding their enemies, by advancing the causes which seek their ruin and impeding those which may safeguard their interests, by promoting moral squalor with a view of inducing inertia and indifference....For instance, a Dr. O. Elthammer of the Stockholm Child Psychiatric Department, who...has "proved conclusively" that pornography does not have a corrupting effect, by showing to some children between the ages of eleven and eighteen a film of a woman being raped by a group of intoxicated louts and then forced to have intercourse with a dog. "None of the children," the doctor triumphantly concluded, "was frightened during and after the film, but a proportion of the older girls did admit to being shocked," while two adults also present "needed psychological treatment for a month afterward."[19]

Outlandish clothes, nudity, and other bizarre activities (even if disgusting) usually are, in themselves, quite innocuous and are not going to produce great stress on society. However, the chain of logical consequences is not over. The process will progress further and some will start to disregard rules of behavior that are fundamental for the survival of society (for example, payment of taxes, military service, support of the government in times of stress). At this point, if a sufficient number of individuals follows this pattern, the survival of the group is in jeopardy.

In conclusion, pornography, although innocuous *per se*, is deleterious to society because, as an expression of the rejection of traditional restrictions, it encourages (and is encouraged by) permissiveness, which is a manifestation of the centrifugal force. The widespread use of pornography becomes, then, a symptom of the group's decline.

Another cause of the increase in permissiveness seems to be affluence. In the discussion earlier in this chapter of the relation between military and economic power, it was noted that power (the purveyor of affluence) is associated with the intellectual "golden age" of the group. It is to be noted now that the same power, through affluence, contributes also to the decline of the group: affluence generates permissiveness, which in turn decreases the will to fight, which in turn produces military weakness with consequent economic decadence and therefore loss of the group's independence. This is one of the mechanisms that check the indefinite growth and survival of countries and civilizations.

Permissiveness, as already mentioned, means lack of discipline, emphasis on the pursuit of pleasure, and a general decrease in importance of the traditional values of a society. Affluence generates permissiveness simply by eliminating the need for discipline, for limitations on the pursuit of pleasure, and for traditional principles. This is because those virtues have a practical value: in a poor society, discipline and restraint will help the individual to earn the necessities of life and to accumulate the necessary credits needed for survival. For the member of the affluent society the necessities of life are guaranteed, the individual feels secure, and the need disappears.[20] This should not be taken as meaning that all poor societies are full of virtuous and disciplined people; we know well that it is not so. In poor societies other factors shape the behavior of the individual. What is underlined here is that affluence produces certain deleterious effects, not that its contrary necessarily produces the opposite.

One of the most obvious characteristics of a permissive, affluent society is its unwillingness to endure hardship. People seem more ready to fight to acquire wealth and security than to maintain them. The application of power always involves hardship, and therefore the permissive, affluent society always embraces a foreign policy of compromise and appeasement. Therefore permissiveness, as an expression of the centrifugal force, tends to accelerate the process of disintegration of the group—that is, the decline of societies and civilizations.

In this discussion the role of religion as a factor that encourages the practice of the traditional virtues has not been mentioned because traditional religion itself is to be counted among the old-time virtues that become neglected by the group in decline. Often there is an increase in the number of bizarre, grotesque, somewhat mystic new cults that is an expression of the incapacity of the group to accept the discipline of the old religion:

> The soul [of the group]...finally, weary, reluctant, cold, loses its desire to be, and, as in Imperial Rome, wishes itself out of the overlong daylight and back in the darkness of proto-mysticism, in the womb of the mother, in the grave.[21]

An intriguing element in the process of decline is the apparently enthusiastic role of the more educated, usually referred to as intellectuals. Again and again we see the groves of academia, for example, proposing and supporting peace at any price, unilateral disarmament, promiscuity, unconventional life-styles, etc., all elements that are at the same time symptoms of and contributors to the decline of the group. Why the intellectuals? Why precisely those who should be the first to understand and at least try to avoid helping the process of decay? In part, of course, it is sheer ignorance. When we say "intellectuals" or "university professors" or "writers" or "historians," we really mean individuals who have some particular knowledge in a field that requires intellectual instead of manual skills. So, for example, the historian knows some history, the sociologist some sociology, the physicist some physics. Because they may even have a reputation in their field, we consider them among the "wise" and expect that their ideas in international politics, for example, should be particularly sound and worthy of respect. Nothing could be farther from the truth, of course. The physicist may have very

Power and Decline 257

fuzzy or naive opinions concerning international relations, and even the professor of history may completely lack the capacity to discern historical patterns and to use historical experience to guide his interpretation of the present. This may, in part, explain the phenomenon. Still, we have seen such a higher percentage of "intellectuals" joining self-destructive causes (e.g., during the Vietnam war, during debates about rearmament or stricter criminal penalties) on so many occassions that perhaps some other mechanism is at work.

After the Second World War, the Western world succeeded in eliminating from its midst all significant authoritarian political systems and opted for democracy; unfortunately, disappointment soon set in. Political freedom, by necessity, involves a loosening of the restraints on individuals, which brings forward some unpleasant traits both in individuals and societies. This explains the large amounts of hypocrisy, vulgarity, stupidity, intellectual dishonesty, superficiality, and mediocrity that are so evident in democratic societies. (All these offensive traits, in addition to other shortcomings, exist also in non-democratic societies, but they are not so evident there because of the lack of freedom that prevents their expression, diffusion, and exposure.) Intellectuals are, by their nature, more sensitive than others and tend to resent more these failings.[22] Because they also have a tendency to be more ready than others to escape from the dreary boundaries imposed by reality, they easily fall prey to dreams. The enthusiastic endorsements and panegyrics of the Soviet Union under Stalin by Bernard Shaw and Julian Huxley are cases in point.[23] The naiveté of reputable scientists in social and political matters is well known. The intellectuals seem to be always the first to take positions against the interests of the group—and, in effect, against their own interests as well—because they have their sensors set at a level that is too high. The result is that they reject the "establishment" without, sometimes, being able to judge objectively its unpleasant traits. On the other hand, when those unpleasant traits become unbearable, even the group's members with a less developed sensitivity resent the shortcomings of society. Manzoni describes this well in *I Promessi Sposi* with Renzo's reaction to a popular uprising:

> Da queste e da altrettali cose che vedeva e sentiva, Renzo cominció a raccapezzarsi ch'era arrivato in una cittá sollevata, e che quello era un giorno di conquista, vale a dire che ognuno pigliava, a proporzione della voglia e della forza, dando busse in pagamento. Per quanto noi desideriamo di far fare buona figura al nosto povero montanaro, la sinceritá storica ci obbliga a dire che il suo primo sentimento fu di piacere. Aveva cosí poco da lodarsi dell'andamento ordinario delle cose, che si trovava inclinato ad approvare ció che lo mutasse in qualunque maniera.[24]

If the elements just discussed explain, in part, the anti-group attitudes of many "intellectuals," the factor that seems to be the most important is the one described earlier in this chapter: the elements that contribute to particularism are usually more easily defensible, from a logical point of view, than those that contribute to cohesion. The intellectual is therefore more prone to follow what, at least at first sight, seems the most logical approach to the problem of the group. It requires an extra effort to realize that the logic supporting particularism is superficial and that it poses a threat to the survival of the group.

In the course of this discussion the expression "if a sufficient number of individuals" is often repeated because it is only when a certain numerical threshold is reached that the general effect follows. In every group one can find small subgroups that behave in unusual ways, but their numerical value, which varies according to fads, usually does not reach the critical threshold, and therefore does not have significant influence on the status quo. However, if a group that disregards the rules of behavior fundamental for the survival of society reaches the numerical threshold, society has two alternatives (not necessarily mutually exclusive): decadence or revolution. Revolution often results in a dictatorship that will try to re-establish the old virtues and values. Julius Caesar started a dictatorship that lasted for half a millennium. When he took power, the old Republic was disintegrating because the ruling classes had abandoned the traditional virtues and permissiveness and corruption were rampant. The early Empire tried to re-establish the ancient virtues by legislation, with very little success. The dictatorship of Benito Mussolini emerged from the decaying body of Italian democracy and tried again, after two thousand years, to do the same. The Communist regimes of Russia and China oppose sexual promiscuity, civil disobedience, disregard of patriotic rituals, etc.; in other words, they try to re-establish the old virtues.

The human need for freedom, which if undisciplined leads to permissiveness and license, is an expression of the centrifugal force and tends, as an extreme consequence of the particularistic process, to generate anarchy, with consequent disintegration of the group. On the other hand, the human need to coalesce into social groups is an expression of the centripetal force and tends, as an extreme consequence of the process of cohesion, to degenerate into fanaticism and tyranny (e.g., Sparta), with the consequent degeneration of the group. The continuous struggle between the two forces is the subject of history; their proper equilibrium results in a stable group, the survival of which, however, depends on discipline and readiness to fight:

> In the main military men have agreed with Donoso-Cortes [1809-1853]...that "when a nation shows a civilized horror of war, it receives directly the punishment of its mistakes. God changes its sex, despoils it of its common mark of virility, changes it into a feminine nation, and sends conquerors to ravish it of its honor."[25]

If we disregard the pomposity, the silly imagery, the machismo, and the reference to the surgical skills of God, one is forced to admit that the essence of the quotation refers to a sequence of events that corresponds to reality. In fact, its message brings to mind the much older and more elegant passage quoted at the beginning of this section:

> Horum omnium fortissimi sunt Belgae, propterea quod a cultu atque humanitate provinciae longissime absunt, minimeque ad eos mercatores saepe commeant atque ea quae ad effeminandos animos pertinent important.[26]

It may be useful to express the structure and evolution of the Centrifugal and Centripetal forces in table form:

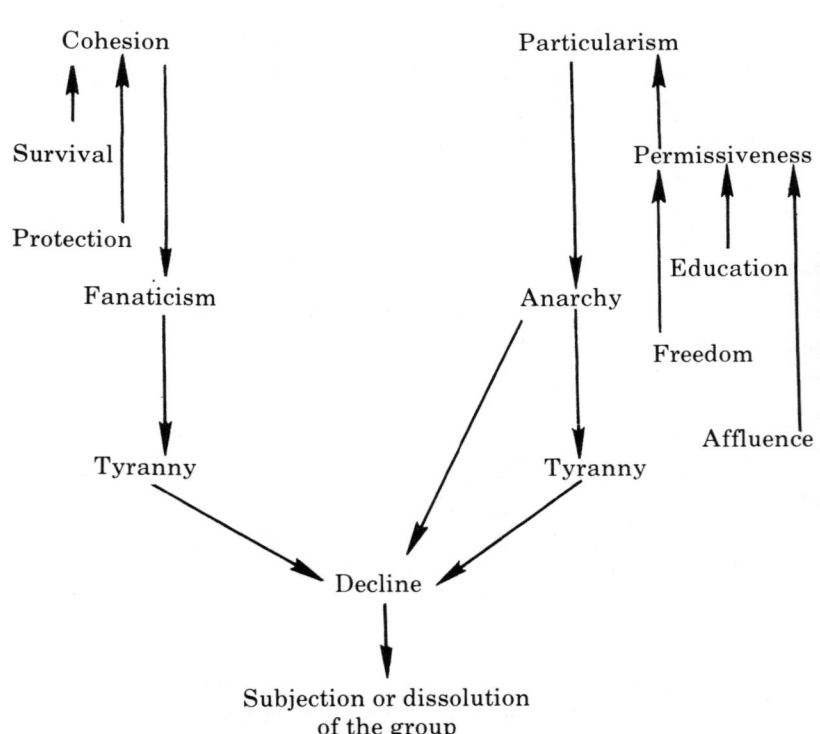

Albrecht Dürer — *Samson Killing the Lion*

Chapter 9

> Porgimi dunque, Febo, de' tua lumi:
> se mai priego mortal da te s'intende,
> fa ch'or la mente mia oscura allumi.[1]
>
> Machiavelli,
> *Rime Varie, Capitolo pastorale*

PROGRESS AND HOPE

(a) Is There Progress?

The capacity to inflict suffering with indifference is characteristic of animals, but not of man. In spite of the many examples, past and present, that would seem to suggest the contrary, there is no doubt that during the arduous and as yet unfinished process of becoming civilized, man is becoming more and more reluctant to inflict suffering. This has been an on-going process since antiquity, but its progress has been so slow that it is difficult to detect if one examines a short historical period. It is, however, evident at once if one compares remote antiquity with the present time. Slavery, human sacrifices, slaughter or sale of prisoners of war, mortal combats for entertainment, public executions, public torture, etc., are examples of acts which were accepted as a matter of course in the past. While examples of similar deeds can be found today, it is obvious that they are no longer part of the usual conduct of human affairs.

The Athenians sacrificed Persian prisoners before the Battle of Salamis (480 B.C.),[2] and the Romans did not hesitate to immolate humans at a critical time during the struggle against Carthage (216 B.C.).[3] The killing of all males who survived the conquest of a city was common in antiquity, and rebels and deserters were usually tortured before being put to death. Hostages were savagely mangled should their fellow-citizens violate their faith, and the tale of Regulus, although apocryphal, may be representative of the manners of the time.

In spite of all the cruelty and the brutality, however, the Romans were the ones who, perhaps more than others, showed some glimmer of humanity:

> ...It is only by comparing the Roman with contemporary non-Roman war-practice that the soldier of the great Republic can fairly be judged. And when we find the Samnites not merely slaying, but previously torturing the men of a town reduced by famine; the Lucianians mutilating in horrible fashion the body of the slain Epirote king Alexander; the Gauls in Northern Italy carrying off as trophies the heads of the slain, and fashioning the skull of a Roman consul into a libation cup for their temple service, we recognize the Roman as a civilizer even in his severity.[4]

It is interesting to note that in the eyes of the Greeks the war-practices of the Romans were particularly mild.[5]

As man became more civilized, he started to feel that generosity and restraint were superior to the opposite. Caesar, in his commentaries, is obviously proud of his reputation as a generous victor. After the almost complete destruction of the Nervii,

> ...ut in miseros ac supplices usus misericordia videretur, diligentissime conservavit suisque finibus atque oppidis uti iussit et finitimi imperavit ut ab iniuria et maleficio se suosque prohiberent.[6]

When the Aduatuci submitted but wanted to keep their arms, they appealed to his well-known generosity:

> Unum petere ac deprecari: si forte pro sua clementia ac mansuetudine, quam ipsi ab aliis audirent, statuisset Aduatucos esse conservandos, ne se armis despoliaret.[7]

Caesar answers:

> Se magis consuetudine sua quam merito eorum civitatem conservaturum, si priusquam murum aries attigisset se dedissent.[8]

And when, finally, he sells all of them as slaves, he makes clear that he did so only because of their perfidious betrayal after he had again shown his generosity by ordering the soldiers out of the town at night so that the inhabitants might suffer no outrage.[9]

In spite of the examples of generosity and the condemnations of cruelty found in ancient history, however, wars were usually fought with great ferocity. Later, the barbarians, even after their formal adoption of Christianity, did not change their war-practices significantly. Procopius records that after the fall of Milan in 539, all the male inhabitants, in the number of three hundred thousand, were massacred by the Gothic conquerors. Totila mutilated prisoners and often put the inhabitants of captured cities to the sword.[10] The Bulgarian Simeon (893-927), warring against the Croats, systematically depopulated their territory, murdering the inhabitants and leaving the land waste and desolate. When he defeated the Byzantine troops he cut off the noses of the prisoners. The contemporary Muscovites not only killed the inhabitants in captured cities, but crucified, burned alive, and otherwise tortured their captives.[11]

The customs of war did not improve very rapidly. Raymond of Toulouse, being attacked on his way to the First Crusade by the inhabitants of Dalmatia, cut off the noses and hands and put out the eyes of his prisoners. Richard Coeur de Lion not only slew thousands of Saracen prisoners, but blinded captive French knights.[12] The execution of prisoners was a common event at Constantinople. Basil II (1014) blinded fifteen thousand Bulgarians, leaving one eye to the leader of every hundred. Thirty years later Saracen marauders were impaled by Byzantine officials.[13] The Greeks of Adramyttium in the time of Malek Shah (1106-16) drowned Turkish children in boiling water,[14] and the crusading Prince of Antioch (1097) cooked human bodies on spits to earn for his men the terrifying reputation of cannibalism.[15] It is to be remembered that, during the crusade against the Albigenses, it was a churchman who, when Béziers fell (1209) and there was some hesitation in massacring the orthodox with the heretical, cried, "Slay them all! The Lord will know his own." In the wars between Saracens and Christians in Spain, the Christians displayed great ferocity. At the Battle of Tolosa (1211) the Christian cavaliers gave no quarter; in Ubeda and other towns subsequently stormed they slew every Moslem without regard to age and sex.[16] Similarly, when Ferdinand of Castile entered into Balma (1232), all the inhabitants were killed. Before the Battle of Guadalete the Christians put to the sword in cold blood a large number of Moslem prisoners.[17] The English gave no quarter at Crécy (1346), the Black Prince massacred the inhabitants of conquered Limoges (1370), and at Agincourt (1415) a false alarm caused the issue of orders for a general slaughter of prisoners.[18]

It was the Moslems who, at the time, showed greater humanity. The inhabitants of towns surrendering to the Saracens were usually allowed to depart, if they so wanted, on the condition that they leave behind all their personal belongings.[19] The instructions given in 963 by Kin El Hakem Ben Abderahman as to the duties of *Moslemah* when going forth to the Sacred War reflect the ancient spirit of the Prophet:

> ...When taking possession of a city, let no man slay women, children, or old men past power of resistance; neither shall any man attack monks vowed to a life of solitude, save in the cases where these latter are making a defense injurious to the Moslemah cause. Do violence to none to whom you have once given promise of security, but be careful to keep all engagements and fulfill all contracts.[20]

The fact that Christian kings, princes, and generals behaved cruelly and ferociously should not be construed as meaning that the Christian message of peace was completely lost and that the Church had no moderating influence on the barbaric customs of the time. It was one of the achievements of Christianity, during the wars of the Middle Ages, to propagate the view that violence against women and children was dishonorable.[21] Perhaps worse practices would have been followed without this moderating effect. Nevertheless, war customs did not significantly improve until the Enlightenment, when, as noted before, a dramatic change took place. War, previously accepted as "natural" and as a "noble art," became "senseless," "brutal," and "unworthy of mankind."[22]

> It was common form in these mid- and later eighteenth-century years to compare their wars with those of earlier, less-enlightened and progressive ages. Mr. Jefferson was effectively casting George III as an unenlightened despot when he included, in the list of grievances of the American colonists, that the British monarch had "endeavored to bring on the inhabitants of our frontiers, the merciless Indian savages, whose known rule of warfare is an indistinguished destruction of all ages, sexes, and conditions."[23]

In Europe, wrote the French author Rabaut:

> Wars are less bloody than among ignorant and savage people: armies slaughter each other politely; heroes salute before killing each other; soldiers of opposing armies pay each other visit before battles, as people lunch together before an outing. No longer is it nations which fight each other, but just armies and professionals; wars are like games of chance in which no one risks his all; what was once a wild rage (*fureur*) is now just silly (*une folie*).[24]

Vattel, the most influential of the publicists, in 1758 wrote:

> At the present day, the nations of Europe almost always carry on war with great forbearance and generosity. These dispositions have given rise to several commendable practices, which exhibit often a high degree of courtesy. Refreshments are sometimes sent to the besieged governor; and the besieger ordinarily refrains from firing upon the quarters of the King or general.[25]

It was this sort of aristocratic bias in the customs of war which led some observers to deny the Enlightenment's achievements:

> So between army staff, before and after battle, there were relations of high courtesy which tempered to a certain degree the ferocity of war....But the men of the eighteenth century, beneath an exterior of polished refinement, were still brutish and violent. While most of them could discourse elegantly on "humanity," very few were humane. "Sensibility" was a mere matter of fashion; they powdered and preened themselves, but at the bottom they retained all the crudity of the previous century....The armies were accompanied by "a crowd of parasites hanging on their flanks" and living on the pillage....Lumbering across the countryside these rapacious caravans infested and ruined the land....[26]

In spite of this acid comment of Sorel, there is no doubt that "Bellona, the goddess of war, really was to some extent tamed in the later Enlightenment."[27] By that time it was normal, in time of war, for "cartels" or conventions to be signed by oppos-

Progress and Hope 269

ing commanders before battle, establishing hospitals for wounded soldiers and guaranteeing their security from attack or molestation. In many cases, not only the wounded were protected, but also medical personnel.[28]

There is no doubt, therefore, that the Enlightenment brought a significant improvement in the conduct of war. One of the causes of such change for the better is perhaps to be found in the emphasis that the Enlightenment put on reason and on the rational approach to the solution of problems. After all, war *is* brutal and unworthy of man; the eighteenth century simply brought this obvious truth to light and gave to it such emphasis that the changes described above were a necessary consequence. In addition, man, although driven relentlessly towards war by his inner urge for survival, has always felt that peace was better than conflict, that clemency was better than cruelty and benevolence better than brutality.

The reason for the subsequent loss of the ground gained in the eighteenth century may be more complex.

> Much of this civility ceased after the [French] Revolution. Since other of the civilities of the later Enlightenment survived and continued, I cannot offer any other explanation for this falling off than a combination perhaps of these factors: the greater rapidity of movement of post-Revolutionary armies, the arousal of national animosities, the rise in the cost of failure, and some reluctance to trust the other side (which certainly played a large part in the failure of many prisoner exchange proposals).[29]

Indeed, the character of armed conflicts changed after the French Revolution: wars, previously games played by kings and generals, became "popular" and "total." In other words, the masses became involved and their status changed from cannon fodder to active protagonist. Before, the people were a passive instrument that allowed the elites to fulfill their needs for immortality. During the post-Revolutionary wars, it was the entire people, the masses, that felt the necessity to fulfill the same need. Nationalism and the ideological war were born:

> ...the war which developed out of the French Revolution was different in kind (as well as in quantity) from every war that had preceded it....There is a case for describing it as the first of the modern "total" and "ideological" wars which have since become familiar...."Our principles are to liberate, that is, to Frencify (*franciser*) the whole of Europe," wrote a very clever person signing himself "Ph. A. Gr." in the *Moniteur*....[At the great session of the National Convention of December 15, 1792] in an atmosphere of terrific excitement, Cambon read the Proclamation designed to be made to each liberated people. It began:
>
> "The people of France to the people of...! Brothers and friends, we have won our liberty, and we shall keep it; our unity and our power guarantee it. We offer to help you too to enjoy this inestimable good, which has always been your right, denied you by your criminal oppressors. We came to chase away those tyrants: they have fled before us; show yourselves now to be truly free, and we will guarantee to protect you from their vengeance, their plotting, and their return...."[30]

Applause, enthusiasm, excitement...And failure to realize that, under those altruistic offers to liberate the neighbors, French nationalism was exploding. Far from being the liberation of the oppressed, the goal of France was their domination, as Napoleon was to make evident later. The words of Cambon have a haunting, contemporary sound.

Why did nationalism and the participation of the masses in "total" and "ideological" conflicts cause the conduct of war to retrogress to pre-Enlightenment times? In the process of becoming more civilized, man learns to moderate the most atrocious aspects of warfare for two main reasons: because he can more easily "identify" with the victim (see Chapter 2), and because he finds it more and more difficult to participate in violence and combat (as discussed in Chapter 8). The moderating process, however, does not affect all men at the same time and in the same measure: the elites, those who had access to education and to the refinements brought by affluent life, were the first to recoil from the worse excesses.[31] For this reason, in the eighteenth century, helped by the philosophical tenets of the Enlightenment, warfare became more moderate. The kings and princes of both sides, often related to each other, came to consider war as a game of chess; serious and deadly, of course, but still a game for the aristocracy, in which the pawns, although sometimes by necessity sacrificed, were to be spared when possible. It was perhaps not for the noblest reasons that atrocities were avoided and suffering limited: perhaps the conquering commander had toward the conquered a feeling akin to the one that urges us to avoid cruelty to animals. Even if this were the case, however, it was a step forward and a great improvement over the orgies of brutality of yore.

At the time of the Enlightenment, this moderating process had not yet reached the masses, who, when they emerged from their brutish existence of terrible poverty and chronic semi-starvation, had to go through the same steps which the elites had taken before, including the channelling of the instinct of survival in the direction of killing and destroying others to assure one's own immortality. Hitherto, the instinct of survival of the individual who was not a member of the elites had been channelled in other directions by two factors: poverty and religion. The extreme poverty in which the majority of the populations of all countries lived was such that almost all their energy was used to find enough to satisfy the most fundamental needs, and if some was left to fuel needs of perpetuation, religion was there to reassure the faithful by guaranteeing him eternal life. Therefore religion, if not opium, was a good tranquilizer.

Before the revolutions at the end of the eighteenth century, it was the elites' urge to survive that was responsible for war. With the nineteenth century, people (at least in the West) started to be less afflicted by poverty, and this made it possible for them to have leisure for activities not immediately related to food and shelter—and among those, for education and speculations about the future. In addition, religion started to exert a less powerful influence on the minds of many, who began to feel dissatisfied with the guarantee of immortality provided by faith. All this made the masses confront problems and feelings that before were only limited to the few. One of the manifestations of this phenomenon was nationalism, the expression of the people's struggle for immortality. In other words, the urge of Caesar and Alexander transferred to the masses.

As the elites eventually become less responsive to this urge for immorality, the masses will eventually do the same after being exposed for a sufficient time to education and to the refinements brought by affluence. It has been discussed before (Chapter 8) how affluence and education are among the main factors that cause the decline of the group, so that the cycle of rise, decline, and fall may continue indefinitely. This means that the process that causes warfare to become more humane and civilized is the same that causes the decline of the group. This does not mean, of course, that affluence and education should be opposed in an attempt to postpone decline; it would be absurd, as absurd as any attempt to prevent the process of growth in children on the ground that it is the very same process that leads to old age and death. These points will be discussed in the second part of this chapter.

In spite of the ground lost after the French Revolution, over the centuries there has been an almost continuous, if slow, progress toward a more civilized warfare. In spite of the most horrible episodes of war brutality, man has shown a constant need for decency and generosity that is illustrated by many episodes reported in all wars. Here are some examples from recent times: from the American Civil War, the First World War, and the Second World War respectively:

> Afterward I saw the ambulance remaining in one place too long a time, as I thought, so I rode over to ascertain the cause of the delay. A rebel soldier was lying on the ground and the surgeon had made a superficial examination. There was a large, ragged shell wound of one knee apparently involving the joint, and a wound on the top of his head, where it was denuded of scalp and where the cranial bones were fractured, with a small piece torn away, leaving the brain exposed. A strange feature of the case was that the man was entirely conscious, instead of dying or dead as we thought he should have been.

His anxiety was to know what we were going to do with him. He repeated his inquiry until the ambulance surgeon, to quiet him, said, "Well, Johnnie, if it were not for the wound on your head we would cut your leg off, and if were not for the wound on your leg we would cut your head off, but we will not do both—so pick him up, boys, and put him in the ambulance." He was never afterwards in condition to justify amputation of either end of his corpus, but he persistently continued to live. His suppurating wounds much reduced his weight, but at last he began to improve, and continued to gain until in about six or seven months he was able to get about the hospital grounds with little help. As it became necessary to protect the wound on his head and thereby guard against accidental injury of the brain, we sought for and found among the hospital patients a working jeweler who could make a cap to cover the lesion if silver to make it could be obtained. That was in the days of fractional paper currency, as some of you may remember, when silver was extremely scarce; but on making his want known, the invalid U.S. soldiers in hospital were quick to contribute their rare and highly prized coins for the purpose. Toward the close of the war orders came to send him with other Confederates to camp in Ohio for exchange. The poor fellow did not want to go, but begged to remain in hospital, where he certainly was given every possible care and comfort—but orders were imperative and he had to go....[32]

While on an individual basis the campaign was fought by both armies with reasonable decency, sometimes hopelessly mangled men were administered the *coup de grâce* by their opponents. In one reported instance a British officer scouting the area came across a horribly wounded enemy soldier. "Shoot him," he said unhappily to his enlisted runner. The German lay watching them in a stupor of agony. The runner unslung his rifle but could not fire, nor could another enlisted man in the little patrol. The officer drew his own pistol, stared in gloom at the German writhing on the ground below, and could do no more. Later he said savagely, "Damn funny, wasn't it? And we just left him there, so I suppose he will die in the mud tonight."[33]

...We found out from the prisoners that if it hadn't been for the Nip peasants who also worked in the mines, many of the Allied prisoners—and there were Americans, English, Dutch, just about every nationality there—would have starved to death. These Jap workers would always try to bring an extra ball of rice down into the mines with them. They could see that the prisoners were hungry as hell and they'd do their best to get them food.

We also knew how to handle that one. We found a large warehouse full of rice. We lined up all the Jap miners we could find. Then we unlocked the warehouse door and told those miners to go to it. It was quite a sight to see.[34]

During the Second World War, the sight of occupying troops playing with children was particularly heart-warming and made the horrors of Otchakof recede into a barbarian past hopefully lost forever. The Americans were particularly prone to engage in such activities:

[After the capitulation of the Japanese] the 2nd Division did go to Japan, but without a shot being fired....When we did go ashore, it was under full battle conditions minus a bombardment. All our weapons were at the ready. We set up our perimeter, dug our foxhole, and waited.

We were attacked the next day all right, by hordes of Japanese kids crawling all over our machine guns. We fought them off with chocolate bars. We felt a little foolish, but the kids had a great time. I remember one of our men, a real hard-nosed guy, shaking his head.

"Christ," he said, "they're just like the kids back home. Why the hell did we have to have a war?"[35]

If individual feats of generosity are common in the history of warfare, rare are episodes of the same nature in which a belligerent government is involved; even rarer those in which the government in question was one more devoid of moral scruples than others:

One of the turning points of the submarine campaign and of treatment of survivors of torpedoed ships came with the sinking of the passenger ship Laconia, an event that gave rise to a grave charge against Doenitz. The Laconia, of 19,965 tons, was torpedoed in the mid-South Atlantic between the West African coast and Brazil on September 12, 1942. She carried 2,732 passengers and crew, including some 1,800 Italian prisoners of war being transported to England from North Africa, where they had been captured. The Laconia was a legitimate target for a U-boat. She mounted two 4.7-inch naval guns of Japanese manufacture from World War I, six 3-inch antiaircraft guns, six 1.5-inch guns, four rapid-fire Bofors guns, and two groups of 2-inch rockets—more than was needed to sink a submarine. Further, on previous voyages she had served as troop ship. This time, in addition to the crew of 463 men, there were 286 British military men, 80 civilian passengers, including women and children (mostly returning home from Suez and the British colonies), the Italian prisoners, and 103 Poles, a company from a division formed in April 1942 in Teheran. They were now acting as jailors for the Italians on board.

The weather was clear, the sea calm, and the Laconia sank slowly enough for everyone except the Italian prisoners of war to get off the ship. The majority of the Italians, who had been locked up in the hold, were caught there, but some 500 managed to break out, having fought off their Polish guards, and most of them got off the ship. Because of the Laconia's list many of the lifeboats and rafts could not be lowered. After the ship went down, Kapitaenleutnant Werner Hartenstein, the commander of the U-156, who had sunk her, saw immediately that hundreds of the survivors would perish in the waters infested with sharks and barracudas unless emergency rescue measures could be taken. He heard calls for help in Italian, and discovered to his dismay that a large number of Italian prisoners of war had been on board. He wirelessed Doenitz: "Sunk...Britisher Laconia...unfortunately with 1500 [actually 1800] Italian war prisoners. Up to now 90 fished out please instruct."

Doenitz, despite the standing rule of all navies that waging war takes precedence over rescuing, detached two submarines, the U-506 and the U-507, underway to missions in the area of Freetown to take part in the rescue operation and requested the Italian commandant stationed at Bordeaux to send the Italian submarine Cappellini, which was operating in the area. The Vichy Government was also asked to send surface ships from

Dakar. Hartenstein with Doenitz's permission sent a radio message in English *en clair* guaranteeing the safety of any Allied vessel that would aid in the rescue providing it did not attack his U-boat. The U-156 took 260 survivors on board, rescuing friend and foe impartially; half of them were transferred to the U-506 when it came a day later. The U-507, arriving soon after, picked up 157 others from the water and overfilled lifeboats, making its decks too crowded. The three submarines each took a row of lifeboats in tow, the U-156 flying a large Red Cross flag, four meters square, to identify the rescue work.

But a four-motor American Liberator bomber spotted the U-156, flew over the scene, and after circling the submarine and the lifeboats went away. When it returned a half hour later, it carried out five bombing attacks on the submarine from a height of eighty meters, despite a radio message from Hartenstein that he had English on board and signals from a RAF officer in a lifeboat using an Aldis lamp. One bomb struck a lifeboat the U-156 was towing, a near hit capsized another; there were killed and wounded, and the submarine was damaged by a bomb hitting amidships directly under the control room. The plane flying at a low level on its first bombing run over the submarine was an easy target for the U-156's antiaircraft gun, but Hartenstein forbade its being used, although he cursed his decision as the plane's last two bombs were aimed at his ship. He wirelessed to Doenitz: "Both periscopes are at present out of order. Breaking off rescue; all off board, putting out toward west, will report." The survivors were put back into the water near lifeboats that could take them on board and Hartenstein had to use what he called "mild force" to get some of the terrified Italians to leave his ship. The Italians, thin and half naked, were in poor physical shape. They had been put on rations of bread and water for days for having violated the no-smoking rule in the hold of the Laconia and for having tried to break into the ship's storeroom. But Hartenstein had to put them off his ship; he then was able to make emergency repairs on the U-156, and he remained on the scene.

Doenitz had to make a soul-searching decision. Hitler got copies of the exchange of messages with the submarine commanders. The Führer had doubtlessly only approved the rescue operation in the first place because of its mollifying effect on

German-Italian relations, but if one of the U-boats should be badly damaged or sunk, Doenitz would have to take full responsibility for the loss of German lives. At the beginning of the operation Admiral Kurt Fricke, telephoning Doenitz in his Paris headquarters from Berlin, told him, "The Führer has been informed of the Laconia affair. He is displeased, and asks you urgently, if you continue the rescue operations, not to take any risks with the U-boats...no risks at all...." Many of Doenitz's own staff opposed continuing the operation after the bombing of the U-156, but he replied, "I can't simply put these people in the water. I will go on as before."

Doenitz ordered only Hartenstein to break off his rescue operations; U-boat commanders Wuerdemann and Schacht in the U-506 and U-507, carrying survivors, continued toward the rendezvous with the French ships from Dakar...Schacht...had on board 1 British officer, 16 children, and 15 women, and was towing seven boats with 330 survivors in them. Wuerdemann had 142 Italians on board and 9 women and children.

On the 17th, the U-506, with its 151 survivors, was bombed by a seaplane. Three bombs detonated near her, but she had dived in time, reached a depth of sixty meters, and was undamaged. Doenitz sent another order telling the two U-boat commanders that only Italians were to be kept on board. Schacht put his British passengers in lifeboats with the exception of two officers he kept as prisoners. He then made off for the rendezvous, where he transferred the Italians and gave the French ships the position of the survivors. Wuerdemann delivered all his passengers to the French sloop Annamite, which had been sent to aid the rescue....

The rescue operation as such was a success: a total of 1,039 men, women, and children were brought on board the Gloire, 42 on the Annamite. The others were brought in by the submarines and lifeboats. The Cappellini rescued 70 or so, some of whom died of shark bites and exhaustion; the rest were transferred to the Dumont-d'Urville, keeping 8 on board (2 Englishmen and 6 Italians). Of the 103 Poles, 73 were rescued, as were 450 Italians out of the 1,800, a few of whom died almost immediately. Pictures were taken of the survivors as they landed in Gibraltar and Casablanca; the German submarine captains were given testimonials of gratitude—they had turned over their officers' quarters to the women and children and had even provided them cold cream, eau de cologne, and the creature comforts they could supply. The submarines returned with their exhausted crews to their home ports.

But on September 17 and again on the 20th, as a result of the bombing of the U-156, Doenitz sent a signal to the commanders of all U-boats, telling them they were under no circumstances to attempt to rescue or to give aid to lifeboats.

...The lesson for Doenitz and the German Navy seemed clear. Obviously no rescue operation could be undertaken without grave danger to the submarines and their crews. That the U-boats were dispatched to save Italians is plain....Nevertheless, the U-boat crews had made no distinction in the nationality of the people they picked up. Doenitz's willingness to detach submarines from their battle stations for a rescue operation and Hitler's tacit approval can only be attributed to the presence of Italians on board the Laconia but once the rescue was started, the Italians were given no priority. The rescue was a spectacular one made under great psychological stress, and Doenitz was its chief organizer.[36]

It is interesting to recall that Doenitz was sentenced to ten years, and that he spent more than eleven years, in confinement.

In conclusion, the evidence shows that, over the ages, there has been progress in the conduct of war. In the ancient world the enslavement of the women and children of the defeated and the slaughter of the men was more or less routine. From the Middle Ages up to the seventeenth century, although prisoners were not routinely enslaved or killed, conquered cities were sacked. During the sack there was, of course, widespread slaughter, rape, and robbery, but it was not a systematic process supervised by the military authorities and it was limited to only a few days. In our time there is no sacking of conquered cities; there is some looting, murder, and rape, but this is done sporadically, and usually against orders, by the criminal elements that exist in every army. There is no question that there has been progress toward a more humane treatment of the civilian population and of the conquered, even if the horror of some episodes of the more recent wars makes us feel that the contrary is true.

In modern times, even the act of killing in battle has changed and now requires less brutality. In the past, in most cases, the enemy was butchered at close quarters and the killer could see the act from the landing of the blow to the last convulsions of agony. In ancient times, this was followed by the stripping of the cadaver, which then became the object of various physical indignities (see the episode of Achilles and Hector in the *Iliad*). As arms became more effective, contact between the killer and the victim became progressively less close because weapons could be used at an increasingly greater distance. Killing became "depersonalized." Today we have reached the point where the killer not only does not see his victim, but not even his physical surroundings. In fact, in the age of intercontinental missiles, the victims are numbers and the cities colored areas on maps.

It is evident that any gruesome act (including killing) is more easily performed when "depersonalized." Imagine a situation in which somebody with no medical training whatsoever is faced with the necessity of performing the amputation of a leg with no anesthesia, a butcher knife, and a saw. It is obvious that very few could do it, no matter how compelling the necessity and how much they might want to save the patient. Suppose, however, that there is an alternative, suppose that the would-be surgeon could order a robot to perform the task and then go away to a place where the screams of agony could not reach him. Most people would be capable of doing this if convinced that it was the only way to save the life of the patient. The reason for the different attitude in the two cases is clear: for a normal person, it is much easier to perform a gruesome act, no matter how necessary, if it is carried out in a way that the senses do not directly perceive the details of the deed. Similarly, the soldier can more easily perform the gruesome acts dictated by the necessity of war by pushing a button than by bloodying his hands. In other words, killing by "pushing the button" requires less crude bellicosity than the same act performed with a knife at close quarters: any of

Genghis Khan's warriors would have loved to be able to chop off a hundred thousand heads in one mighty swing, but the pilot who dropped the atomic bomb on Hiroshima would have been horrified at the thought of killing so many people with his own hands.

Our being able to kill large numbers by "pressing the button" but not by direct means is a step toward the day when our descendants will study with wonder and horror our capacity for killing each other.

(b) Is There Hope?

A few centuries before Christ, having conquered the Italian peninsula, Rome turned toward the Mediterranean and met Carthage. The two giants locked in a struggle that lasted more than one hundred years and ended with the destruction of the African power. Rome became the master of the world.

Why did they not pursue politics of peaceful coexistence? The immense destruction and suffering of the Punic Wars would have been avoided. The energy and wealth spent to fight each other could have been used to explore and spread civilization in Africa and in the immense unknown territories of Europe and Asia. Peaceful coexistence would have generated prosperity for all, whereas the results of the wars were the destruction of Carthage and, in Italy, ravages of such magnitude that their consequences were felt for centuries. True, by eliminating Carthage, Rome became *caput mundi*, but surely the world was large enough for two *capita mundi*. Carthage could have colonized Africa, and Rome Europe. It would have been the golden age for mankind.

Why did they choose to fight? Simply because it was the natural and normal thing to do. Since the beginning of history, whenever two groups become dominant, conflict follows. The Romans and the Carthaginians were not abnormal or insane; on the contrary, had they chosen to live in peace, they would have behaved in an abnormal and unusual way.

Two thousand years later, in our time, two giants watch

each other across oceans that, because of modern technology, are smaller than the ancient Mediterranean. Under usual circumstances, conflict would be inevitable. Other conflicts would follow in an unending series. War would be eliminated only in the very distant future, after man has climbed another step in his evolutionary scale.

This is what would happen under usual circumstances. The circumstances are not usual, however: for the first time in history, the country contemplating starting an all-out atomic war has the absolute certitude that at the end it will be among the losers. There is no doubt that this is, by far, the most powerful restraint that has ever interfered with man's propensity to wage war. It is easy to imagine that Hannibal would have become the most ardent advocate of peaceful coexistence if, when crossing the Alps, he would have become absolutely certain that the war against Rome was going to result in his suicide and the final destruction of Carthage. There is no doubt that the certainty of losing would have made lambs of Hitler and Genghis Khan.

For centuries, wise men and religious leaders have repeated that war is an abomination that makes all men and all countries the losers in the long run, and that peace would give humanity marvelous opportunities for progress. Wise words forever admired and ignored. The inner drive toward war was too strong to resist. Now, however, the nuclear age insures instant and complete extinction. In fact, war, instead of a means to achieve survival, becomes a means to assure the death, not only of individuals and families (a price often paid before), not only of countries and civilizations (a price occasionally paid before), but also of humanity and of the whole planet, an intolerable price. Therefore war shall be eliminated.

As a means that has become unable to achieve its end, war loses its imperviousness to ethics and logical reasoning and to religious convictions. Although its elimination will be ascribed to such reasoning and convictions and to deeply felt ethical principles, in reality it is the result of fear. Fear of extinction. War is abolished because atomic weapons have changed the terms of the equation: the old one was WAR = SURVIVAL, the new is WAR = DEATH. Now the instinct of survival is against war, and peace is inevitable because it is dictated not by logic, a weak persuader, but by an instinct, an irresistible one. Finally the old dream has become reality: war will be no more.

The war abolished by the existence of nuclear weapons is, of course, all-out war among the superpowers, and the question could be asked whether this represents any advantage over the old ways. In the past, it is true, great powers used to fight each other, but at least the very existence of humanity was not in danger. Today, even if the hydrogen bomb imposes restraint, there is always the possibility of the terrible consequences of a miscalculation or a mistake.

Is it better or worse? The question is idle.

In the first place, nuclear weapons are here to stay and little is gained by speculating about whether it would be better if they were not. Second, we must get used to the idea that technological progress will put at the disposal of man more and more energy, which, if misused, will wipe out larger and larger portions of the universe. If we extrapolate into the future the ever-growing capacity of man to manipulate energy, it is not only conceivable but probable that one day he will be able, not just to sterilize the earth's surface, but to disintegrate the planet itself and to wipe out the rest of the solar system. Therefore, it would appear advisable to stop worrying, accept the fact that man has at his disposal tremendous energies—that he will have more in the future, and make sure that accidents and miscalculations do not occur. We cannot turn the clock back to the pre-nuclear age and we may as well accept this as a fact.

If this is the case, we must accept the principle that each superpower, for the foreseeable future, will have enough atomic weapons to obliterate the world. This, on the other hand, by keeping man in a continuous state of fear will make him avoid major wars. Fear is a great pacifier. This may seem demeaning to our dignity, but we must remember that, in the past, peace was always maintained through fear. The *Pax Romana* and the *Pax Britannica*, for example, were imposed by the swords of the legions and the guns of the Royal Navy.

The *Pax Atomica* will be maintained by the hydrogen bomb.

One cannot know what the Cold War would have been like if there had been no nuclear weapons, but it is hard to believe that such an intense contest between such powerful states, involving political stakes as important as Western Europe, would have been so readily contained beneath the threshold of general war had it not been for the prospect of nuclear devastation.[37]

The thesis that nuclear weapons have made war obsolete is presented most fully and explicitly by Walter Millis. It is implicit in the copious peace literature since World War II; for example, the writings of Bertrand Russell, Charles Osgood, Erich Fromm, and Seymor Melman. The idea, however, is not confined to the peace group. General Douglas MacArthur, for example, declared that the science of destruction in the nuclear age has transformed the abolition of war from a moral question to a political necessity. President Johnson affirmed what every post-World War II President and many other heads of state have said in similar words when he declared: "There is no real comparison between the attitudes of most of the world's governments today and twenty-five years ago on the role of warfare as an instrument of national policy. War is obsolete, obsolete because there can be no winner....The question is not whether the world can eliminate war. The question is when—when all nations will have the courage and the good sense to do so." This kind of hyperbole differs from the view of the peace group because it assumes that, until war is eliminated by some unspecified means, the war system must go on the same as ever, except that states must be especially cautious to avoid wars with a high risk of becoming nuclear. But it shares the basic assumption that war is obsolete because it must entail cataclysmic costs that are grossly disproportionate to any conceivable gains.[38]

It is evident that peace, even a peace imposed by fear, is better than war, and even if small conflicts continue, nightmares like the First and Second World Wars will be eliminated.
Even if nuclear weapons prevent the superpowers from

making war on each other, that does not mean, of course, that wars among small countries or so-called "proxy wars" are not possible and that the superpowers will not make war on small countries. The existence of nuclear weapons, however, has also modified this aspect of the dynamics of international relations.

If a superpower attacks a small country, the probability of all-out nuclear war is remote. When Russia invaded Afghanistan, it would have been absurd for the U.S. to even consider the possibility of a nuclear threat on the issue. When the United States invaded Grenada, Russia likewise refrained from bellicose threats. One could think that this would lead to frequent attacks of the superpowers on small countries. Yet this is not the case because the effect that a country's actions have on world opinion is important. The final purpose of each superpower is to convince the rest of the world that its system is superior, so that the resulting "ideological infiltration" may help in undermining the strength and prestige of the other superpower. In addition, it is in the interest of each superpower to reassure the other (as much as possible) concerning bellicosity and aggressive intentions. This is for various reasons, one of the most important being the following: deterrence does not work in an all-or-nothing way; there are degrees of deterrence which are proportional to the power of the deterrent country. In other words, if both superpowers have enough nuclear weapons to destroy each other, but one has just enough and the other ten times more than enough, the two opposing forces do not have equal deterrence. This is so because possible errors, malfunctions, miscalculations, unexpected occurrences, new discoveries, etc., will influence less the destructive capability of the country with the larger nuclear arsenal. It is in fact to be expected that in a serious crisis, all other elements being equal, the country with the smaller stockpile would have to give in. This being the case, each superpower wants to reassure the government of the other so that the latter will be less stimulated to increase its stockpiles.

International trust for a given country depends on two factors: military power (in this case trust means international confidence in the capacity of the country to apply military power effectively when necessary) and restraint in using power (in this case trust means international confidence in the "benignity" of the country). In the case of superpower politics, invasion of a small country tends to decrease the amount of international trust, as shown by the Vietnam and Afghanistan wars; the intensity of this effect depends, of course, on circumstances and on the effectiveness of superpower propaganda. It must be underlined, however, that, as far as world opinion is concerned, effective application of military power is more important than other considerations and that, therefore, the biggest decrease in trust, in the two examples above, was caused not so much by the conflicts *per se* but, for the Americans, by the loss of the war and, for the Russians, by their failure, so far, to win.

Clearly, if nuclear weapons have eliminated all-out war, they have not eliminated its deep cause, namely the instinct for survival. This being the case, man will find effective substitutes for war. As discussed before (Chapter 1), war (victorious war, of course) brings survival by making the group capable of imposing on others its language, its values, and its way of life. Because man's nature and needs have not changed, the same results will be sought by other means such as ideology, science and technology, and economic predominance.

If Chinese were to become the language of science and technology, for example, and if the Chinese brand of Communism were to become the most successful political system, this would represent an accomplishment equivalent to victory in many wars. Every educated person would speak Chinese—at least as a second language, China would become the standard to imitate, and the survival of the "Chinese way of life" would be assured for a long period.

Substitutes for war, like ideological infiltration, the technology race, and attempts at economic dominance, therefore, are, like war, based on a powerful subconscious drive. For this reason it is useless to oppose them with ethical arguments. For example, how often have we heard that with the amount of money spent for landing a man on the moon we could have bought so many millions of tons of milk for starving children and built so many hospitals for the poor and so many houses to shelter the needy, etc. Inane arguments. The groups that will be more successful in the exploration and colonization of space may hope to obtain the same result as those groups that were most successful in the exploration and colonization of earth: survival (in the sense already discussed). The same applies also to ideological and economic dominance and to any other means that our subconscious will perceive as a substitute for war in the pursuit of immortality. The arms race, in this context, will be discussed later.

Considering how effective nuclear weapons are in preventing war, the question could be raised as to whether it would be advisable to distribute atomic stockpiles to all countries.

Many groups are at a primitive technological level and the sudden acquisition of nuclear weapons would find them psychologically unprepared. There is no historical precedent to indicate what the reaction of a backward country would be to the sudden acquisition of military power several orders of magnitude above what it possessed before. Perhaps we may consider some of the Middle East nations which suddenly became rich with the sale of oil as examples of countries that have suddenly acquired enormous power (although economic in this case and not military). It would appear that, in some cases at least (e.g., Iran under the Shah), the sudden wealth may have been a destabilizing factor. We may assume, therefore, that the sudden acquisition of enormous military power would create an even more unstable, dangerous situation. On the other hand, if nuclear weapons are obtained as the result of long, slow technological progress, the government and the ruling class will have had more time to adjust to the responsibility of power.

It is evident, therefore, that the spread of atomic weapons should be limited as much as possible among the countries that do not have nuclear capabilities, even if this means that those countries will continue to engage in war. After all, a conventional war between Libya and Albania, let's say, would be of less concern than their possession of atomic weapons. As for the countries with nuclear capability but no weapons, they are performing a tactical maneuver dictated by political circumstances. It is evident, for example, that Canada has not acquired nuclear weapons not because of ethical scruples but because it finds it cheaper, and politically advantageous, to rely on the U.S. nuclear deterrence.

While an all-out confrontation between the superpowers is kept in check by the Pax Atomica, wars between non-nuclear countries and conventional wars in which the superpowers are more or less directly involved will continue for a long time to come. The disappearance of "Great Wars" or "World Wars," however, is to be considered a tremendous step forward. The fear of nuclear annihilation is the price that we have to pay. There is no doubt that in the third century B.C., the possibility that humanity could perish was more remote than now. On the other hand, if Rome and Carthage had nuclear weapons, Carthage would still exist.

What about nuclear disarmament? Like ritualized dances, disarmament conferences have no value other than psychological. The thought that governments are involved in discussions to reduce the stocks of nuclear weapons, with the goal of eliminating them altogether, gives us reassurance. In reality, of course, the governments involved know very well that, under no circumstances, will nuclear weapons be eliminated and that eventual agreements will only be on marginal details with no great impact.

Besides insurmountable problems of verification, the abolition of nuclear weapons would create a very unstable situation: first, by throwing the world back to the pre-nuclear age when high risks were taken, in the political arena, because the worst that could happen was a conventional war for which the country taking the risk was prepared; second, by increasing the danger of nuclear war because, as mentioned before, even if nuclear weapons were eliminated, the capacity to produce them would not be, and a conventional war would cause the resumption of their production and their use; third, by increasing the possibility that any country, especially a third-rate one, could surreptitiously prepare a few nuclear weapons and use them in relative security from retaliation.

In addition, the existence of nuclear weapons generates the nuclear arms race, which, contrary to common belief, contributes to the maintenance of peace. While the arms races of the past were preparations for war, the nuclear arms race *replaces* war. The race consists, of course, not so much in accumulating more and more weapons but, more importantly, in a competition to achieve technological breakthroughs. When one is achieved by one side, everything else being the same, it becomes the equivalent of winning a battle or, in exceptional cases, even a war, because, depending on the importance of the breakthrough, the side with the new technological edge may gain an advantage so substantial that it may be able to impose its will on the other side. Which, of course, is the objective of war, in this case reached without violence. The drive toward war (discussed in Chapter 1) is, in this way, channeled toward technological competition instead of violent conflict. In addition, the capacity for winning the arms race is related to power and to all other elements that make a group more capable of competing with other groups (see Chapter 8). The arms race is, therefore, a valid substitute for war and, as such, replaces it.

Even if nuclear weapons have the capacity of eliminating all-out war, they have no influence on the decline of the group because, as discussed before (Chapter 8), decadence, in most cases, is not caused by war or peace but by permissiveness and its three main roots: affluence, education, and freedom. It would appear that if the process of decline is to be stopped (or at least delayed), permissiveness should be avoided, or at least contained.

One of its roots is freedom; freedom from external interference (what has been called negative freedom[39]), which is a natural aspiration of man. Early humans, exposed to the dangers of a hostile environment, must have realized that it was advantageous to limit the range of their impulses in exchange for the security offered by living in a group. Social life and the necessary limitation of freedom that it demands were therefore dictated by the desire for security or, which amounts to the same, by fear.

As long as man lived a precarious, marginal existence, his desire for freedom was covered by layers of other worries, including the search for immediate necessities. When society became relatively affluent and sophisticated, however, the need for security decreased while the yearning for freedom increased, as in the Athens of Pericles and the Rome of Brutus. During the first centuries of the Roman Empire the desire for freedom was soon snuffed out again by fear—fear of civil war under Augustus, fear of the Prince's ruthlessness later, and fear of the barbarians pressing at the borders still later. In the Middle Ages, there was another kind of fear—fear of damnation. The limitations imposed by a demanding Church were accepted as necessary to avoid eternal damnation, a concept somewhat incongruous to us but terrifying for Medieval man. As religious fear began to abate in the late Middle Ages, the Medieval communes came into existence in the relatively affluent (and more secure) milieu of the emergent middle class, as an expression of the same yearning for freedom. Later, the desire for freedom erupted in the American and French Revolutions, and afterward generated the Western democracies.

It is interesting to note that, in our days, oppressive regimes tend to magnify external danger so that fear may again help to make the imposed constraints more acceptable. It is also worthy of note that the limitations on individual freedom imposed by Communist regimes are resented more in the affluent, advanced societies of Eastern Europe than in others where poverty and ignorance are more widespread.

If we accept the proposition that the desire for freedom is a natural aspiration and that limitations are tolerated only if forced by fear and by the need for security, we must conclude that constraints imposed simply to avoid permissiveness would be resented and, pitted against a natural aspiration, would be bound to fail. We must, therefore, turn to another root of permissiveness.

Affluence, as discussed before, tends to reduce the need for discipline. After a few generations the members of the affluent group lose contact with the harshness of the environment and tend to take for granted what their forefathers had earned with sweat and toil. This in turn tends to cause the disregard of what we could call "the old virtues" and the adoption of a way of life that in times of hardship would not have been possible. The tolerance of the affluent group for permissiveness is in reality an acknowledgment of the decreased importance of the group itself as a provider of security. Affluence, in other words, provides security by a means other than the ancestral one: discipline within the group.

In affluent societies, isolated voices condemning permissiveness are not lacking. During the Roman Empire the virtues of the old Republic were often contrasted with the lack of discipline of the society of the time, and in our days, in the United States, some deplore mores that would have been unthinkable at the time of the pioneers. Only in a society as affluent as ours is it possible to see such relatively large numbers of young people dedicated only to non-productive activities—as were, for example, the so-called "hippies" of the Sixties. Also the pursuit of pseudo-religious cults or pseudo-philosophical or pseudo-artistic dreams is possible only when the rest of society can afford to pay the bill. It must be underlined, however, that, although the behavior of those who choose to "drop out" of the mainstream of society is the most striking, permissiveness also affects the rest of the group. A member of the affluent society of today works less and enjoys more leisure than in the less affluent past. This in itself tends to relax those rules of behavior that we call "old virtues," which are the response of the individual and group to a more demanding environment.

According to legend, Lucius Quinctius Cincinnatus was plowing his small farm when he was notified that the senate had made him dictator so that he could save the fatherland from the menace of the Aequi. He defeated the enemy, entered Rome in triumph, and promptly returned to his plow. A society composed of Cincinnati could indeed avoid decline and be affluent at the same time. The gods, however, have lost the mold of Cincinnatus and the voluntary renunciation of affluence (associated with maintenance of discipline) may be observed only in isolated cases without social impact. It would be unrealistic, however, to think that it is possible to enforce an artificial harshness for the purpose of eliminating the deleterious consequences of affluence. It would appear, therefore, that the second root of permissiveness (affluence) is as untouchable as the first one (freedom).

Since Socrates, it has been a widely accepted tenet that education is the panacea for most if not all the problems of humanity. It should be evident by now that this is not the case, at least as far as political problems are concerned. A cursory glance at the history of the West shows that there seems to be no parallelism between education and political wisdom. The point could be raised that it is so because education, for most, has not reached the hypothetical critical threshold necessary for enlightenment. In fact, in Chapter 8 we have seen that education (in the sense of cultural refinement) fosters permissiveness and, therefore, the decline of the group. Because, obviously, the spreading of education cannot and should not be stopped, we are confronted with the same seemingly insoluble problem: education must be encouraged and promoted, and yet, by so doing, we foster the development of permissiveness, one of the major causes of decay of the group.

The three major roots from which permissiveness is generated (freedom, affluence, and education) are not only desirable in themselves, but the intensity of man's struggle to acquire them seems to indicate that their fulfillment is one of his inner drives. To attempt their elimination, therefore, would be dangerous and futile. The question that we must now ask ourselves is: if the roots of permissiveness cannot be eliminated, in fact, if they are to be encouraged, and if permissiveness invariably causes decline, how can we avoid or at least retard decline itself? To answer the question we must first decide if, independently of any time-scale, decline is theoretically inevitable.

When we say that, for man, death is inevitable, we are asserting one of the best-established biological principles. Yet our conclusion is only based on statistical evidence and not on any knowledge of an inherent characteristic of living matter. We are sure that all individuals will eventually die because all men have died in the past; our degree of certitude is extremely high because, given the number of men that have lived, not a single exception has been observed.

Is the life cycle of the group (rise, zenith, decline, death) as we have observed it over the last five or six thousand years inevitable? The number of individual human beings that have lived and died is much larger than the number of groups that have gone through the same cycle; for this reason our statistical conclusion is stronger in the case of the death of the individual than in the case of the decay of the group. In addition, if a certain series of events has always taken place in a certain time-scale, there is no reason to believe that it will always continue to do so. For example, until now all things made by man were condemned to disappear in a relatively short time. Even what is made of the most durable materials will disappear in a few hundred thousand (or perhaps a few million) years: the pyramids, the Parthenon, the Coliseum, our stainless steel, non-biodegradable plastics, all.[40] However, the spacecraft Pioneer 10, launched in 1972, left the solar system on June 13, 1983 and, barring accidents, could travel on, they say, for one hundred billion years. One hundred billion years is not eternity but, for the human mind, it is almost indistinguishable from it.

It must be conceded, however, that the fact that throughout recorded history not a single group has lasted as a dynamic organized structure more than a relatively short time is convincing evidence that the possibility of the indefinite survival of any group is so remote that, for all practical purposes, we may consider it non-existent.

If decline and fall cannot be avoided, can they at least be retarded? Because we have identified permissiveness as the main factor that causes decline, the problem arises whether permissiveness can be controlled in spite of the fact that its causes cannot and should not be eliminated but preserved and encouraged.

At first sight the problem seems insoluble; we must consider, however, that the same causes do not produce the same effects in all circumstances. For example, the same caloric intake will produce obesity in the sedentary but not in the active person, and the same exposure to *Diplococcus Pneumoniae* may produce pneumonia in the weak and enfeebled but may have no effect on the person in good physical condition. In addition, although not proven, it is possible that once the mechanism of a certain behavior is known, it becomes easier to modify the behavior itself. Freud and his followers, for example, consider this one of the basic axioms of their doctrine. Therefore, once we realize how permissiveness is deleterious to the group, it may be possible, without interefering with its causes, to curb it. For example, we could continue to enjoy freedom without pornography, affluence without lack of discipline, and education without derision of traditional values. After all, to use the same examples, it should not be difficult to understand that pornography is not exactly a noble art, that lack of elementary discipline is not something particularly enjoyable, and that derision of traditions is not an intellectual achievement. Under ordinary circumstances, except for a few in the lunatic fringe, no member of a group wants its decline. Many among the prophets of permissiveness, therefore, may preach their credo without realizing its implications. If the implications of permissiveness are made clear and are understood by all members of the group, decline may be retarded.

Another element that may contribute to the postponement of decline is enlightened self-interest, which is to be distinguished from simple self-interest. According to the latter, everyone pursues his advantage without regard to others. This is the rule in the biological world. Each animal implements it with the blind purpose of securing, for example, food for himself, sometimes for his young, and usually with no concern for others. The concept of simple self-interest (for a country as for the individual) is clear: a certain action is in the country's interest when it produces immediate advantages that outweigh the immediate disadvantages; self-interest is the positive result of the algebraic sum of the advantages (positive) and disadvantages (negative) *at any given time.*

In a group system, in which the elements are interrelated, the advantages of a few members, gained at the expense of the others, may deprive some to the point that the system collapses with consequent loss for every component element. This may seem obvious but it is only in the last century or so, for example, that a certain degree of redistribution of wealth among the members of the group was recognized as a legitimate social need—with results advantageous to all. On the international level, the same need, coupled with the necessity of helping the recovery of the conquered, was recognized only after the Second World War.

Enlightened self-interest modifies the concept of simple self-interest by mitigating the need for immediate advantage and by including the proposition that the advantage of some may result in advantage for all by making the group (or the international order) more stable. It is to be noted that this "altruistic" component is not based on any ethical consideration.[41] The simple algebraic addition of positive (advantageous) and negative (disadvantageous) forces is still the essence of the principle of enlightened self-interest, but, in this case, it is to be calculated *in a longer time-frame.* The difficulty consists, of course, in the identification of all the forces involved and in the assessment of their relative value in the long run as opposed to the primitive, immediate gratification of simple self-interest.

Enlightened self-interest is, therefore, a step forward in the progress of civilization and, because man usually follows ethical principles in his utterances and utilitarian ones in his acts, its utilitarian aspects reflect reality.

The centripetal force has acted throughout history on larger and larger groups, from the tribe to the city-state to modern nations. As modern technology has reduced the difficulty inherent in a process of identification encompassing large distances and peoples of different languages and customs, the centripetal force may start to act on an even larger group: the entire civilization. Until now we in the West, for example, have recognized that we belong to a single civilization, but this has not prevented us from slaughtering each other and from depicting each other as subhuman. Even if, in the past, our fury may have prevented us from realizing that most of our wars were in reality civil wars, the time has come for us to do so now. We may have already started. Nowadays the idea that there may be a war between the U.S. and England or between Spain and Italy strikes us as absurd. Military and economic reasons may be in part responsible for our reaction, but the feeling that we belong to the same culture, to the same civilization, undoubtedly plays a role. The Second World War was not only the last all-out war but also the last civil war of Western civilization. This does not mean that minor wars between some smaller countries (e.g., in South America) will not take place; what we will not see again, as a first step, are major wars among the more developed members of our civilization.

It would be even better, of course, if we were to realize that, as all civilizations are part of the Human Civilization, all wars are civil wars. Unfortunately, for the moment, this is only an intellectual understanding that does not reach our inner drives, and it is premature to hope that we will behave accordingly in the foreseeable future. We must therefore rely on something else (namely the fear of atomic annihilation) to prevent the recurrence of the "World Wars" of the past.

CONCLUSIONS

At the beginning of the twentieth century, Europe was the hub of the world and England was the leading country. France considered itself second by trying desperately to remember Napoleon and to forget Sedan. In reality Germany was second, and soon an age-old process repeated itself: the second challenged the first for the leading position. The First World War started.

Thus far, all had proceeded according to millenary rules. A subtle change, however, started to take place at this point; a change that was to have profound consequences for the rest of the century. At about that time, many started to feel that war, the old evil, could be eliminated. This was not a new concept, as we have seen in Chapters 5 and 7; what was new was that enough people began to believe in it so that it was no longer the dream of only a few.

In becoming a common belief, the idea of perpetual peace was oversimplified and trivialized. It became accepted wisdom that war could be avoided, simply and easily, by basing relations between countries upon the same ethical principles that govern (or should govern) the relations between individuals: good will, honesty, generosity, brotherly love, justice, etc. At the end of the war, with the enthusiastic support of the United States, the League of Nations was created as a forum for the implementation of international justice.

In the meantime, the idea that in this way conflict could easily be avoided continued to work its way into the cultural substrate of the Western world. This spawned strong movements (especially among the "intellectuals") advocating pacifism and peace at any price, so that when Hitler started to play the international game according to the old rules, the rest of the Western world was scandalized, shocked, and psychologically unprepared to react.

The Fascists and the Communists were the only ones who understood the naiveté of the peace movement of the time. The Fascists, out of ideological fervor and arrogance, proclaimed their contempt loudly and clearly; the Communists, more cleverly, supported pacifist movements everywhere because inside Russia they had no weight, and in all other countries they were useful as debilitating factors.

When World War II began and Germany overran Europe, the United States Government was faced with a dilemma: either let Germany win and be confronted by a powerful Japan in Asia and an even more powerful Germany in Europe or convince the American people to fight to re-establish the status quo.

Because it was in the obvious interest of the United States to do so, its government decided to follow the latter course. This, however, presented formidable difficulties after so much encouragement, for many years, of the idea that the evil of war was easily avoidable. The obstacle could be overcome only if the people were to be convinced that this was not a war like the others but a special one. The propaganda machine started to push the idea that this special war was not fought for reasons of national interest but for a much nobler one: the defense of freedom and justice. The same justice that, as everybody knew, would soon eliminate the evil of war.

In spite of great efforts, however, this argument did not go very far (many remembered that the previous war was the war to end all wars) and resistance to intervention remained strong in the United States. Then Pearl Harbor and the persecution of the Jews tilted the balance in favor of intervention. The Nazis' racial atrocities were so abhorrent that they did not need any "retouching" by the propaganda machine; Pearl Harbor was, of course, depicted as an act of ultimate evil and the American people were finally convinced that the war was being fought for freedom and justice.

The Americans won the war. They had to pay, however, a very high price: their reconfirmed conviction that the Second World War was a special war fought only for freedom and justice and that war in general was an easily avoidable evil in which only wicked countries engage. The Nuremberg Trials were both the result of these beliefs and a major factor in reinforcing them.

Curiously enough, by that time even the American leaders seemed to believe more and more in their own propaganda and, with the self-righteousness of the unsullied, they set out to make the rest of the world see the light and accept the same beliefs. By then the United States was the undisputed leader of the Western world, and old Europe, devastated by the war and, even worse, by political and social ills, was simply following the leader.

Soon a feeling of uneasiness started to be felt by more and more Americans. This was due to several factors. It became increasingly evident, for example, that one of the allies, Joseph Stalin, was as evil as Adolf Hitler, the Enemy. Some pointed out that the dropping of the atomic bomb on Japan, without at least some warning, was not exactly in keeping with the much-flaunted ethical principles. Even military necessity became less and less acceptable as a justification because, according to the "laws" applied at the Nuremberg Trials, it was subordinate to moral principles to the point that, even in time of war, each individual had to decide carefully if a given order was moral or immoral—and therefore valid or invalid.

In addition, the beliefs that with justice, good will, brotherly love, etc., war could easily be avoided and that conventional ethics should govern international relations (together with the principles established at the Nuremberg Trials) could not fail to have devastating consequences for the Western countries—especially for the United States—where those same beliefs were being taken seriously. The stage was set for a resounding military defeat of the West. When the Korean war started, the rout of the West was only postponed by the imposing stupidity of the other side. The invasion of South Korea was prepared and executed with such disregard of political precautions that the war could still be sold as another special one fought not so much for the interest of the West, but in defense of the most noble principles and with God on our side. The conflict ended in a stalemate.

In the meantime, the leaders of the Western world continued to act (out of conviction, domestic political considerations, or both) as if conventional ethical principles were valid in international relations. Therefore, when an American spy plane, for example, was shot down over a hostile country, the world saw the singular spectacle of the President of the United States apologizing and promising that such acts of treachery would not happen again.

The *redde rationem* came with the Vietnam war.

From the beginning, Western leadership attempted, as usual, to label it as another war fought for the most noble principles and not (as it was) for the interests of the Western world. The chances for this attempt to succeed were already small but, to reduce them to zero, a new element entered into the picture: the media. Now the war could be brought into each citizen's house. In "living color" and right in the living room, bloody massacres, maimed youngsters, small girls engulfed in flames, mothers crying over the bodies of children, blundering military officers, etc., suddenly revealed to the American public the horrors of war.

The revelation was the more shocking because, during previous wars, the populace was led to believe that only the enemy committed horrible deeds. As was to be expected, the public started to identify such repulsive details with that particular war and the conclusion was reached that that particular war was unjust and brutal and had to be stopped at all costs.

Military authorities and government officials tried, of course, to limit the dissemination of such details by limiting accessibility to the facts, by covering or perhaps distorting them, and by other means. The newsmen, as a reaction, developed a self-righteous sense of being knights in shining armor, anointed discoverers of the Truth. The American media developed a delusion of grandeur that is still one of the elements contributing to the instability of the Western world. The situation in Vietnam was further complicated when many came to the conclusion that the South Vietnamese government, defended in the name of freedom, justice, etc., was cruel, corrupt, and immoral. This, of course, clashed with the efforts to push the concept of the noble and just war.

In the meantime, the Nuremberg principle that each man had the obligation to refuse to obey ethically wrong orders gained momentum, with the result that refusal to be drafted for the "immoral" war became a crusade and a protest against the wicked leadership of the United States. The circle was soon completed: the American leadership was immoral, the Vietnam war (in contrast to others) was immoral, and, by the logic of opposites, the enemy was right and morally superior. At that time, the sight of Americans demonstrating in favor of the enemy was not unusual.

The Vietnam war became for the United States (that is, for the Western world) a major disaster. The most powerful country in the world lost a war (not a battle but a war!) against one of the smallest and most backward. The military defeat, in itself, would not have been serious if it were not that it contributed substantially to damaging the very structure of Western society. To understand why this was the case we must appreciate the special place of the United States in Western civilization.

For Western man after World War II, and even more for the average American, the United States had started to become the concretization of Western civilization itself, perceived, more or less consciously, as just, invincible, and eternal (a role played in antiquity by Rome, in the Middle Ages by the Church, and up to the twentieth century by the individual fatherlands). As such, the United States could not lose a war or engage in an unjust one or show obvious signs of decay, dishonesty, and ineptitude. When it became common belief that it did, the consequences were profound. If the United States was so much at fault, then to support it (that is to say, to be patriotic) was wrong, and if patriotism was to be rejected, then all the other principles on which the ethos of the West rested had to be re-examined. And so the destruction of what were now perceived as sacred cows began: patriotism, obedience to the laws, observance of religious rituals, discipline, the work ethic, conventional sexual mores, etc., were all questioned and rejected by large sections of the population, especially among the young. On the other hand, principles that were resisted by the more conservative (e.g., racial equality) were eagerly embraced.

Since Greek times, racial discrimination has not been a tenet of the Western ethos, as shown by Roman history and later by Church history. The periods in which discrimination was practiced are therefore to be considered temporary aberrations. In the United States, de facto acceptance of racial equality was already well under way before the Vietnam war, but there is no doubt that the "revolution of the Sixties" accelerated the process. This was the only positive result. The rejection of other ethical principles had deleterious consequences. By far the most serious of those consequences was the rejection, by many, of two of the principles on which society rests: the principle of proportionality between merit and reward and the recognition of the preeminence of transindividual values (which is an expression of the centripetal force).

The first was sacrificed at the altar of equality (racial and otherwise) when equality of opportunity was transformed into some vaguely defined and dimly perceived equality of achievement and when, in a paroxysm of righteousness, it was decided that equality of opportunity was not enough to expiate the sins of the past.

Acceptance of the preeminence of trans-individual values manifests itself in religiousness, obedience to the law, and sacrifice for the common good. These principles were abandoned in favor of a pathetic, intellectually primitive hedonism in which great emphasis was laid on drugs, sexual promiscuity, and license.

It is interesting to note that all this was not the result of some wicked ideology but of a well-intentioned attempt to improve the lot of mankind by the application of moral principles perceived as self-evident. It was felt, for example, that equality of opportunity was really not enough because it would result in unequal rewards (an "unjust" outcome), while equality of achievement would be "just" because it would tend to result in equal rewards. As for trans-individual values, again it was felt that it was somehow "unjust" and oppressive to expect from the individual anything else than the free pursuit of his own hedonistic inclinations. As an individual had no right to impose on another his own views of right and wrong, society had no right to impose, on the individual, limitations, constraints, and regulations, especially if they concerned ethics and behavior not immediately harmful to others.

This tendency to transfer ethical principles from the individual to society has affected various subgroups as well. In the case of organized churches this has produced stresses among the faithful and within the hierarchy. In the Catholic Church, for example, contradictory positions have been officially taken by the bishops on certain political problems such as nuclear deterrence:

> Nuclear weapons were also on the minds of France's Roman Catholic bishops last week. Meeting in Lourdes the prelates took a searching look at the concept of nuclear deterrence—and came out roundly in favor of it. By a vote of 93 to 2, the bishops endorsed a 5,000-word document entitled "Winning Peace," which declared among other things that "nuclear deterrence is

still legitimate" and strongly disavowed the idea of unilateral disarmament by the West.

The firm French stand contrasted sharply with that of Roman Catholic bishops in the U.S., who last May called for a halt in the production, testing, and deployment of nuclear weapons.[1]

Historically, in the treacherous fields of politics and international relations, the Church may have been sometimes wrong but it was never in doubt. Now, racked by doubt and dissent, it tries to regain a relevancy that some among its members (especially in America) fear lost. Some suggest a path of renewal that goes through dreams of rejuvenation by returning to the pristine simplicity of yore. This often involves moving, again, to the outside of the "establishment" and embracing revolutionary causes and pacifist movements advocating disarmament at all costs. What the future of the Church will be we are unable to predict, but it is indeed a sign of its crisis that, at least in its temporal mode, it may be both wrong and in doubt.

It is to be hoped that the rejection of the principles just discussed (proportionality between merit and reward and preeminence of trans-individual values), although deleterious for our society, was not part of the general process of decline discussed in Chapter 8, but the result of particular factors affecting the Western world at that time. Unfortunately, some of those factors are still at work. Among the most important in the political field is the persistent belief that international relations are regulated by conventional individual ethics. Another, less important perhaps but very deleterious, is the attitude of the media, which, in a blind race to report and interpret what they perceive to be The Truth, disregard completely the damage inflicted on the group. It is doubtful, for example, that the United States could have won the Second World War if the media could have shown, night after night, children and civilians massacred by Allied bombing, destruction of cities and villages, suffering of wounded and maimed soldiers, episodes like the Laconia affair, etc.

As for nuclear deterrence, we have concluded that, at present, it is our best hope for the elimination of war. So far, prophecies of doom have been proven wrong. In 1960, the novelist and scientist C. P. Snow said:

> Within, at most, ten years, some of those [nuclear] bombs are going off. I am saying this as responsibly as I can. *That* is the certainty. On the one side [arms control], therefore, we have a finite risk. On the other side [arms race] we have a certainty of disaster. Between a risk and a certainty, a sane man does not hesitate.[2]

It is evident that the mistake of Mr. Snow was to think in the old manner. He thought of atomic bombs not as entirely new weapons but as more powerful, old-fashioned bombs—and, of course, if it were so, he would have been right. On the other hand, Benjamin Franklin clearly perceived the advantages of an entirely new weapon:

> In November 1783, King George III and the court at Windsor were treated to an exhibition of a hydrogen balloon....The potential value of the balloon in warfare, however, was recognized quickly....Benjamin Franklin expressed the situation clearly in a letter dated soon afterward:
> "The invention of the balloon appears, as you observe, to be a discovery of great importance. Convincing sovereigns of the folly of wars may perhaps be one effect of it, since it will be impossible for the most potent of them to guard his dominions. Five thousand balloons, capable of raising two men each, could not cost more than five ships of the line, and where is there a prince who could afford to cover his country with troops for its defense as that ten thousand men descending from the clouds might not in many places do an infinite amount of damage before a force could be brought together to repel them?"[3]

It is evident that the idea that man can be scared out of war is not new. Benjamin Franklin was wrong simply because balloons, as weapons, turned out to be not as dangerous as it was thought. Nuclear weapons, however, *are* as dangerous as we think; therefore all-out wars will be no more. One of the great dreams of mankind has become reality, and we may perhaps realistically start to hope that the day when all wars will be eliminated may not be too far away.

NOTES

INTRODUCTION

[1] "Without anger and without partisan spirit." Tacitus, *Annales* I, I.
[2] There are also differences, of course. Nobody, for example, has ever maintained that cancer is good and that certain types of cancer are to be supported, while some have maintained that war is good and others that there is such a thing as "just war."
[3] *Scientific American*, September 1983, p. 28.
[4] The doctrine of double effect, which could be applied to this example, will be discussed in Chapter 7.
[5] Anscombe, G.E.M., quoted by Yehuda Melzer, *Concepts of Just War*. Leyden: A.W. Sijthoff, 1975, p. 164.
[6] Robert E. Osgood and Robert W. Tucker, *Force, Order, and Justice*. Baltimore: Johns Hopkins Press, 1979, pp. 304, 305.
[7] Barrie Paskins and Michael Dockrill, *The Ethics of War*. Minneapolis: University of Minnesota Press, 1979, pp. 152, 160, 166.
[8] The objection that a qualitative (and not quantitative) difference is introduced by the extinction of the human species can be easily rejected by replacing total elimination with elimination of 95 percent or 99 percent of humanity.
[9] Jacques Maritain, *Man and the State*. Chicago: University of Chicago Press, 1951, pp. 1-19.

Chapter 1

THE NATURE OF WAR

[1] "...man being able to make himself secure only with military power..." Translation by P. Prioreschi.
[2] John Keegan and Joseph Darracott, *The Nature of War*. New York: Holt, Rinehart and Winston, 1981, p. 135.
[3] Ibid., p. 44.
[4] Associated Press, *Omaha World Herald*, August 21, 1983.
[5] Keegan and Darracott, *The Nature of War*, p. 43.
[6] Quoted by Gaston Bouthoul, *Traité de polémologie*, Paris: Payot, 1970, p. 105. "War is not in defiance of nature. It is not against nature for the male to kill his fellow male. The law that rules the relations between males of the same species is a law of murder and risk. War is a chapter of love." Translation by P. Prioreschi.
[7] Quincy Wright, *A Study of War*. Chicago: Midway Reprint, University of Chicago Press, 1983, pp. 105, 106, 107.
[8] Margaret Mead, "Warfare Is Only an Invention—Not a Biological Necessity," *Asia*, XL, August, 1940. Quoted by Robert E. Osgood, *Force, Order, and Justice*. Baltimore: Johns Hopkins Press, 1967, p. 8.
[9] Quoted by Keegan and Darracott, *The Nature of War*, p. 43.
[10] Quoted by Bouthoul, *Traité de polémologie*, p. 72. "While I am talking to you, there are one hundred thousand animals of our species, wearing hats, killing another one hundred thousand wearing turbans, for some heap of mud the size of your foot...to know if it will belong to a certain man named Sultan or to another called, I do not know why, Caesar.... Almost none of these beasts have ever seen the animal for whom they are killing each other." Translation by P. Prioreschi.
[11] Wright, *A Study of War*, pp. 26, 27.
[12] "Some, upon the courage of a fruitful issue, wherein...they seem to outlive themselves, can with greater patience away with death." Thomas Browne, *Religio Medici*. London: William Pickering, 1845, XLI, p. 104.
[13] Horace, *Carmina*, III, XXX. "I shall not altogether die, a great part of me shall escape the goddess of death: I shall continuously be reborn, young with my future glory. I shall be famed as long as the Pontiff ascends the Capitol with the silent Vestal virgin...[= as long as Rome shall exist]." Translation by P. Prioreschi.
[14] Wright, *A Study of War*, pp. 37, 42.
[15] Quoted by Wright, *A Study of War*, pp. 39, 40.
[16] Wright, *A Study of War*, p. 41.
[17] Quoted by Wright, *A Study of War*, p. 41.
[18] Dian Fossey, "Imperiled Giants of the Forest," *National Geographic*, Vol. 159, No. 4, April 1981, pp. 501-523. Quotations on pages 511-512.

¹⁹ Jane Goodall, "Life and Death at Gombe," *National Geographic*, Vol. 155, No. 5, May 1979, pp. 592-621. Quotations on pages 594, 611.

²⁰ Bouthoul, *Traité de polémologie*, pp. 112, 113, 114. "In this way the Asiatic rat has succeeded in eliminating completely the races that existed before in Europe. Everywhere similar events have been reported. The Argentinian ant, wherever it arrives and prospers, succeeds in suppressing all other species of ants that were orginally in the invaded regions....The opposition between two species that are neighbors and concurrent looks like a state of almost perpetual war. All means are used to provoke the destruction of the other species. Besides violence, one of the principal means to reach the goal is the securing of all sources of food and the expulsion of the less strong species from all healthy, fertile, and advantageous areas, where it is supplanted by the stronger one....So every lion has its particular domain where it does not tolerate intrusions. Other animals have the tendency to take over for their own use a pasture or hunting ground and to control it by force....But the ants show the most characteristic bellicose tendencies...." Translation by P. Prioreschi.

²¹ David J. Mossman and William A.S. Sarjeant, "The Footprints of Extinct Animals," *Scientific American*, January 1983, p. 75.

Chapter 2

THE SOLDIER

¹ "Whence we often see that if somebody decides to take the shilling, he immediately...rids himself of all civilian manners; because he does not believe that he who must be quick and ready for all kind of violence can have a civilian attitude." Translation by P. Prioreschi.

² Robert Gardner and Karl G. Heider, *Gardens of War: Life and Death in the New Guinea Stone Age*. New York: Random House, 1968, pp. 135, 136.

³ Michael Grant, *The Army of the Caesars*. New York: Charles Scribner's Sons, 1974, p. XV.

⁴ Pliny the Elder. Quoted by Grant, *The Army of the Caesars*, p. XV.

⁵ Grant, *The Army of the Caesars*, p. XXI.

⁶ Tacitus, *The Annals*, Cambridge: Harvard University Press, 1969, p. 146 (footnote by John Jackson).

⁷ Grant, *The Army of the Caesars*, p. XXIII.

⁸ Tacitus, *The Annals*, p. 146 (footnote).

⁹ Ibid., p. 146. "...were beginning to feel the strain of short rations and hardship—they had been reduced to keeping starvation at bay by a flesh diet." Translation by John Jackson.

¹⁰ Caesar, *The Gallic War*. Cambridge: Harvard University Press, 1970, pp. 402, 404. "...so that for several days the troops were without corn, and

staved off the extremity of famine by driving in cattle from the more distant hamlets." Translation by H.J. Edwards.
[11] Josephus, *Jewish War*, III, translation of H. St. J. Thackeray. Quoted by Grant, *The Army of the Caesars*, pp. XXVII, XXVIII.
[12] Peter Connolly, *Greece and Rome at War*. Englewood Cliffs, N.J.: Prentice-Hall Inc., 1981, p. 140.
[13] Edward Gibbon, *The Decline and Fall of the Roman Empire*. London: Methuen and Co., 1909, Vol. II, pp. 191, 192.
[14] Alfred Vagts, *A History of Militarism, Romance and Reality of a Profession*. New York: W.W. Norton and Co., 1937, pp. 39, 40.
[15] Ibid.
[16] André Corvisier, *Armies and Societies in Europe 1494-1789*, translated by Abigail T. Siddal. Bloomington and London: Indiana University Press, 1979, pp. 6, 7, 8, 9, 41, 54, 132-134.
[17] Ibid.
[18] Ibid.
[19] Ibid.
[20] Ibid.
[21] Ibid.
[22] Herbert Langer, *The Thirty Years' War*. Dorset: Blanford Press, Poole, 1980, pp. 97, 98.
[23] Ibid.
[24] Ibid.
[25] Corvisier, *Armies and Societies*, pp. 6, 7.
[26] Ibid.
[27] John Keegan and Joseph Darracott, *The Nature of War*. New York: Holt, Rinehart and Winston, 1981, p. 8.
[28] Corvisier, *Armies and Societies*, pp. 41-54, 132-134.
[29] Ibid.
[30] Keegan and Darracott, *The Nature of War*, p. 170.
[31] Ibid.
[32] Corvisier, *Armies and Societies*, pp. 13, 14.
[33] Ibid.
[34] Ibid.
[35] Ibid., pp. 82-86.
[36] Ibid.
[37] Ibid.
[38] Ibid.
[39] Ibid.
[40] Ibid.
[41] Ibid., pp. 22, 23.
[42] Geoffrey Best, *Humanity in Warfare*. New York: Columbia University Press, 1980, p. 88.
[43] Vagts, *A History of Militarism*, p. 89.
[44] Corvisier, *Armies and Societies*, p. 184.

45 Vagts, *A History of Militarism*, pp. 70, 72, 73.
46 Ibid., pp. 306, 307.
47 Ibid.
48 Ibid.
49 Connolly, *Greece and Rome at War*, p. 44.
50 Tacitus, *Histories*, I, XLVI. "The troops also demanded that the payments usually made to centurions to secure furloughs should be abolished, since they amounted to an annual tax on the common soldiers. A quarter of each company would be away on furlough or loafing about the camp itself, provided the soldiers paid the centurion his price....Moreover the richest soldiers would be cruelly assigned to the most fatiguing labor until they bought relief." Translation by Clifford H. Moore.
51 Christopher Hibbert, *Waterloo, Napoleon's Last Campaign*. New York: The New American Library, 1967. p. 84.
52 Ibid., p. 113.
53 A.J. Barker, *Prisoners of War*. New York: Universe Books, 1975, p. 29.
54 Unknown, *A German Deserter's War Experience*. New York: B.W. Huebsch, 1917, pp. 124, 125.
55 Robert I. Burns, S.J., "The Medieval Crossbow as a Surgical Instrument: An Illustrated Case History," Bull. New York Acad. Med. 48, 983, 1972.
56 Louis Bakay, *The Treatment of Head Injuries in the Thirty Years' War (1618-1648)*. Springfield, Ill.: Charles C. Thomas, 1971. p. 39.
57 Ibid.
58 Owen H. Wangensteen et al., "Wound Management of Amboise Pare and Dominique Larrey, Great French Military Surgeons of the 16th and 19th Centuries," Bull. Hist. of Med. 46, 207, 1972.
59 Ibid.
60 Francis R. Packard, *Life and Times of Ambroise Paré with a New Translation of His Apology and an Account of His Journeys in Divers Places*. New York: Benjamin Blom, Inc., 1971 (first published in 1921), p. 163.
61 Richard Wiseman, Sergeant Surgeon to Charles II, *Of Wounds, of Gun-shot Wounds, of Fractures and Luxations*, a facsimile of Books V, VI, and VII of "Severall Chirurgicall Treatises" (first published in 1676). Bath: Kingmead, 1977, p. 437.
62 Ibid.
63 Packard, *Life and Times of Ambroise Paré*, pp. 64-65.
64 William Beaumont, *Experiments and Observations on Gastric Juice, and the Physiology of Digestion*. Plattsburgh: F.P. Allen, 1833, pp. 9-17.
65 Possibly because of pleural adhesions resulting from previous pleuritic episodes which were common at that time.
66 Concerning the "carbonated fermenting poultice," a textbook of pharmacology published in 1854 (Jonathan Pereira, *The Elements of Materia Medica and Therapeutics*, Philadelphia: Blauchard and Lea, p. 86)

explains:

> CATAPLASMA FERMENTI, L; *Cataplasma Fermenti Cerevsiae; Yeast Poultice*....It is applied, when cold, to fetid and sloughing sores as an antiseptic and stimulant: it destroys the fetor, often checks the sloughing, and assists the separation of the dead part. It should be renewed twice or thrice a day. I have frequently heard patients complain of the great pain it causes. The carbonic acid [liberated by the fermentation] is supposed to be the active ingredient.

As for Muriate of Ammonia, our Ammonium Chloride, it was thought to be a weak antiseptic (see Albert H. Buck, *A Reference Handbook of the Medical Sciences*, Vol. I. New York: William Wood and Company, 1885, p. 255), while vinegar was used for its capacity to stop bleeding (see Perevia, *The Elements of Materia Medica*, p. 945):

> In *Hemorrhages*, as from the nose, lungs, stomach, or uterus, it is particularly beneficial for its refrigerant, sedative, and astringent qualities. It diminishes excessive vascular action, and promotes contraction of the bleeding vessels.

"Aq. acet. am." is probably the aqueous solution of ammonium acetate that was used to "allay headache, especially headache of pyrexia [fever], to quiet an uneasy stomach, or to promote gentle diaphoresis [perspiration] or diuresis [increased excretion of urine] in fever...." (See Buck, *A Reference Handbook*, pp.136, 137) Camphor, on the other hand, was used as remedy for a variety of afflictions: "fever...inflammatory diseases...mania, melancholia, and other forms of mental disorder...spasmodic affections...irritation of the urinary and sexual organs...poisoning...cholera..." (See Pereira, *The Elements of Materia Medica*, pp. 401, 402, 403.)

[67] Beaumont, *Experiments and Observations*.
[68] Ibid.
[69] Ibid.
[70] Ibid.
[71] Keegan and Darracott, *The Nature of War*, p. 203.
[72] John D. Imboden, "The Confederate Retreat from Gettysburg," in *Battles and Leaders of the Civil War*. New York: Century Co., 1888, Vol. 3, p. 424.
[73] Keegan and Darracott, *The Nature of War*, pp. 204, 205, 206.
[74] John Keegan, *The Face of Battle*. New York: Viking Press, 1976, p. 197.
[75] Christopher Hibbert, *Waterloo, Napoleon's Last Campaign*. New York: New American Library, 1967, p. 236.
[76] Best, *Humanity in Warfare*, pp. 126, 127.
[77] Lieut. Col. Fielding H. Garrison, *Notes on the History of Military Medicine* (reprinted from the *Military Surgeon*, 1921-22). Washington: Association of Military Surgeons, 1922, p. 95.

Notes 313

78 Inspecteur Général Sieur, "Histoire des tribulations du corps de santé militaire depuis sa création jusqu' à nos jours," Bull. de la Soc. Française d'Histoire de la Médecine, XXII, March-April 1928, pp. 100, 101.
79 Ibid.
80 Best, *Humanity in Warfare*, pp. 148, 149, 150.
81 Ibid., pp. 151, 152.
82 Keegan, *The Face of Battle*, p. 267.
83 Henry Berry, *Semper Fi, Mac*. New York: Arbor House, 1982, p. 309.
84 Corvisier, *Armies and Societies*, pp. 186, 187.
85 A devout Italian girl murdered in 1902 while resisting rape. She was canonized in 1950.
86 Bernard Millot, *Divine Thunder: The Life and Death of the Kamikazes*. New York: McCall, 1971, p. 228.
87 Captain Rikihei Inoguchi, Commander Tadashi Nakajima, and Roger Pineau, *The Divine Wind: Japan's Kamikaze Force in World War II*. Annapolis: United States Naval Institute, 1958, pp. 200, 201.
88 Carl von Clausewitz, *On War*, translated by Michael Howard and Peter Paret. Princeton: Princeton University Press, 1976, p. 101.
89 Berry, *Semper Fi*, p. 26.
90 Ibid., p. 50.
91 *The Iliad of Homer*, translated by Alexander Pope. New York: Thomas Y. Crowell, no date, Book II, p. 79.
92 Orazio, *Carmina, Iambi, Sermones, Epistulae*. Turin: Petrini, 1972, footnote by Morpurgo, p. 67.
93 Ibid.
94 Catullus, *Poems*, LVII.
95 "With thee I knew Philippi's day and its headlong rout, leaving my shield ingloriously behind." From Horace, *The Odes and Epodes*, translation by C.E. Bennett. Cambridge: Harvard University Press, 1978, p. 123.
96 Berry, *Semper Fi*, p. 278.
97 Ibid., p. 189.
98 Michael Walzer, *Just and Unjust Wars*. New York: Basic Books Inc., 1977, p. 314.
99 Keegan and Darracott, *The Nature of War*, p. 203.
100 J. Glenn Gray, *The Warriors: Reflections on Men in Battle*. New York: Harper and Row, 1967, p. 52.
101 Ibid., pp. 52, 53.
102 William Broyles Jr., *Esquire*, Vol. 102, No. 5, November 1984, p. 61.
103 Quoted by Gray, *The Warriors*, p. 55.
104 Don Congdon, ed., *Combat WW II: European Theater of Operations*. New York: Arbor House, 1983, p. 120.
105 Berry, *Semper Fi*, p. 208.
106 Corvisier, *Armies and Societies*, p. 6.
107 Albert Sorel, *Europe and the French Revolution: The Political Traditions of the Old Regime*. London: Collins, 1969 (first pub. 1885), p. 112.
108 Keegan and Darracott, *The Nature of War*, p. 231.

109 Congdon (ed.), *Combat WW II*, p. 404.
110 Guy Chapman, *A Passionate Prodigality*. New York: Holt, Rinehart and Winston, 1966, pp. 99, 100.
111 Robert Graves, *Good-bye to All That*. Garden City, N.Y.: Doubleday and Company, Inc., 1957, p. 131.
112 Walzer, *Just and Unjust Wars*, p. 308.
113 J. Christopher Herold, *Bonaparte in Egypt*. New York: Harper and Row, 1962, p. 274.
114 Vagts, *A History of Militarism*, pp. 78, 79.
115 Hans Jacob Christoffel von Grimmelshausen, *Simplicissimus*, translated by A.T.S. Goodrick. London: George Routledge and Sons, no date, pp. 33, 34.
116 Telford Taylor, *Nuremberg and Viet Nam: An American Tragedy*. Chicago: Quadrangle Books, 1970, p. 9.

Chapter 3

WAR, FAMINE, AND PESTILENCE

1 "...war...an art by which men cannot ever live honestly..." Translation by P. Prioreschi.
2 "Lord, protect us from pestilence, famine, and war."
3 Hans Zinsser, *Rats, Lice and History*. New York: Bantam Books, 1965, p. 89.
4 Ibid., p. 101.
5 Frederick F. Cartwright, *Disease in History*. New York: Thomas Y. Crowell, 1972, p. 13.
6 Zinsser, *Rats, Lice and History*, p. 104.
7 Edward Gibbon, *The Decline and Fall of the Roman Empire*. London and New York: G. Virtue, no year, II, p. 104.
8 Cartwright, *Disease in History*, p. 37.
9 *Encyclopedia Britannica*, 1971, IX, p. 58A.
10 Ralph A. Graves, "Fearful Famines of the Past," *National Geographic*, XXXII, July 1917, p. 70.
11 *Encyclopedia Britannica*, 1971, IX, p. 58A.
12 Associated Press, in *Omaha World Herald*, September 12, 1984, p. 4.
13 Graves, "Fearful Famines of the Past," p. 81.
14 Karl von Clausewitz, *On War*. New York: Random House Inc., 1943, p. 3.
15 Coleman Phillipson, *The International Law and Custom of Ancient Greece and Rome*. London: Macmillan, 1911, pp. 203, 204, 205, 206, 207, 208.
16 Albert Sorel, *Europe and the French Revolution: The Political Traditions of the Old Regime*. London: Collins, 1969 (first pub. 1885), pp. 111-113.

17   Johann Wolfgang von Goethe, *Faust*, Prologue in Heaven.
18   John Keegan and Joseph Darracott, *The Nature of War*. New York: Holt, Rinehart and Winston, 1981, p. 169.
19   Lieut. Col. Fielding H. Garrison, *Notes on the History of Military Medicine* (Reprinted from *Military Surgeon*, 1921-22). Washington: Association of Military Surgeons, 1922. pp. 60-61.
20   Ibid., p. 106, 107.
21   Ibid.
22   Ibid.
23   Gaston Bouthoul, *Traité de Polémologie*. Paris: Payot, 1970, pp. 256, 257, 258, 260, 262.
24   Fareed Haj, *Disability in Antiquity*. New York: Philosophical Library, 1970, pp. 92-93.
25   Garrison, *Military Medicine*, pp. 60-61.
26   Bouthoul, *Traité*.
27   Garrison, *Military Medicine*, pp. 106, 107.
28   Ibid.
29   *Encyclopedia Britannica*, XXIII, 1971, p. 199.
30   Garrison, *Military Medicine*, p. 169.
31   Giovanni Bonalumi, *Esposizione Sommaria del Servizio Santitarioo Di Guerra Secondo I Più Recenti Ordinamenti*. Milan: Fratelli Rechiedei, 1880. p. 61
32   Bouthoul, *Traité*.
33   Ibid.
34   Ibid.
35   Ibid.
36   Ibid.

Chapter 4

PRISONERS AND MILITARY OCCUPATION

1   "For, among other evils that being disarmed brings to you, it makes you contemptible." Translation by P. Prioreschi.
2   Coleman Phillipson, *The International Law and Custom of Ancient Greece and Rome*. London: Macmillan, 1911, pp. 251-263.
3   Ibid.
4   Ibid.
5   Horace, *Epistulae*, I, XVI, 69.
6   Flavius Josephus, *The Complete Works*, translated by William Whiston. Chicago and New York: Donohue Brothers, no date, pp. 599, 600.
7   "The far-seeing mind of Regulus wanted to avoid this when he rejected the shameful terms and, from such precedent [the proposed exchange], he foresaw moral ruin in the future unless the prisoners, who did not deserve

compassion, were allowed to perish. 'With my own eyes have I seen, hanging in Carthaginian temples, our eagles and our weapons taken without bloodshed from our soldiers,' he said. 'With my own eyes have I seen the arms of free Roman citizens chained behind their backs, and gates open wide and fields, once depopulated by our warfare, tilled again. Our soldiers bought back with gold will fight with renewed valor indeed! Loss embraces shame: faded wool does not regain the lost colors even if dyed again, nor can honor, once lost, be restored to the dishonored....He who has trusted the perfidious enemy, he who tamely felt the thongs on his tied arms, he who was afraid to die, will he be brave, will he be able to defeat the Carthaginian in another war? He who, not knowing how to live, mixed tameness with war?' " Translation by P. Prioreschi.

[8] Phillipson, *International Law and Custom*, pp. 263-264.
[9] Ibid., pp. 251-263.
[10] Ibid., pp. 263-264.
[11] "There is no law that spares the prisoner or protects him from penalty."
[12] "What is not forbidden by law is forbidden by decency."
[13] Phillipson, *International Law and Custom*, pp. 263-264.
[14] John Keegan and Joseph Darracott, *The Nature of War*. New York: Holt, Rinehart and Winston, 1981, p. 206.
[15] Herbert Langer, *The Thirty Years War*. Dorset: Blandford Press Poole, 1980, p. 105.
[16] Francis R. Packard, *Life and Times of Ambroise Paré with a New Translation of his Apology and an Account of his Journeys in Divers Places*. New York: Benjamin Blom, Inc., 1971 (first published in 1921), pp. 219-220.
[17] André Corvisier, *Armies and Societies in Europe 1494-1789*. Bloomington and London: Indiana University Press, 1979, p. 186.
[18] Jean Christopher Herold, *Bonaparte in Egypt*. New York: Harper and Row, 1962, pp. 276, 277.
[19] *Samuel* II, I, 5-10.
[20] Josephus, *Complete Works*, p. 704.
[21] John Bagot Glubb (Glubb Pasha), *The Lost Centuries*. Englewood Cliffs, N.J.: Prentice-Hall Inc., 1967, p. 180.
[22] Michael Levien ed., *Navel Surgeon, the Voyages of Dr. Edward H. Cree, Royal Navy, as Related in His Private Journals, 1837, 1856*. New York: E.P. Dutton, 1982, pp. 102, 105.
[23] Christopher Hibbert, *The Great Mutiny—India 1857*. New York: Viking Press, 1978, pp. 138, 313, 379.
[24] Jack Lindsay, "Mass Suicide after Mass Murder." *London Tribune*, August 25, 1944.
[25] Donald Knox, *Death March: The Survivors of Bataan*. New York and London: Harcourt Brace Jovanovich, j1981, pp. 339-340.
[26] Josephus, *Complete Works*, p. 602.
[27] Geoffrey Best, *Humanity in Warfare*. New York: Columbia University

Press, 1980, pp. 155, 156.
²⁸ Keegan and Darracott, *The Nature of War*, p. 207.
²⁹ Caesar, *De Bello Gallico*, I, XXXVI, XLIV. "It was the right of war that the conquerors dictated as they pleased to the conquered....he took the tribute by the right of war, as customarily imposed by the victor on the conquered....all the cities of Gaul had come to attack him and had mobilized against him; he had beaten and conquered all those forces in a single battle. If they wished to try again, he was ready to fight again; if they wanted to enjoy peace, then it would be unjustified to refuse the payment of tribute...." Translation by P. Prioreschi.
³⁰ Steven Runciman, *The First Crusade*. Cambridge: Cambridge University Press, 1980, pp. 88-89.
³¹ Albert Sorel, *Europe and the French Revolution: The Political Traditions of the old Regime*. London: Collins, 1969 (first pub. 1885), pp. 109, 110.
³² Best, *Humanity in Warfare*, p. 65.
³³ Ibid.
³⁴ Ibid., pp. 89-95.
³⁵ Ibid.
³⁶ Ibid.
³⁷ Ibid.
³⁸ Ibid., p. 100.
³⁹ Ibid., p. 168.
⁴⁰ Ibid., p. 223.
⁴¹ John Master, *The Road past Mandalay*. New York: Harper and Brothers, 1961, pp. 274, 275.
⁴² Herold, *Bonaparte in Egypt*, pp. 366, 367, 368.
⁴³ Gary Gordon, "Soviet Partisan Warfare, 1941-44: The German Perspective." University of Iowa Thesis, 1972, p. 30, 31. Quoted by Best, *Humanity in Warfare*, p. 228.
⁴⁴ Eugene Davidson, *The Trial of the Germans*. New York: Macmillan Company, p. 569.
⁴⁵ Herman Neubacher, the German foreign office plenipotentiary in SE Europe, to Field Marshal von Weichs, apropos of the Klissura massacre. Quoted from Telford Taylor in Best, *Humanity in Warfare*, p. 234.
⁴⁶ Corvisier, *Armies and Societies*, p. 78.
⁴⁷ Davidson, *The Trial of the Germans*, p. 575.
⁴⁸ David Pryce-Jones, *Paris in the Third Reich: A History of German Occupation, 1940-1944*. New York: Holt, Rinehart and Winston, 1981, p. 10. Caption under a photograph of two German Soldiers shopping in a Paris shoe Store: "Like so many tourists, German soldiers after the 1940 campaign swarmed into shops in search of goods unobtainable at home." It is interesting to compare this behavior of soldiers who "like tourists" politely go into the shop and pay for the goods, with the behavior of occupying soldiers of other times.
⁴⁹ *Webster's Third New International Dictionary*, 1976.

50 Pryce-Jones, *Paris in the Third Reich*, pp. 206, 207.
51 Indro Montanelli, *L'Italia Della Guerra Civile*. Milan: Rizzoli, 1983, pp. 338, 339.
52 Theodor Mommsen, *The History of Rome*. London: Richard Bentley and Son, 1877, II, pp. 309, 310.

Chapter 5

LAWS OF WAR AND PEACE

1 "You must realize that there are two ways of fighting: by law or by force; the first is proper to man, the second to beasts." Translation by P. Prioreschi.
2 Geoffrey Best, *Humanity in Warfare*. New York: Columbia University Press, 1980, p. 40.
3 Arthur Nussbaum, *A Concise History of the Law of Nations*. New York: Macmillan, pp. 90-93.
4 Ibid.
5 Ibid.
6 Ibid.
7 Ibid., pp. 102-114.
8 Yehuda Melzer, *Concepts of Just War*. Leyden: A.W. Sijthoff, 1975, p. 13.
9 Nussbaum, *Concise History of the Law*, pp. 102-114.
10 Ibid.
11 Ibid.
12 Ibid., p. 3.
13 Ibid., p. 1.
14 Ibid., pp. 3, 4, 5.
15 Aristotle, *Politics*, in *On Man in the Universe*. Roslyn, N.Y.: Walter J. Black, Inc., 1971, p. 259.
16 Nussbaum, *Concise History of the Law*, pp. 3, 4, 5.
17 Frederick L. Shuman, *International Politics*. New York: McGraw-Hill, 1953, p. 37.
18 Vergil, *Aeneid*, VI, 847, 848. "Excudent alii spirantia mollius aera... vivos ducent de marmore vultus."
19 Nussbaum, *Concise History of the Law*, pp. 10, 11.
20 Ibid., pp. 12, 13, 14, 15.
21 Tacitus, *Annales*, XII, XVII. "Next day the beseiged sent deputies to ask for quarter offering, in exchange, ten thousand as slaves. The victors refused because, they said, it would be cruel to slay them when prisoners, but it would also be difficult to guard such a multitude; better they should

perish by the law of war. The signal for no mercy was therefore given to the soldiers, who were already on the ladders." Translation by P. Prioreschi.

22   Nussbaum, *Concise History of the Law*, pp. 12, 13, 14, 15.
23   Ibid., pp. 3, 4, 5.
24   Ibid.
25   Ibid.
26   Nussbaum, *Concise History of the Law*, pp. 17-27.
27   Ibid.
28   Ibid., pp. 45-54.
29   Ibid.
30   Ibid., pp. 61-70.
31   Ibid., pp. 115-118.
32   Nicolas Cheetham, *Keepers of the Keys*. New York: Charles Scribner's Sons, 1983, p. 224.
33   Nussbaum, *Concise History of the Law*, pp. 129-131.
34   "It is more than a crime, it is a mistake."
35   Nussbaum, *Concise History of the Law*, pp. 120, 121.
36   Ibid., p. 196.
37   Ibid., pp. 227, 228, 231.
38   Ibid., pp. 17-27.
39   Ibid., pp. 61-70.
40   Eugene Davidson, *The Trial of the Germans*. New York: Macmillan Company, 1966, p. 588.
41   Best, *Humanity in Warfare*, pp. 331, 332.
42   John Keegan and Joseph Darracott, *The Nature of War*. New York: Holt, Rinehart, and Winston, 1981, pp. 3-7.
43   Isaiah, 2:4.
44   Keegan and Darracott, *The Nature of War*, pp. 3-7.
45   Joshua Prower, in the foreword of the reprint of *Liber Secretorum Fidelium Crucis*, by Marinus Sanutus. Toronto: University of Toronto Press, 1972, p. VII.
46   Nussbaum, *Concise History of the Law*, pp. 42-44.
47   Ibid.
48   Ibid., pp. 77, 78.
49   Ibid., pp. 142-144.
50   Best, *Humanity in Warfare*, pp. 77-82.
51   Ibid.
52   Ibid.
53   Ibid.
54   Ibid.
55   Nussbaum, *Concise History of the Law*, pp. 142-144.
56   Raymond Aron, *Peace and War*. New York: Frederick A. Praeger, 1968, p. 18.
57   Keegan and Darracott, *The Nature of War*, pp. 3-7.
58   Ibid.
59   Ibid.

60 Hans J. Morgenthau, *Politics among Nations, the Struggle for Power and Peace.* New York: Alfred A. Knopf, 1956, pp. 368-370.
61 Ibid.
62 Ibid.
63 Ibid.
64 Ibid., p. 373.
65 Ibid., p. 386.
66 Ibid., p. 387

Chapter 6

ETHICS AND WAR CRIMES

1 "Very rarely are men capable of being altogether bad or altogether good." Translated by P. Prioreschi.
2 Quoted by Jacob Bronowsky, *The Ascent of Man.* Boston: Little, Brown and Company, 1973, p. 118.
3 Edward Gibbon, *Decline and Fall of the Roman Empire.* London: Methuen and Co. 1909, I, p. 93.
4 Bertrand Russell, *Power: A New Social Analysis*, quoted by John Kenneth Galbraith, *The Anatomy of Power.* Boston: Houghton Mifflin Co., 1983, p. 1.
5 Thucydides, *The Peloponnesian Wars*, V, 84-115, translated by Benjamin Jowett. Oxford: Clarendon Press, 1900, pp. 169-177.
6 Ibid.
7 Fénelon, *Écrits et lettres Politiques*. Quoted in Robert E. Osgood and Robert W. Tucker, *Force, Order, and Justice.* Baltimore: Johns Hopkins Press, 1967, p. 100.
8 Quoted by Barrie Paskins and Michael Dockrill, *The Ethics of War.* Minneapolis: University of Minnesota Press, 1979, pp. 9, 10.
9 Telford Taylor, *Nuremberg and Vietnam: An American Tragedy.* Quadrangle Books, Chicago, 1970, p. 31.
10 Louis FitzGibbon, *Katyn.* New York: Charles Scribner's Sons, 1971, pp. 23, 24.
11 Michael Walzer, *Just and Unjust Wars.* New York: Basic Books Inc., 1977, pp. 225, 226.
12 Ibid., pp. 270, 271.
13 Paul Ramsey, "A Political Ethics Contest for Strategic Thinking," in Morton A. Kaplan, ed. *Strategic Thinking and Its Moral Implications.* Chicago: 1973, pp. 134, 135. Quoted in Walzer, *Just and Unjust Wars*, p. 272.
14 Osgood and Tucker, *Force, Order, and Justice*, p. 238.

[15] William J. Bosch, *Judgment on Nuremberg*. Chapel Hill: University of North Carolina Press, 1970, p. 183.
[16] Ibid., p. 184.
[17] Ibid., pp. 186, 187, 188.
[18] Ibid.
[19] Walzer, *Just and Unjust Wars*, p. 240.
[20] Ibid., p. 245.
[21] Paskins and Dockrill, *The Ethics of War*, pp. 24, 25.
[22] Noble Frankland, *Bomber Offensive: The Devastation of Europe*. New York: 1970, p. 41. Quoted by Walzer, *Just and Unjust Wars*, p. 255.
[23] Walzer, *Just and Unjust Wars*, pp. 255, 256, 261.
[24] Osgood and Tucker, *Force, Order, and Justice*, p. 200.
[25] Walzer, *Just and Unjust Wars*, pp. 317, 318.
[26] Michael Walzer, *War and Moral Responsibility*, quoted by Paskins and Dockrill, *The Ethics of War*, p. 286.
[27] Alessandro Manzoni, *I Promessi Sposi*, Milan: Hoepli, 1945, pp. 461, 462.
[28] Ibid., p. 474. Translation by P. Prioreschi.
[29] Taylor, *Nuremberg and Vietnam*, p. 24.
[30] Bosch, *Judgment on Nuremberg*, p. 225.
[31] Eugene Davidson, *The Trial of the Germans*. New York: Macmillan Company, 1966, pp. 586, 587.
[32] Rebecca West, Foreword, in Airey Neave, *On Trial at Nuremberg*. Boston: Little, Brown, and Company, 1978, p. 5.
[33] Sydney D. Bailey, *Prohibitions and Restraints in War*. Oxford: Oxford University Press, 1972, pp. 42, 43.
[34] William Henry Chamberlin, "The Bankruptcy of a Policy," in Harry Elmer Barnes, ed., *Perpetual War for Perpetual Peace*. Caldwell, Idaho: Caxton, 1953, pp. 533, 535. Quoted in Bosch, *Judgment on Nuremberg*, pp. 151, 152.
[35] Gange, *American Foreign Relations*, p. 258. Quoted by Bosch, *Judgment on Nuremberg*, pp. 151, 152.
[36] William Henry Chamberlin, *Beyond Containment*. Chicago: Regnery, 1953, p. 73. Quoted by Bosch, *Judgment on Nuremberg*, pp. 151, 152.
[37] Eugene Davidson, *The Trial of the Germans*, p. 587.
[38] Robert E. Conot, *Justice at Nuremberg*. New York: Harper & Row, 1983, pp. 516, 517.
[39] Ibid.
[40] Neave, *On Trial at Nuremberg*, pp. 56, 331.
[41] Richard H. Minear, *Victor's Justice: The Tokyo War Crimes Trial*. Princeton: Princeton University Press, 1971, p. 6.
[42] Bosch, *Judgment on Nuremberg*, p. 14.
[43] Ibid.
[44] Ibid., pp. 43, 44, 45.
[45] Ibid.
[46] Ibid., p. 182.

[47] Taylor, *Nuremberg and Vietnam*, p. 86.
[48] Davidson, *The Trial of the Germans*, p. 381.
[49] Minear, *Victor's Justice*, pp. 95, 96.
[50] Ibid.
[51] Ibid., pp. 136, 137.
[52] Paskins and Dockrill, *The Ethics of War*, pp. 269, 270.
[53] Ibid.
[54] Ibid.
[55] Yehuda Melzer, *Concepts of Just War*. Leyden: A.W. Sijthoff, 1975, p. 30.
[56] John Keegan and Joseph Darracott, *The Nature of War*. New York: Holt, Rinehart and Winston, 1981, pp. 208, 209.
[57] Hans J. Morgenthau, *Politics among Nations: The Struggle for Power and Peace*. New York: Alfred A. Knopf, 1973, p. 239.
[58] Minear, *Victor's Justice*, p. 100.
[59] Davidson, *The Trial of the Germans*, pp. 381, 382, 383, 384.
[60] Ibid.
[61] Luis FitzGibbons, *Katyn*. New York: Charles Scribner's Sons, 1971, p. 183.
[62] Davidson, *The Trial of the Germans*, p. 83.
[63] Ibid., pp. 32, 33.
[64] Ibid., p. 575.
[65] Taylor, *Nuremberg and Vietnam*, p. 56.
[66] Gordon Wright, *The Ordeal of Total War 1939-1945*. New York: Harper and Row, 1968, p. 128.
[67] Alfred Vagts, *A History of Militarism, Romance and Reality of a Profession*. New York: W.W. Norton Company, 1937, pp. 250, 251.
[68] Margret Boveri, *Treason in the Twentieth Century*. New York: G.P. Putnam's Sons, 1963, pp. 35, 36.
[69] Taylor, *Nuremberg and Vietnam*, p. 16.
[70] Ibid., p. 47.
[71] A. Frank Reel, *The Case of General Yamashita*. New York: Octagon Books, 1971, pp. 91, 92.
[72] Taylor, *Nuremberg and Vietnam*, pp. 91, 92.
[73] Ibid.
[74] Ibid.
[75] Walzer, *Just and Unjust Wars*, p. 320.
[76] Reel, *The Case of General Yamashita*, p. 109.
[77] Taylor, *Nuremberg and Vietnam*, p. 90.
[78] Ibid.
[79] Courtney Browne, *Tojo, the Last Banzai*. New York: Holt, Rinehart and Winston, 1967, p. 255. Quoted by Minear, *Victor's Justice*, p. 211.
[80] Conot, *Justice at Nuremberg*, pp. 521, 522.
[81] Bosch, *Judgment on Nuremberg*, p. 23.
[82] Winston S. Churchill, *The Second World War*. Vol. V, *Closing the Ring*.

Boston: Houghton Mifflin Co., 1951, pp. 374, 375. Quoted Morgenthau, *Politics among Nations.* p. 234.
[83] Davidson, *The Trial of the Germans*, p. 18.
[84] Reel, *The Case of General Yamashita*, pp. 242, 243.
[85] Julius Stone, *Aggression and World Order: A Critique of United Nations Theories on Aggression.* Berkeley: University of California Press, 1958, pp. 138-39. Quoted by Bosch, *Judgment on Nuremberg*, pp. 46, 47.
[86] Taylor, *Nuremberg and Vietnam*, p. 182.
[87] Quoted in Reel, *The Case of General Yamashita*, p. 324.

Chapter 7

JUST WAR AND PACIFISM

[1] "The night of Pier Soderini's death
his soul went to the mouth of Hell;
Pluto shouted: what Hell? silly soul,
go to Limbo with the other children."
Translation by P. Prioreschi.
[2] Thomas Alfred Walker, *A History of the Law of Nations.* Cambridge: Cambridge University Press, 1899, p. 47.
[3] Coleman Phillipson, *The International Law and Custom of Ancient Greece and Rome.* London: Macmillan, 1911, pp. 179, 180, 181, 182.
[4] Titus Livius, *Ab Urbe Condita*, XLV, 22. "...you are those Romans who believe that your wars are successful because they are just, and who take pride not so much in the way they end because you win, but in the way they begin because you do not start them without a just cause." Translation by P. Prioreschi.
[5] Phillipson, *International Law and Custom*, pp. 179, 180, 181, 182.
[6] Ibid.
[7] Sydney D. Bailey, *Prohibitions and Restraints in War.* Oxford: Oxford University Press, 1972, p. 2.
[8] Origenes, *Contra Celsum*, V, 33. From *Contre Celse*, French translation by Marcel Borret. Paris: Les Éditions du Cerf, 1969, Tome III, p. 99. Translation from the French by P. Prioreschi.
[9] Tertullianus, *De Corona Militis*, quoted by Bailey, *Prohibitions and Restraints*, p. 2.
[10] Origines, *Contre Celse*, Tome IV, pp. 347, 349. Translation from the French by P. Prioreschi.
[11] Bailey, *Prohibitions and Restraints*, pp. 3, 4.
[12] Ibid.

[13] Arthur Nussbaum, *A Concise History of the Law of Nations*. New York: Macmillan Company, 1954, pp. 30-37.
[14] Ibid.
[15] Thomas Aquinas, *Summa Theologica*. Rome: Forzani, 1894, Vol. III, p. 314, 315. "...for a certain war to be just, three things are required. *First*, the authority of the prince, on whose order the war is to be fought: it is not legitimate for a private person to start a war....*Second*, a just cause is required, so that those who are attacked may deserve the attack on account of some fault; in fact Augustine says... 'just wars are defined as those that revenge injuries, if the people or a city that is to be punished did not take appropriate measures if some citizen had committed a fault, or if they do not restitute what has been unjustly taken.' *Third*, it is required that the intention of the belligerent be right; which means, of course, that it must intend to promote the good or avoid the bad....In fact it can happen that, although the authority of he who declares the war may be legitimate, and the cause may be just, nevertheless the war may be illicit because of perverse intention: Augustine says:...'lust for inflicting injury, cruelty in punishing, bellicosity and lack of compassion, savageness in renewing a war, lust for power, and similar faults make a war unjust.' " Translation by P. Prioreschi.
[16] National Conference of American Catholic Bishops, *The Challenge of Peace: God's Promise and Our Response, a Pastoral Letter on War and Peace*. Washington: United States Catholic Conference, 1983, pp. 28-31.
[17] Nussbaum, *Concise History of the Law*, pp. 48, 49.
[18] Gaston Bouthoul, *Traité de polémologie*. Paris: Payot, 1970, pp. 51, 52. "Heavenly sights...in the church and in the entire city the people were rendering grace unto God." Translation by P. Prioreschi.
[19] Bailey, *Prohibitions and Restraints*, pp. 17, 18.
[20] Yehuda Melzer, *Concepts of Just War*. Leyden: A.W. Sijthoff, 1975, p. 13.
[21] Mao Tse-tung, *On Revolution and War*. New York: 1970, p. 66. Quoted by Melzer, *Concepts of Just War*, p. 13.
[22] Ibid.
[23] Geoffrey Best, *Humanity in Warfare*. New York: Columbia University Press, 1980, pp. 313, 314.
[24] Melzer, *Concepts of Just War*, p. 13.
[25] Dietrich Shindler and Jiri Toman, eds., *The Laws of Armed Conflicts*. Leyden: A.W. Sijthoff, 1973, p. X.
[26] Nussbaum, *Concise History of the Law*, pp. 73, 74.
[27] Best, *Humanity in Warfare*, pp. 308, 309.
[28] Most authors use the spelling *jus* possibly consecrated by habit and tradition. We consider *ius* the correct spelling. See Oxford Latin Dictionary, Oxford, 1982.
[29] Best, *Humanity in Warfare*, pp. 310, 312.
[30] Robert E. Osgood and Robert W. Tucker, *Force, Order, and Justice*. Baltimore: Johns Hopkins Press, 1967, p. 292.

Notes 325

31   Ibid., pp. 293, 294.
32   Ibid., pp. 296, 298, 299.
33   Ibid., pp. 299, 300, 301.
34   Ibid., pp. 293, 294.
35   Ibid., p. 312.
36   Philippa Foot, "*The Problem of Abortion and the Doctrine of Double Effect*" in Rachels, ed., *Moral Problems*, New York: 1971, p. 34, 35. Quoted by Melzer, *Concepts of Just War*, p. 160.
37   It would not do, at this point, to argue that the possibility of the destruction of humanity changes the situation by making it a case of self-defense because humanity includes "us." It would not do because the argument could be easily changed to state that the tyrant threatens to destroy three quarters of humanity or all of humanity except "us" living in a self-sufficient moon colony.
38   Jacques Maritain, *Man and the State*. Chicago: University of Chicago Press, 1951, p. 73.
39   American Catholic Bishops, *The Challenge of Peace*, pp. 28-31.
40   Edward Gibbon, *The History of the Decline and Fall of the Roman Empire*. New York: Harper and Brothers, 1850, VI, pp. 262, 263.
41   Ibid.
42   Ibid.
43   Vergil, *Eclogue* IV. "Uncalled, the goats shall bring home their udders distended with milk, and the flocks will not fear the great lions." Translation by P. Prioreschi.
44   *Encyclopedia Britannica*, Vol. 13, 1978, p. 848.
45   Dante, *Divina Commedia*, I, 103-104. "...will not crave land and riches, but wisdom, love, and virtue." Translation by P. Prioreschi.
46   Max Scheler, *Die Idee Des Friedens Und der Pazifismus*. Berlin: 1933. Quoted by Raymond Aron, *Peace and War, A Theory of International Relations*. New York: Frederick A. Praeger, 1968, p. 704.
47   Plinio Prioreschi, *Omaha World Herald*, July 20, 1982, p. 7.
48   Melzer, *Concepts of Just War*, p. 135.
49   Maurice Cranston, *Pacifism as an Ideology*. Quoted by Melzer, *Concepts of Just War*, p. 143.
50   Malcom Muggeridge, *Things Past*. New York: William Morrow and Co. 1979, p. 226.
51   Vilfredo Pareto, *The Rise and Fall of the Elites*. Totowa, N.J.: The Bedmister Press, 1968, pp. 60, 61.
52   Sidney Hook, *The Hero in History*. New York: 1943, p. 256. Quoted by Best, *Humanity in Warfare*, p. 15.
53   Daniel C. Maguire, *Death by Choice*. New York: Doubleday, 1974, p. 110.
54   *Time* Magazine, January 24, 1983, p. 30.
55   National Broadcasting Corporation, radio news, January 12, 1985.
56   Encyclopedia Britannica, Vol. 6, 1971, pp. 758, 759.

⁵⁷ Interview of Franklin E. Zimring, Director of the Center for Studies of Criminal Justice at the University of California at Berkeley, as reprinted from *The Washington Post* in the *Omaha World Herald* of February 20, 1984.
⁵⁸ *The Wall Street Journal*, July 26, 1984, p. 1.

Chapter 8

POWER AND DECLINE

¹ "There one can see Memphis and Thebes conquered
and, with them, Babylon, Troy and Carthage,
Jerusalem, Athens, Sparta and Rome.
  There it is shown how beautiful they were,
tall, rich, powerful; and how, finally,
fortune gave them to their enemies."
                    Translation by P. Prioreschi.

² Raymond Aron, *Peace and War*. New York: Frederick A. Praeger, 1968, p. 47.
³ Quoted by Aron, *Peace and War*, p. 52.
⁴ Ibid.
⁵ Ibid., p. 54.
⁶ Edward Gibbon, *The Memoirs of the Life of Edward Gibbon with Various Observations and Excursions by Himself*. London: Methuen and Co., 1900, p. 32.
⁷ Ibid.
⁸ For a privileged class, survival and perpetuation of the group signify also perpetuation of a privileged status. This may have played a part in the patriotism of the privileged.
⁹ Horace, *Epistles*, II, I, 156. "Conquered Greece conquered the coarse victor."
¹⁰ Diffusion of ethno-marked influences is proportional, of course, to the time during which power is exerted. A group very powerful for a short time (e.g., the Median Empire, 635-555 B.C.) would have slight ethno-marked influence.
¹¹ Robert E. Osgood, *Force, Order, and Justice*. Baltimore: Johns Hopkins Press, 1967, p. 13.
¹² Caesar, *De Bello Gallico*, I, 1. "Of all these people the Belgians are the strongest, because they are farthest away from the culture and civilization of the [Roman] province [i.e., Gallia Narbonensis] and most rarely are visited by merchants who bring the goods that make for effeminacy." Translation by P. Prioreschi.

¹³ Arthur A. Stein, *The Nation at War*. Baltimore: John Hopkins Press, 1980, p. 9.
¹⁴ Henry Berry, *Semper Fi, Mac*. New York: Arbor House, 1982 pp. 216-217.
¹⁵ Stein, *The Nation at War*, pp. 38-53.
¹⁶ Occasionally decline can occur when the system of international forces undergoes such a radical change that a given country becomes a secondary power by necessity. An example in point is England after the Second World War. The prominence of the two superpowers in the East and in the West gave England no chance to maintain her prominent status independently of the relationship between her centrifugal and centripetal forces.
¹⁷ Isaiah Berlin, *Two Concepts of Liberty*. Oxford: Oxford University Press, 1958, p. 11.
¹⁸ Plinio Prioreschi, "On the Abuse of Marihuana and Other Drugs," *Medical Hypotheses* 3, 265, 1977.
¹⁹ Malcom Muggeridge, *Things of the Past*. New York: William Morrow and Company, 1979, pp. 202, 234.
²⁰ It may be objected that, in every society, this need should persist because the individual always strives to achieve something. When affluent, for example, he may strive to become rich. True, but the struggle for the superfluous is not invested with as much energy as the struggle for the necessary. In addition, it involves a smaller percentage of the population. Many of those who have the minimum to live a decent life resign themselves to the idea that they will never be millionaires, but very few of those who lack the necessary resign themselves to the idea that they will never be free of want.
²¹ Oswald Spengler, *The Decline of the West*. New York: Modern Library, 1965, p. 75.
²² In non-democratic societies the intellectuals are also the most vocal opponents of the establishment because they are more sensitive to the other shortcomings of the system—as, for example, indoctrination, lack of individual freedom, and oppression.
²³ Muggeridge, *Things of the Past*, pp. 27-34.
²⁴ Alessandro Manzoni, *I Promessi Sposi*. Milan: Hoepli, 1945, p. 179. "From those and other things that he had heard and seen, Renzo began to realize that he had arrived in a rioting city and that that was a day of grabbing; that is to say, that everyone would grab according to his will and strength, giving blows in payment. Although we would like to show our poor peasant in a good light, historical truth forces us to say that his first feeling was of pleasure. He had so few reasons to be happy about the way things were usually going that he was inclined to approve any change no matter which." Translation by P. Prioreschi.
²⁵ Alfred Vagts, *A History of Militarism, Romance and Realities of a Profession*. New York: W.W. Norton and Company, 1937, p. 427.
²⁶ Caesar, *De Bello Gallico*, I, 1. (See footnote 12 for translation).

Chapter 9

PROGRESS AND HOPE

[1] "Oh Apollo, give me some of your light,
and if you ever listen to mortal prayer,
illumine what in my mind is dark."
Translation by P. Prioreschi.

[2] Thomas Alfred Walker, *A History of the Law of Nations*. Cambridge: Cambridge University Press, 1899. p. 42.

[3] Nigel Davies, *Human Sacrifice*. New York: William Morrow and Company, Inc. 1981, p. 47.

[4] Walker, *A History of the Law*, p. 49.

[5] Ibid.

[6] Caesar, *De Bello Gallico*, II, 28. "...so that mercy would be shown toward the wretched and the supplicants, he was most careful for their safety and ordered them to return to their territory and towns, and commanded their neighbors to restrain themselves and their dependents from attack and outrage." Translation by P. Prioreschi.

[7] Caesar, *De Bello Gallico*, II, 31. "For one thing only were they praying and entreating: if because of his clemency and mercy, of which they had heard from others, he would decide to save the Aduatuci, that he would not despoil them of their arms." Translation by P. Prioreschi.

[8] Caesar, *De Bello Gallico*, II, 32. "He would spare them more because that was his custom than because they deserved it, if they surrendered before the battering ram touched the walls." Translation by P. Prioreschi.

[9] Caesar, *De Bello Gallico*, II, 33.

[10] Walker, *A History of the Law*, pp. 66, 72.

[11] Ibid., pp. 123-127.

[12] Ibid.

[13] Ibid.

[14] Ibid.

[15] Ibid.

[16] Ibid.

[17] Ibid.

[18] Ibid., p. 133.

[19] Walker, *A History of the Law*, pp. 66, 72.

[20] Ibid., pp. 123-127.

[21] John Keegan and Joseph Darracott, *The Nature of War*. New York: Holt, Rinehart and Winston, 1981, p. 208.

[22] Alfred Vagts, *A History of Militarism, Romance and Reality of a Profession*. New York: W.W. Norton and Company, 1937, pp. 89, 95.

23 Geoffrey Best, *Humanity in Warfare.* New York: Columbia University Press, 1980, p. 36, 37, 126-27.
24 Ibid.
25 Ibid.
26 Albert Sorel, *Europe and the French Revolution.* London: Collins, 1969 (first pub. 1885), pp. 109, 111.
27 Best, *Humanity in Warfare*, pp. 36, 37, 126-127.
28 Ibid.
29 Ibid.
30 Ibid., p. 84, 85, 86.
31 "The declining elite becomes softer, milder, more humane...." Vilfredo Pareto, *The Rise and Fall of the Elites.* Totowa, N.J.: Bedminster Press, 1968, p. 59.
32 Stanley B. Weld and David A. Soskys, "The Reminiscences of a Civil War Surgeon, John B. Lewis," J. Hist. Med. 21, 47, 1966.
33 Leon Wolff, *In Flanders Fields: The 1917 Campaign.* New York: Ballantine Books, 1969, p. 207.
34 Henry Berry, *Semper Fi, Mac.* New York: Arbor House, 1982, pp. 248-49.
35 Ibid., p. 248.
36 Eugene Davidson, *The Trial of the Germans.* New York: Macmillan Company, 1966, pp. 403, 404, 405, 406, 407.
"The mystery of what happened on the Allied side has not to this date been fully cleared up....It is known that the messages were received by the British Admiralty and that Allied ships were in the neighborhood. A later British report said that rescue attempts were planned and that the Liberator attack had taken place because of a misunderstanding." (p. 407.)
37 Osgood and Tucker, *Force, Order, and Justice*, pp. 142-143.
38 Ibid., pp. 15, 16
39 Isaiah Berlin, *Two Concepts of Liberty.* London: Oxford University Press, 1958, p. 7.
40 James R. Chiles, "Engineers versus the Cons, or How Long Will Our Monuments Last?" Smithsonian, 14, March 1984, pp. 56-67.
41 This is not easily acknowledged; man prefers to appeal to loftier tenets; to recognize that his motivations are not based on justice, generosity, altruism, and other exalted principles is considered demeaning and unworthy. From the discovery that our planet was not the center of the universe, to the realization that we were not suddenly created (in the image of God) some four thousand years ago, from the acknowledgment that our animal ancestors crawled out of the mud of the primeval swamps, to the Principle of Uncertainty, our egos have been battered and bruised. To comfort our depressed ego, we want therefore to crown ourselves with attributes that, we feel, are noble.

CONCLUSIONS

[1] *Time*, November 21, 1983, p. 43. The statement of the American Catholic Bishops in favor of a nuclear "freeze" is in *The Challenge of Peace, God's Promise and Our Response, a Pastoral Letter on War and Peace.* Washington: United States Catholic Conference, 1983, p. 60.

[2] "The Moral Un-neutrality of Science," *Science*, January 27, 1961, vol. 133, pp. 255-262, quotation on p. 259.

[3] Arthur F. Scott, "The Invention of the Balloon and the Birth of Modern Chemistry," *Scientific American*, January 1984, p. 129.

INDEX

Abortion, 212
Adler, Alfred, 144
Affluence, effects of, 255, 260, 272, 290, 291, 293
Afghanistan, Russian invasion of, 156, 240, 284, 285
Aggression, as a war crime, 176, 177, 178
  Soviet Union and Japan, 177
Agile, Raymond d', 201
Albigenses, 266
Alcaeus, 53
Alcohol, abuse of, 251
Alexander, 9, 233, 272
Alexis St. Martin, 37
Ambassadors, exchange of, 120
American media, 301, 304
American Revolution, 289
Amoral, definition, 148
Amorality of the first order (or degree), 148, 149
  of the second order (or degree), 148, 149, 151, 152, 158, 211-213

Anacreon, 53
Anarchy, 260
Andromache, 85
Angell, Norman, 135
Appeasement, 221, 256
Archilochus, 53
Ariovistus, 95
Aristotle, 113
Armenian Church, 119
Arms race, xiii, xiv, 286, 288
  as a substitute for war, 288
Augustus, 3
Australia, 231
Ayala, Balthasar, 112

Battle
  of Actium, 4
  of Agincourt, 266
  of Cannes, 84, 86
  of Chaeronea, 3
  of Crécy, 266
  of Marathon, 233
  of Pavia, 24, 171

of Poitier, 120
of Salamis, 233
of Sedan, 297
of Solferino, 124
of Waterloo, 31, 43
Beaumont, William, 37
Belgium, 231
Belleau Woods, 51
Belli, Pietro, 112
Bellicosity, 55-58
Bellona, 268
Bellum iustum et pium, 114
Bezoar, 36
Bismarck, 242
Bizarre activities and lack of discipline, 254
Black Death, 170
Blood tax, 25
Bombing of civilians in Second World War, 167, 179
Bravery, 47, 48
Byzantine Empire, 117

Caesar, 9, 86, 95, 171, 259, 265, 272
Canada, 231
   American invasion of, 156, 231
   Communist takeover of, 238, 239
Cannibalism in war, 266
Canon Law, 116
Capitalism, 98
Carthage, 4, 280
Catholic Church, its attitude toward nuclear weapons, 303
Catullus, 53
Central America, xiii
Centrifugal Force, 52
Centripetal Force, 52
Cervantes, 29
Charlemagne, 9
Charles Martel, 120
Charles V, 171

Chinese language, 285
Christine of Sweden, 26
Church States, 25
Churchill, Winston, 189, 190
Cicero, 200
Cincinnatus, 290
Civilians, bombing of in Second World War, 167, 179
Civilization, as defense against death, 7
   as survival, 9
   Greco-Roman, 9
   Western, 9
Class struggle, 100
Clausewitz, Karl von, 154
Code of Manu, 115,
Cohesion, 247, 249, 250, 260
Collaborationism, 104
Collaborators, 107
Colonial wars as just wars, 152
Commando Order, 179, 180
Communism, 98
Communist Party, Italian, 239
Communists and the peace movement, 298
Comte, Auguste, 135
Condottieri, 22, 24, 25
Conformism, 229, 253
Conformity, *see* Conformism
Congress of Vienna, 124
Constantine, 117, 198
Constantine Paleologue, 118
Constantinople, 117, 266
Continental Blockade, 123
Country, as defense against death, 7
Courage in battle, 51
Cowardice in battle, 47
Credibility, American, after Vietnam, 161, 162
   in international relations, 162
Crime, in the United States, 225
   murders of Interstate 57, 223
Crimes against humanity, as war crimes, 179
Crossbow, 33, 116
Crucé, Emeric, 131
Cruelty, in war, 59, 62, 72, 73, 74, *see also* War, atrocities

Cuban missile crisis, 206
Cultural influences, as measured by language diffusion, 232, 234

Dani, of New Guinea, 16
Dante, 9, 216, 232
"Dead Army", 26
Death, lines of defense against, 7, 8
Death wish, pacifism as an expression of, 225
Decadence, *see* Decline
Declaration of Human Rights and retroactive laws, 191
Declaration of Paris of 1856, 126
Declaration of war, Soviet Union on Japan, 177
Decline, of the group, 240, 250, 256, 288, 291
  inevitability of, 292
  postponement of, 293
Deditio, 114
"Degree of freedom," 239, 240
Deserters, 241
Deterrence, degree of, 284
  nuclear, 281-283
Dialogue of Melos, 146
Diplomatic immunity, 120
Disarmament, xiii, 136-139, 141
  nuclear, 137, 140, 141
  poison gases, 140
Discipline, 252, 254, 255, 290, 291, 293
Dissolution or subjection of the group, 260
Divina Commedia, 233
Doctrine of the Just War, *see* Just War Doctrine
Doenitz, Admiral, 176
Donoso-Cortes, Juan Francisco Maria, 259
Double effect, principle of, 208-213
Douhet, Giulio, 147
Drive for war, subconscious, 6
Drugs, abuse of, 250
Dubois, Pierre, 131

Duke of Enghien, 123
Duke of Sung, 151
Dunan, Jean Henri, 44, 124

Earth, as defense against death, 7
Economic prosperity and military power, 231
Education, effects of, 260, 272, 291, 293
Elites, effeteness of, 222
Elizabeth I, 26
Emich of Leisingen, Count, 95
End justifies the means, xv, xix, 166, 168, 169, 179
"Enemy goods, enemy ship", 125
"Enemy ship, enemy goods", 125
English language, diffusion of, 234
Enlightenment, 96, 122, 267, 270, 271
  conduct of war during, 268, 269
Ethics
  and international relations, 147, 150, 156, 157
  and mass, 163
  and necessity, 212
  and nuclear deterrence, 153, 154
  and war, 166, 167
  principle of double effect, 208-213
Eusebius Pamphili, 197
Expansion of the group, 143
Expansive pressure of the group, 144
Experimental method, 235

Family, as defence against death, 7
Famine, stele of, 70
Famines, 71
Fanaticism, 260
Fascism, 98, 236
Fascists and the peace movement, 298
Fénelon, 147
Fear, 282, 289
  religious, 289
Ferdinand of Castile, 266

334 MAN AND WAR

Fetiales, 114, 196
Field hospitals, 44
First Crusade, 95, 171, 266
Flag, national, 252
Flavius Josephus, 18, 88, 92
Florence, 25
Florence Nightingale, 44
France, 25, 297
Francis I, 131, 171
Franklin, Benjamin, 305
Freedom, 250, 260, 288-291, 293
Freeze of nuclear weapons, xiii
French Revolution, 97, 98, 123, 133, 134, 269, 270, 272, 289
Freud, Sigmund, 293
Fundamental drives of behavior, 6

Galileo, 233, 234
Geneva Convention of 1949, 149
Genghis Khan, 55, 89, 280, 281
Gentili, Alberico, 112
Geometry, and morality, 148
Geopolitics, 238
Germany, 25, 297
Gibbon, Edward, 144, 229, 245
God, as defense against death, 7
Goering, Hermann, 181
Goethe, 9
Golden Age, 215, 235
  of Greece, 3
Goretti, Saint Maria, 48
Graecia capta ferum victorem coepit, 233
Granada, Spain, 120
Greek Orthodox Church, 117, 119
Grenada, U.S. invasion of, 238, 284
Grotius, Hugo, 112, 202
Group, definition, xix
Guerilla warfare, 98, 99, 106
Gustavus Adolphus, 42

Hague Conventions, V and XIII, 126
Hague Peace Conference, the first, 124

Hannibal, 84, 86
Hector, 85
Henry VIII, 131
Heroism, in battle, 47
Hindi language, 232
Hippies, 290
Hirota, Koki, 187
Hitler, Adolf, 9, 281, 298, 299
Hobbes, Thomas, 4
Holocaust, 205
Homer, 9
Homicides, in the United States, 225
Honor, 28, 29
Horace, 9, 53, 83
Hostages, execution of, 183
Human sacrifices, 264
Humanity, as defense against death, 7
Huns, 55
Hydrogen bomb, 282

Ideological infiltration, 284
Immortality, 7, 8, 144
Individuality, 7
Inevitability of death, 292
Influence of a group on others
  cultural, 234
  ethno-marked, 234, 235
  ethno-neutral, 234, 235
Innocent X, Pope, 121
Inquisition, 253
Instinct of survival, 7
Intellectuals
  as pacifists, before World War II, 217, 298
  role in the process of decline, 256-258
International law, 111
Invulnerability, 7
Isidore of Seville, 200
Islam, at the time of the Byzantine Empire, 118
Islamic law on international relations, 118

Index 335

Italian language, diffusion, 232
Italy, 25, 53
  in World War II, 160
Ius ad bellum, 204
Ius gentium, 115
Ius in bello, 204

Janissaries, 21
Japan, 53
Japanese suicides in World War II, 243
Jericho, 3
Jews, 119, 205, 236, 299
Jim and Pedro, case of, xvii
Just War Doctrine, 109, 110, 117, 195, 199, 201-204, 206, 207, 213, 214
Justin Martyr, 197
Justinian, 117

Kamikazes, 48, 49, 241
Kant, Immanuel, 134
Katyn Massacre, 181
Kellogg Pact, or Treaty (also called Kellogg-Briand Pact), 135, 178, 205
Killing, depersonalized, 279
Kim, Vietnamese girl, 223
Koran, 119

Laconia affair, 274-278
Lactantius, 197
Languages, diffusion, 232
Lansquenets, 23
Lateran Council, Second, 116
  Third, 116
Latin language, 9, 121, 232, 234
Laws of war, milestones, 127-129
League of Nations, 135, 205, 298
Leclerc, Charles, General, 42
Leo X, Pope, 117, 131
Leviathan, 4
Lieber Code, 93, 94
Livy, 196

Louis XIV, 9, 21, 44
Louis XVI, 222
Luigi da Porto, 5

MacArthur, Douglas, General, 64, 159
Macedonian War, Third, 105
  see also War
Machiavelli, xv, 24, 166
Maltese language, 232
Manzoni, Alessandro, 69, 258
Mao Tse-tung, 151, 201
Marathon, battle of, 233
Martyrdom, 198
Mary of Scotland, 120
Masada, 88
Mass and ethics, 163, 211
Means, the end justifies the, xv, xix, 166, 168, 169, 179
Media, American, 301, 304
Melos, dialogue of, 146
Military occupation, 99
  and collaborationism, 104
  and collaborators, 107
  and retaliation, 101-103
  resistance to, 106
Military power, analogy with money, 236
Military pressure, 145
Mohammed II, 117
Montesquieu, 112
Morality, *see* Ethics
Moscow, as the third Rome, 118
Murcare, 19
Murci, 19
Murders, in the United States, 225
Mussolini, Benito, 161, 259
Mutiny, The Great, of India, 90

Napoleon, 9, 25, 98, 123, 297
National anthem, 252
National flag, 252
Nationalism, 269, 270

as people's struggle for immortality, 272
Nazis, atrocities, 299
Necessity, in ethics, 212
  in war, 100, 163
Neutrality, 126
  of Switzerland, 126
  violations in First and Second World Wars, 126, 127
Newton, Isaac, 48
Nicaragua, American support for the guerillas in, 240
Nuclear deterrence, 281-283
  and ethics, 153, 154
Nuclear disarmament, 137, 140, 141, 287
  verification, 287
Nuclear pacifism, unilateral, 220
Nuclear weapons
  acquisition of, 286
  Catholic Church attitude, 303
  freeze, xiii
  spread of, 286, 287
Nuremberg principles concerning obedience to orders, 158-160, 301
Nuremberg trials, 158, 167, 173-176, 181, 184, 185, 188-191, 299
  Indictment counts, 175
  tu quoque defence, 182

Obedience to military orders, 158, 160, 184
Occupation, military, 99
"Old virtues," 290, 293
Opium War, 89
Orders, obedience to, 158, 160, 184
Origen, 197

Pacifism, 111, 130, 222, 215, 216, 218, 219
  absolute, 217, 219
  and crime, 223-225
  as the expression of a death wish, 225
  of the Early Church, 197-199
  nuclear unilateral, 220
  relative, 217
Pacifists, moral superiority of, 222
  their attitude toward crime violence, 223-225
Pact of Paris of 1929 (Kellogg Pact), 135, 205
Paine, Thomas, 192
Paré, Ambroise, 35, 86
Pareto, Vilfredo, 221
Particularism, 247, 249, 258, 260
Patriarch of Constantinople, 117
Patriotism, 27, 229-231, 302
Pauline teaching on the use of evil to achieve good, xvii
Pax Atomica, 283, 285
Pax Augusta, 216
Pax Britannica, 282
Pax Romana, 216, 282
Peace movement, in the United States, 161, 163
Peace, perpetual, 130-135, 297
  universal, 131
Pearl Harbor, 205, 236, 299
Penn, William, 132
People's war, 98
Permissiveness, 252, 254, 255, 260, 289-291, 293
Perpetual peace, 130-135, 297
Pestilence, 67, 68, 69
Pétain, General, 107
Pillaging, imperial ordinances about, 121
Pioneer 10, 292
Plague, 67-69
Plato, 113
Poison gases, disarmament, 140
Poisoned weapons, 116
Pornography, 250-254, 293
Power, 144, 145, 227, 235, 240
  and force, 145, 228
  and potentiality, 228
  as energy source for group pressure, 145, 228
  as the springboard of the expansive force, 145, 228

economic, 145, 228
Greek and Roman, 233
military, 145, 228
of ancient Greece, 234
of Renaissance Italy, 233
psychological, 228
Prisoners of war, 81
cruelty toward, 94
killing of, 59-61, 82, 86, 89, 91, 115
mistreatment, 181
sacrifice of, 264
suicide of, 91, 93
Professional soldiers, 21
Propaganda, 54, 63, 236, 238, 298
Protection of the individual by the group, 260, 289
Public opinion, 157, 236, 239
Punic Wars, 244, 280, *see also* War
Pus bonum et laudabile, 33

Quisling, Abraham Johnson, 107

Racial discrimination, 302
equality, 302
Raeder, Admiral, 177
Rayneval, Gérard de, 96
Red Cross, 44, 124
Regulus, 83, 264
Religion and the soldier, 46
Renaissance Italy, power of, 233
Resistance to military occupation, 106
Retaliation, 102, 103
Retroactive laws, 191
Revolution, 134, 259
Richelieu, Cardinal, 44
Rise and decline of the group, 241
Roman legionary, 17
Roman war practices, 264, 265
Romance languages, 234
Rome, 280
Roosevelt, Elliot, 189
Roosevelt, Franklin Delano, President, 190
Russell, Bertrand, 144, 217

Russian language, diffusion, 232

Sacrifices, human, 264
Saint-Pierre, Abbé de, 132
Saint-Simon, 245
Salamis, *see* Battle of Salamis
Scipio, Africanus, 86
Second Coming, 198
Second World War as a special war, 299
Security provided to the individual by the group, 289
Sedan, *see* Battle of Sedan
Self-interest, enlightened, 293, 294
in international relations, 156
simple, 294
Self-perpetuation, 7
Seneca, 86
Shakespeare, 9, 233
Sherman, William Tecumseh, 109
Simplicissimus, 22
Slave trade, 124
Slavery, 264
Snow, C.P., 305
Socrates, 113, 291
Solar system, as defense against death, 7
Sorel, Albert, 268
Space, colonization of, 286
Spain, 25
Sparta, 31, 259
Spengler, Oswald, 245
Spheres of influence, 238
Spying, as a criminal activity, 149
St. Augustine, 117, 199
St. Thomas Aquinas, 117, 200
Stalin, Joseph, 189, 190, 299
Suarez, Francisco, 111
Subjection or dissolution of the group, 260
Suffering, capacity to inflict, 263
Sully, Duke of, 131
Surrender, in Roman law of war, 114
Survival, as a root of cohesion, 7, 145, 260

instinct of, 7, 13
Sweden, 231
"Swedish drink", 86
Swift, Jonathan, 230
Switzerland, 231

Tacitus, 9, 114
Tamerlane (Timour), 215
Temple of Janus, 4
Terror bombing, in Second World War, 167, 179
Tertullian, 197
Theodosius I, 117, 199
Thersites, 53
Thirty Years War, 23, 26, 69, 86, 121, 172
Thucydides, 146
Timour (Tamerlane), 215
Tokyo trials, 187-191
Torquemada, 253
Torture, as a justifiable means, 169, 264
Toussaint l'Overture, 42
Toynbee, Arnold Joseph, 245
Traditional values, 290, 293, *see also* "Old virtues"
Treaties, between groups, first examples, 113
Treaty, American-Prussian, of 1785, 122
  of Paris, 1929, 135, 205
  of Tilsit, 124
  of Versailles, 204
Triage, of wounded, in war, 46
Truces and compacts, first examples, 113
Truman, Henry, President, 159
Truman-MacArthur controversy, 159
Tyranny, 260

Universe, as defense against death, 7
Universal peace, 131
Untori (smearers), 170
Urban II, Pope, 171

Valhalla, 52
Valor, in battle, 47
Vattel, Emmerich, 203, 268
Velasquez, 235
Venice, 25
Vercingetorix, 171
Vergil, 9, 114
Versailles, Treaty of, 204
Vikings, 55
Violence and pacifism, 224, 225
Vitoria, Francisco de, 111

Wallenstein, General, 42
War
  among primates, 11
  and cancer, xiii
  and necessity, 100, 163-167, 169, 183
  atrocities, 59, 72-74, 182, 183, 264, 266, 267
  bellum iustum, 196
  bellum pium, 196
  Boer, 42
  brutality in, 279
  cannibalism in, 266
  casualties, 76-79
  causes of, 4
  colonial wars, 152
  cruelty in, 127, 201
  decency and generosity in, 272-277
  defensive, 207
  depersonalized killing in, 279
  doctrine of just war, *see* Just War Doctrine
  drive for, 6
  end of all-out wars, 306
  ethics, 166, 167
  Falkland, 155
  just and unjust, *see* Just War Doctrine
  Korean, 94, 243
  laws of, 127-129
  Macedonian, Third, 105
  motivation for, 13
  Opium, 89

Peloponnesian, 146
Persian (480-479 B.C.), 3
principle of proportionality in, 207, 208
"proxy wars", 284
Punic Wars, 83, 244, 280
Sacred War, Moslem, 267
substitutes for, 285
Thirty Years War, 23, 26, 69, 86, 121, 172
Vietnam, xiii, 54, 94, 153, 157, 158, 160-162, 191, 205, 218, 223, 236, 237, 242, 243, 257, 285, 300-302
WAR=DEATH, 282
WAR=SURVIVAL, 281
War Crimes
 aggression, 176-178
 bombing of civilians, 179
 crimes against humanity, 179
 execution of hostages, 183
 Holocaust, 205
 Katyn Massacre, 181
War Criminals, 170
 in World War I, 172
 in World War II, 172
Western Civilization, 302
 wars within, 295
Westphalia, peace of, 121
Wilson, Woodrow, President, 205
Wolsey, Cardinal, 131
World wars, 295
Wounds
 pain, 37
 treatment of, 33-35, 37

Yamashita, General, 185-187